Color

and

Fiber

Color
and
Fiber

Patricia Lambert
Barbara Staepelaere
Mary G. Fry

West Chester, Pennsylvania 19380

Acknowledgements

In 1977, we sat down with the tentative hope of putting together a book about color just for people who worked with fiber. We never dreamed the experience would be as challenging and involved, nor that it would give us the opportunity of working with so many gifted artists. Countless people have been involved with the project as a whole, and we are profoundly grateful to them—especially to the artists who contributed examples of their work, and to our students who were always willing to experiment with ideas and to give of their time and talent so generously. Although we cannot cite everyone, we would like to express our special indebtedness and appreciation to a few by name.

Our thanks to Antonia Kormos, a dyer of extraordinary ability, patience, and endurance and our illustrators, Scott Dustman, Anthony Conway, and Alexander Lee; to our colleagues Paul Berendsohn, Barry Cohen, Lois Dougherty, Johathan Harris, M.D., Betty Louis, Mary Nelson, Joyce O'Neill, Kunio Owaki, Gladys Rosen, Audrey Rosenthal, and Chet Kalm, Director of the Foundation Program at the Parsons School of Design, for their interest, support, and contributions of technical and aesthetic expertise; and to our families and friends who gave us so much encouragement—to Franklin D. Fry, Anne, Mary, Christine, Martha and Franklin G., Ruth and Wolf Levine, and Nora and Roger Shattuck.

This project would never have become a reality without Nancy Green, who helped us bring it together with our editors David Sachs and Steven Gray; and to Heide Lange, our agent—along with her strong right arm, David Black—our gratitude for their faith and friendship. Our heartfelt thanks also to Ellen (Sue) Taylor, Lyngerda Kelley and to Nancy and Peter Schiffer, who thought they saw a light.

Printed in the United States of America.
ISBN: 0-88740-065-5
Published by Schiffer Publishing Ltd.
1469 Morstein Road
West Chester, Pennsylvania 19380

This book may be purchased from the publisher.
Please include $1.50 postage.
Try your bookstore first.

Cover: **Color Blanket**
Artist: Carol Russell
Photo: Patricia Lambert

Frontispiece: **Directional light produces value changes in draped satin.**
Photo: Patricia Lambert

iv

Foreword

Any serious student of fabrics sooner or later experiences a moment of discovery of the special, tangible nature of color in fibers and fabrics. In that moment, color is experienced as a vital sensation inextricably connected to texture, pattern, and meaning—as a sensational cushion in the connection between the individual and the surrounding world. Color can thus be seen as a means to extend ourselves into our surroundings.

Today, as more and more fabric artists, designers, and craftspeople assume increased responsibility for the quality of works they produce, there is a growing need for information about the unique properties of color in building structures and images. *Color and Fiber* presents, for the first time, a concise and accessible explanation of color as related to fiber. By understanding the basis upon which the sense of color operates, the artist is able to appreciate how much of color experience is physiological and how much is cultural; that is, how much of the process of using color is determined by the nature of human eyesight and color perception and how much is based upon values and experience shared with other people. By focusing on the interaction between color and fiber, the authors have revealed many special characteristics of this relationship that are often ignored or overlooked. Cumulatively, the information forms a strong and secure foundation, encouraging insight, appreciation, and inspiration for new approaches and developments in the use of color.

This is not simply a craft book, but a thorough treatment of an involved subject carefully and clearly explained. It has been beautifully illustrated with photographs and drawings which reinforce concepts in the text.

Patricia Lambert, Barbara Staepelaere, and Mary G. Fry have arrived at their observations through careful research and experimentation in their own work as artists and designers, as well as through their years of experience as teachers. Anyone who carefully follows the contents of this book from beginning to end will benefit from a treatment of the theoretical and practical aspects of the subject that is commensurate with the best college-level course in color available today. *Color and Fiber* is destined to become a standard text for those involved in structured programs, as well as for those studying independently.

Gerhardt Knodel
Chairman, Fiber Department
Cranbrook Academy of Art
Bloomfield Hills, Michigan

Dedication

To our students.

*He Who Has Imagination Without Learning Has Wings
But No Feet.*   Chinese Proverb

Contents

Introduction

This book concentrates on the use and control of color by and for the fiber artist. Whether you stitch, quilt, weave, work in macramé, hook rugs, knit, crochet, or experiment in mixed media and fiber, your work can benefit from the information in this text. Our goal is to help you realize your greatest potential for self-expression through the use of color and fiber and to provide easy access to specific facts and techniques for solving color problems. You can use this book to lay the foundation needed to control color artistically, and you can make continued use of the more advanced ideas as sources for your own expression.

In classes and discussion groups, beginning fiber artists often question the need to learn specific information about color. Some beginners feel that knowing theory and facts inhibits their ability to produce spontaneous work. They grow anxious that they may be jamming their heads too full of non-essential facts, creating a situation where ideas cannot flow. But a firm intellectual base does just the opposite. Creativity is always enhanced by knowledge; and when information is thoroughly absorbed, it can help to inspire and support new ideas and directions.

Color and Fiber is divided into three sections. Part One, The Language of Color, presents essential terminology, ideas, and definitions about light and color, and discusses the aesthetics of reflected color. This section prepares you for problems, projects, and more advanced ideas.

Part Two, Fiber Structure and Color, describes how light, dyes, and pigment work with the specific physical structures and properties of individual fibers. Fibers, yarns, and fabrics differ in their responses to light and color; the importance of this fact cannot be over-emphasized. Fiber is a unique art form, and the ability to solve color problems depends on the artist's having a thorough understanding of its relationship to light as well as to color.

Part Three, Color and Fiber, discusses the practical application of the information presented in the first two sections. Besides offering some new thoughts about color mixing and special color effects, such as iridescence and opalescence, this section examines projects and problems that the individual, the small group, or the large class can do. Subjects in this section include expanding color palettes, producing different spatial effects, controlling small and large areas of color to achieve greater emotional impact, and developing color systems. Although this section completes the book, it by no means signals an end to the subject; it is only a beginning to a rich and varied field.

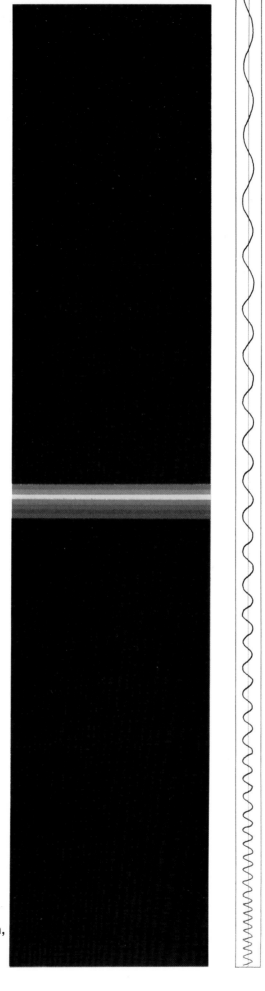

radio waves

infrared light

visible light

ultraviolet rays

X-rays

gamma rays

(not in proportion)

1-1. **Light waves and the electromagnetic spectrum, showing the relative portion of visible light.**

9

Part One

The Language of Color

Every discipline has its own language; color is no exception. The only way to become truly comfortable and conversant with it is to understand it as completely as possible. This section offers a preparation in the language of color, laying a foundation for visual communication and creating a degree of order and clarity from which to work.

The nomenclature of color theory and application has always seemed a bit enigmatic. In fact, it sometimes presents real problems of communication among people in the visual arts because names of colors and many terms are often confused or misleading. Over the years, however, many people in the field of color have made successful inroads toward standardizing color terminology. It is one of the goals of this text to provide another positive step in the evolution and standardization of the language of color—here, as related to fiber.

Chapter 1

Color and Light

The phenomen of color depends on four factors: the presence of light; colorants (pigments and dyes) contained in substances; the quality of surfaces, and structures that may or may not contain colorants; and the mechanism of color perception contained in the viewer's eye and brain. Only the first two factors need concern us here.

Light

Light is radiant energy; although we cannot see the actual vibrations of this energy, we perceive our world in color because of it. Where light is absent, there is no color. Thus, the nature of light contains the essence of color.

Visible light constitutes a very small part of an enormous spectrum of wave energy known as electromagnetic radiation (see Figure 1-1 on page nine). The spectrum of electromagnetic radiation includes all the energy wavelengths that bombard our planet—from miles-long radio waves to cosmic rays measuring 0.000000000000394 of an inch. All electromagnetic radiation travels in wave motion at the speed of light, 186,000 miles per second. The waves are measured from crest to crest, and each particular kind of radiant energy consists of waves having a characteristic length and frequency.

There are several ways of expressing wavelength. The unit most commonly used in measuring wavelengths in the band of visible light within the electromagnetic spectrum is called the nanometer, a length equal to 1 billionth of a meter. Our eyes are sensitive only to radiant energy of wavelengths between 700 and 400 nanometers. We do, however, feel the effects of infrared waves as heat, and ultraviolet waves which produce chemical and physical changes in our skin; in addition, we can observe the effects of other types of radiation such as X rays and radio waves.

Sir Isaac Newton was among the first scientists to explore light in a systematic manner, laying the foundation of our contemporary understanding of color. In 1676, concerned with the nature of light and lenses, Newton focused a beam of sunlight (white light) at a prism; the prism bent (refracted) the beam of light, separating it into a band of brilliant colors (see Figure 1-2). To prove that white light itself was made up of the colors revealed by refraction, Newton reorganized the band of colors into white light by directing them through a second prism, held upside down. He identified seven principal groups of color: red, orange, yellow, green, blue, indigo, and violet. These became known as spectral hues and served as identifying names within the colored band of the visible spectrum, the limits of which are red (at 700 nanometers) and violet (at 400 nanometers). Wavelengths outside this range are invisible to human beings.

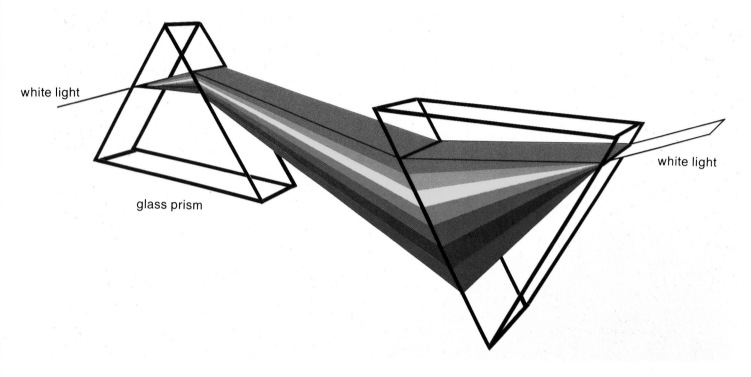

1-2. **The refraction of white light: Newton's experiment.**

Additive Color Mixing: Color Mixing with Light

The broadest bands of color seen in the visible spectrum are those belonging to *red-orange, green,* and *blue-violet.* These colors are known as the light primaries. When all three are projected and overlapped, their specific wavelengths mix together to produce white light (see Figure 1-3). In areas where only red-orange and blue-violet light are overlapped, the result is magenta—a red-violet that is lighter (that is, closer to white) than either of the parent colors. In areas where only red-orange and green light are overlapped, the result is yellow—again a lighter color than either of the two original colors. Similarly, the overlapping of green and blue-violet light produces cyan—a relatively light

blue-green. *Magenta, yellow,* and *cyan* are known as the light secondaries. This demonstration in which wavelengths of light are added to one another as different colored lights re-creates Newton's experiment, without using the prisms, and shows clearly that colored lights combine directly (or *additively*) and that the final result is white light.

When the spectrum is arranged in a circle, the light primaries and secondaries are easily visualized, each color having a partner that appears opposite it. Red-orange lies opposite cyan; blue-violet lies opposite yellow; and green lies opposite magenta. These pairs of light colors (each consisting of one primary and one secondary color) are known as complementary pairs of spectral hues. Each pair, when combined, produces white light.

12

Among the modern applications of additive color mixing is color television. The fluorescent face, or screen, of the television's cathode ray tube is composed of tiny dots of three kinds of phosphors. A phosphor is a substance, usually of mineral origin, that fluoresces or emits light when excited by radiation. In this case, the radiation is provided by electrons fired from three guns (one for each primary color) situated at the anterior end of the picture tube. One type of phosphor emits red light when radiated, one emits green light, and one emits blue light. When the screen is scanned by electrons, it becomes a mosaic of tiny red, green and blue dots that are too small to see individually. Mixed in the proper proportions as colored lights, these dots produce the colored forms perceived as images on the screen. If a group of all three types of phosphors is stimulated equally, the viewer sees that portion of the screen as white; if just the red and green phosphors are radiated, the viewer sees yellow; and so on.

In color television, nonspectral colors such as brown and pink are the result of changes in total light level (light intensity), as well as of changes in excitation of the specific phosphors involved. The greater the light intensity, the lighter the color; and conversely, the lower the light intensity, the darker the color.

Other disciplines that involve the production of color through additive mixing include stage lighting, interior special effects lighting, and lighting for fountains, sculpture, fiber art, and buildings.

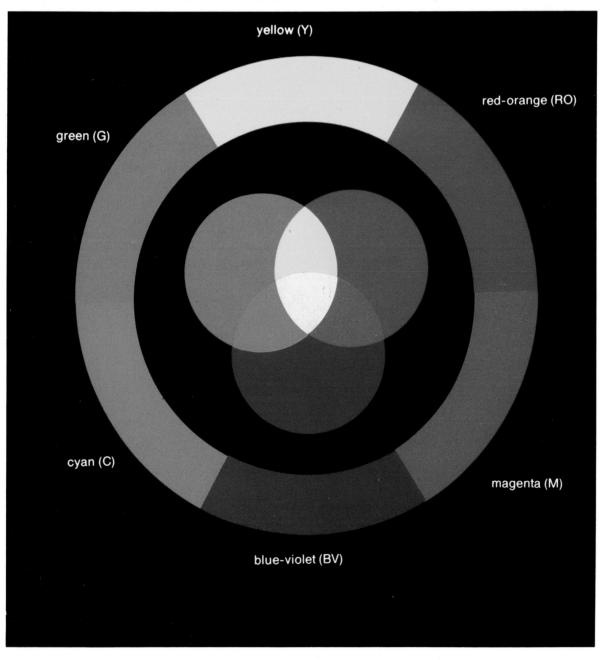

1-3. **The additive mixing of light.**

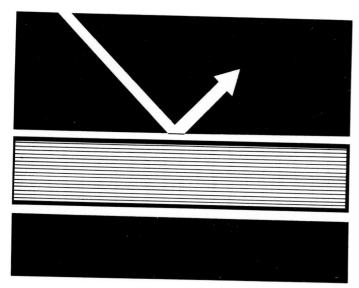

1-4a. reflection

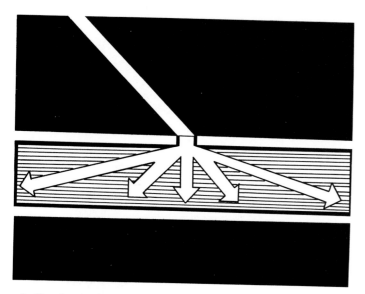

1-4b. absorption

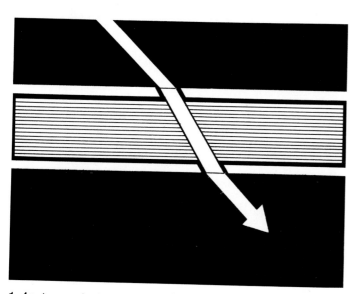

1-4c. transmission

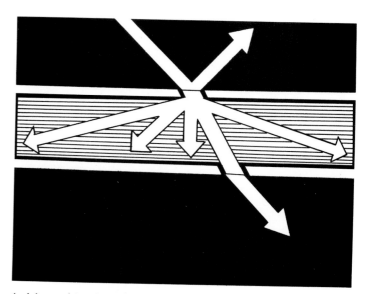

1-4d. combination of reflection, absorption, and transmission

Even if the actual vibrations of light energy were visible, the sensation of color would not be. White can only be broken into its component wavelengths by special structures such as prisms or by substances known as colorants—that is, pigments and dyes.

Pigments are relatively insoluble colored substances that are contained in a liquid medium such as water, oil, or acrylic resin. They are spread over a receiving surface in the way that paint or printing ink is (both are examples of pigments). Dyes, on the other hand, are generally soluble in their vehicle—usually water—and produce color effects by being absorbed into the receiving substance. Both pigments and dyes have molecular structures that reflect, absorb, and transmit specific wavelengths of light easily.

Depending on the particular molecular structure of a colorant and surface, light may be: reflected back to the viewer; absorbed into the molecular surface and dissipated as heat; transmitted through the surface; or subjected to some combination of reflection, absorption, and transmission. One of the three processes always dominates, however, and this in turn produces a specific color effect (see Figure 1-4).

When a surface reflects light in the red part of the visible spectrum and absorbs light in all other parts of it, the color seen is red. Observed colors represent the wavelengths of light reflected by or transmitted through an object—never the wavelengths that are absorbed. These phenomena are known, respectively, as selective or chromatic reflection and selective or chromatic transmission.

1-4. **Surface structure and the behavior of light.**

Black, white, and gray are technically not colors; rather, they are *values.* Grays represent percentages of either reflection or absorption of total available light. A surface having 100 percent absorption appears as opaque black. Such a surface can be described as having 0 percent reflection. If all available light is reflected—that is, if the surface has 100 percent reflection—the surface appears as opaque white and can be described as having 0 percent absorption. Most workers in the visual arts identify grays as percentages of light absorbed. Thus, a 5 percent gray is one that has little total light absorption and is a very light gray, while an 80 percent gray has much more total light absorption and is a dark gray (see Figure 1-5). Black, white, and the various grays demonstrate nonselective or achromatic reflection.

Not only is the visual sensation of color a response to selective and nonselective reflection and transmission, it is a response to the amount or strength of total light present. A color placed in very bright light reflects more total light and consequently looks lighter and somewhat paler than it does in average illumination. The same color placed in very dim light looks duller (that is grayer) and bluer.

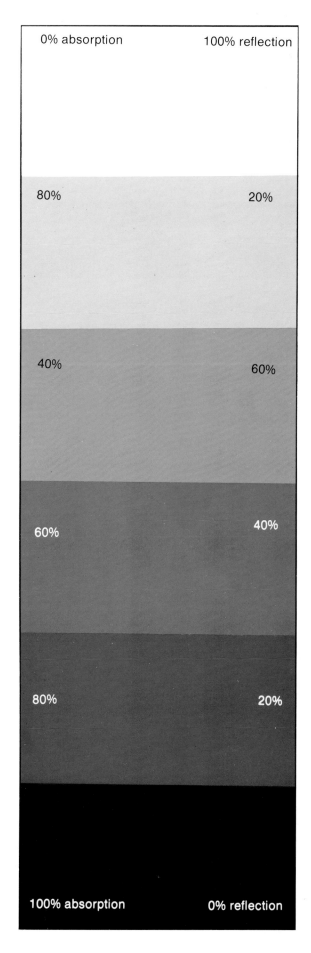

1-5. **Absorption of light, and the value scale (grays represent percentages of absorption of total available light).**

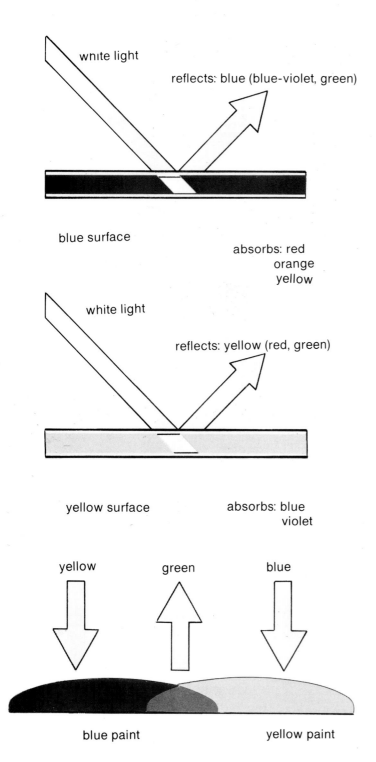

white light

reflects: blue (blue-violet, green)

blue surface

absorbs: red
orange
yellow

white light

reflects: yellow (red, green)

yellow surface

absorbs: blue
violet

yellow green blue

blue paint   yellow paint

1-6. **Subtractive color mixing with paint.**

When paints or dyes are mixed or when transparent or translucent colored substances (such as glass, fiber, or acetate sheets) are overlaid, the resulting color is known as a *subtractive color mixture.* Rather than adding wavelengths of light together to form new colors—as happens with mixtures of colored lights—colorant combinations form new colors by removing or subtracting reflected or transmitted wavelengths of light from the mixture.

When a blue pigment, dye, or transparent material is mixed with a yellow colorant of the same material, the result is a green whose specific character depends on the proportions and qualities of the parent colors. In analyzing this phenomenon, we can reach a clear understanding of the term *subtractive.* A blue colorant absorbs the long (red and orange) wavelengths of visible light, as well as most of the medium (green) wavelengths, while reflecting the shorter (blue) wavelengths predominantly. A quantity of green is reflected, too, but the blue wavelengths dominate, so we see blue. Yellow absorbs the shorter (blue and blue-violet) wavelengths and reflects the middle and longer wavelengths, including red and green, to produce the sensation of yellow (see Figure 1-6). When blue and yellow are mixed, they nullify (subtract) each other's characteristic wavelengths so that the only series of wavelengths consistently reflected—that is, not absorbed or subtracted—is green.

Colored glass, sheets of acetate or gelatin, and photographic filters offer further examples of subtractive mixtures. A magenta filter or any other magenta-colored transparent material allows red and blue wavelengths of light to be transmitted through it, while it absorbs (subtracts) all other (predominantly green) wavelengths that constitute white light; a cyan filter transmits blue and green wavelengths and absorbs red and other longer wavelengths; a yellow filter transmits red and green wavelengths but absorbs blue ones (see Figure 1-7).

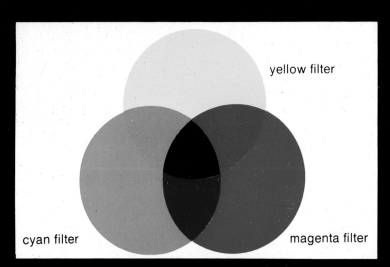

1-8. Subtractive mixing of secondary light hues.

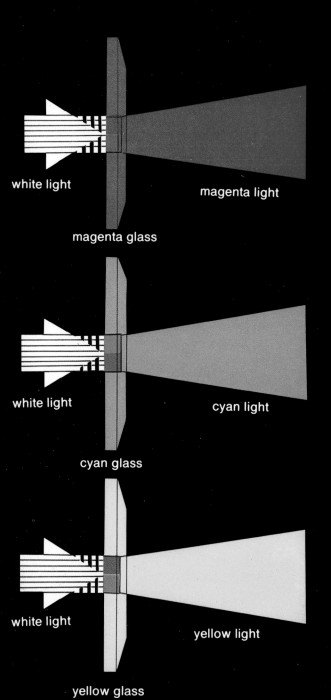

white light

magenta light

magenta glass

white light

cyan light

cyan glass

white light

yellow light

yellow glass

1-7. Filters and subtractive mixing.

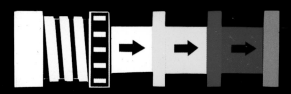

white light is projected through yellow, magenta, and cyan filters

subtracting all wavelengths from the visible spectrum; thus no light is transmitted

These facts contrast markedly with additive mixtures of light, where the projection of these three colors in combination produces white light. If filters of these three colors are placed on a single projector, every wavelength in the visible spectrum is absorbed or subtracted, and no light is transmitted (see Figure 1-8). If these three colors are mixed as pigments or dyes, the same thing happens; the mixture is seen as black because no wavelength remains unabsorbed and able to be reflected back to the viewer.

Structural Colors

Structural colors are produced by the interaction of light with the physical structure of a substance, rather than by the interaction of light with a colorant or with subtractive mixtures of colorants. Structural colors may be classed as iridescent, opalescent, or luminescent. Each has specific color qualities and effects.

Iridescence produces brilliant colors that shine and glitter with constantly changing spectral or rainbow hues as the viewer's angle of vision changes. These colors sometimes appear metallic, simulating the reflectance of bronze, copper, and gold.

Opalescence is a cloudy version of iridescence, more delicate and translucent in appearance. Although spectral hues do appear in opalescent material, they may be dark and glowing or pale and milky. The name originated as a descriptive term for the milky quality of colors found in the opal.

Luminescence means specifically "light without heat," but it is used generally to describe light and color emanating from an object that lacks any evident light or color source. The color effects are often brilliant and glow with an eerie, unreal quality.

The color effects of iridescence and opalescence are produced by the action of three types of light behavior: refraction diffraction, and interference.

Refraction, the bending of light as it passes from one medium such as air to another such as glass, has already been discussed in Newton's classic experiment. The structure of a prism causes light to be refracted and separated into its component wavelengths; violet wavelengths are bent the most, red wavelengths are bent the least, and the other spectral or prismatic hues fall at various locations in-between. The most dramatic example of natural refraction is the rainbow. Its colors are formed by light refracted through billions of water droplets, which act as tiny prisms refracting light from a single source in one direction.

Diffraction is the deflection or spreading of light as it passes through closely situated, equidistant lines or slits. These structures, known as diffraction gratings, break a beam of light into individual wavelengths, thereby making spectral hues visible (see Figure 1-9). The intense metallic colors of brilliant iridescence seen in some birds are produced by the diffraction of light through millions of slits or holes in the feathers. The minute, regularly stacked impurities in an opal act as a diffraction grating that produces color variations as the angle of vision changes.

Refraction and diffraction produce the same color effects; only the physical structures causing them are different.

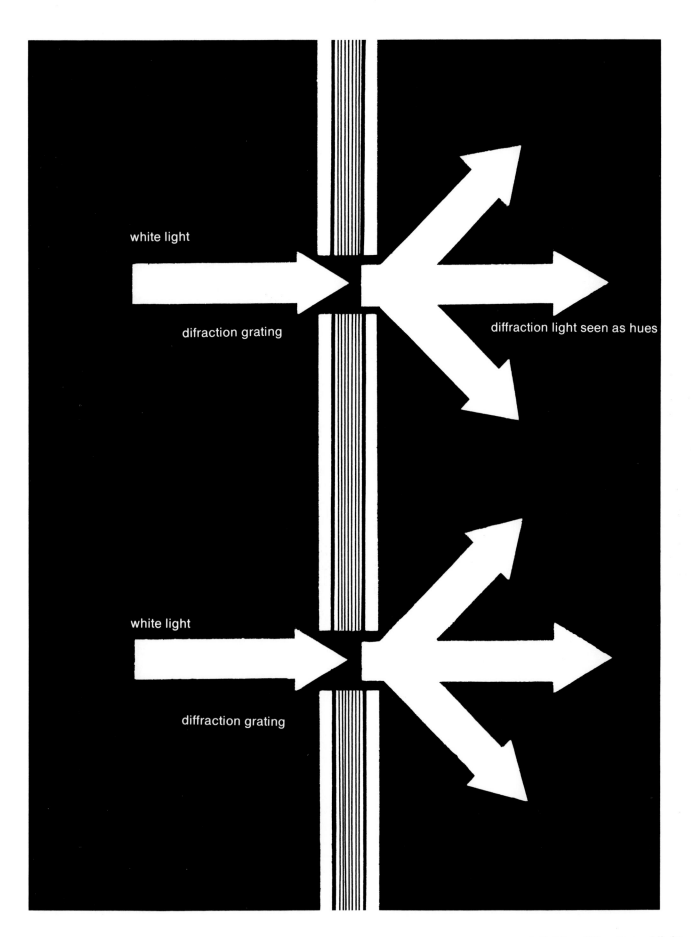

white light

difraction grating

diffraction light seen as hues

white light

diffraction grating

1-9. **The diffraction of light.**

Interference is a term used to describe the interaction of different wavelengths of light. A good analogy for light-wave interference is the behavior of water waves at the beach or along a river. If two waves move together with the same frequency, with the same length, and with their peaks and troughs coinciding, they reinforce each other and produce a stronger, more intense wave. On the other hand, if two waves meet, and the peak of one coincides with the trough of the other, they cancel each other. If the peaks and troughs just miss, neither coinciding with nor canceling each other, the result is a weakened wave.

Light waves behave in the same way. Whenever waves of light interfere with one another—by reinforcing, weakening, or canceling each other—different spectral hues appear as stronger, weaker, or colorless areas that change with the angle of vision. Light hitting an oil film on water is an example of interference. Some light is reflected from the upper surface of the film, and some from the lower surface (see Figure 1-10). The two sets of light waves interfere with one another so that individual waves reflected at one point in a given direction are strengthened, weakened, or canceled and different spectral hues appear. Interference can also occur with prolonged beams of light just as it does with single waves. When interference patterns of this nature are produced by reinforced or canceled beams, the effect is a light-dark pattern and patterns of hue change.

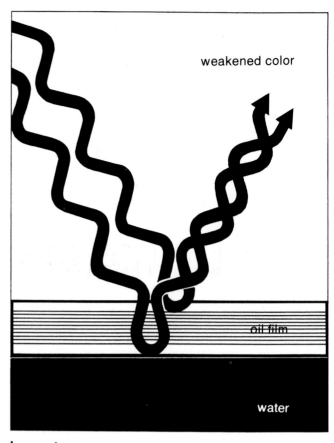

b. weakened waves;

1-10. **Interference:**

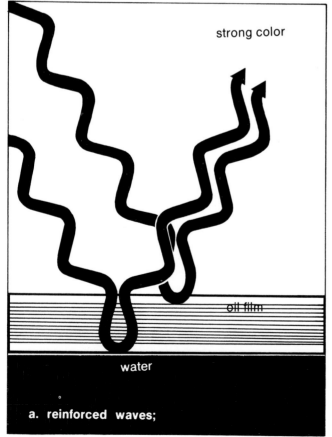

a. reinforced waves;

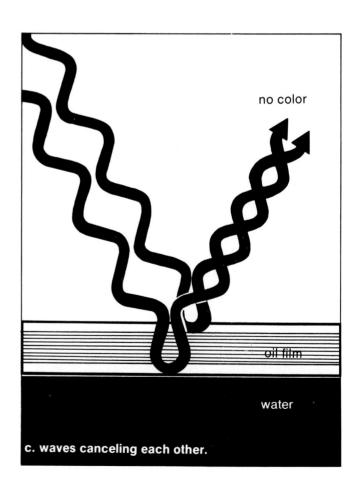

c. waves canceling each other.

20

Luminescence results from light and color effects produced by chemical and electrical activity as well as by the interaction of light and physical structure. Two common examples of luminescence are fluorescence and phosphorescence.

Solids, liquids, and gases that have the ability to emit visible light only while absorbing some other kind of electromagnetic radiation, such as ultraviolet light, are said to be *fluorescent*. Fluorescent lighting tubes make use of this phenomenon to produce white or colored light; the tubes are coated internally with a fluorescent material that emits light when the mercury vapor inside the tubes gives off ultraviolet radiation.

Fluorescent material can be added to paints and dyes. The fluorescent colorants then absorb invisible ultraviolet rays present in sunlight and emit longer wavelengths that we see as color. When this fluorescent material is added to the regular color of a paint or dye, it creates a color whose luminosity and brilliance cannot be matched by conventional colorants. These colors eventually lose their fluorescent quality, however, so permanence is a problem. Day-Glo colors and certain dyes found in marking pens are excellent examples of fluorescent materials; when used appropriately, they produce exciting color effects.

Phosphorescence is fluorescence that continues to glow for a period of time after the radiation that caused it has ceased to bombard it. Materials known as phosphors exhibit this characteristic and can be found in some minerals that continue to glow in the dark for a period of time after being exposed to ultraviolet light. Various tiny organisms that live in the ocean and on certain fish also contain phosphors in their bodies; the term *bioluminescence* is generally applied to light emitted from an organism, regardless of the nature of its production.

The majority of structural colors are found in the natural world. The most prevalent are the iridescent feathers of such birds as peafowl and ring-necked pheasants. Reptile and fish scales and the bodies and wings of specific insects (particularly butterflies) also show startling color effects that are produced only by structure and light.

The hardened nacreous material found on the insides of shells and known as mother-of-pearl offers one of the most striking displays of opalescence found anywhere. Some shells have opalescent exteriors—again composed of layers of nacre through which light is reflected and refracted.

Often refraction, diffraction, and interference work together. Narrow slits not only produce colors by means of diffraction of light from a light source, they can also refract light reflected from a nearby structure. The refracted waves may then interfere with waves diffracted by another slit, and so on. The myriad microscopic structures found in nature produce a limitless array of structural color.

The light quality produced by different types of light—such as daylight, artificial light, and secondary reflections—influences the way we see surface color.

Most light sources, when analyzed, show a continuous spectrum; that is, all wavelengths of the visible spectrum are present. But except for white light, which shows a balance of all wavelengths, different kinds of light show a *dominance* or greater proportion of wavelengths in one part of the spectrum, producing light that has a particular color quality. The wavelengths dominant in a particular light source will enhance or reinforce colors that are similar in character to the light and will dull colors that are dissimilar. When a red surface is seen under the light of an ordinary incandescent bulb (tungsten illumination), the red appears to be a richer, redder color because tungsten light has a dominance of longer or red wavelengths. When the same red surface is seen under a fluorescent light source, which has a dominance of shorter or blue wavelengths, the red will appear duller because the quantity of red wavelengths to be reflected back by the color are simply not present in the light.

Light that reinforces red, orange, and yellow colorants is described as *warm* light; light that enhances blue, green, and violet colorants is described as *cool* light.

DAYLIGHT

Daylight is excellent for viewing color because all the wavelengths in the visible spectrum are balanced. Any color can be viewed accurately, and the light level is comfortable—neither too bright nor too dim—making optimum selective reflection of all colors possible. Individual variations in daylight still show balanced light but tend to shift the spectrum to some degree. Hence, pure sunlight is relatively warm and glaring, while pure northlight is cooler. A mixture of northlight and open sky tends to be the coolest in quality because atmospheric particles such as dust, water, pollution, and air molecules scatter light of wavelengths closer to the blue and violet end of the spectrum.

At sunrise and sunset, daylight is quite distorted toward the red end of the spectrum. The sunlight must travel through more layers of atmospheric pollution containing large particles that absorb the shorter wavelengths of the spectrum and leave mostly the longer wavelengths visible. This accounts for the red quality of daylight at these hours.

ARTIFICIAL LIGHT

The term *artificial light* applies to several types of illumination. The type most frequently encountered is the incandescent tungsten light—the ordinary household light bulb with the screw-in base. This type of bulb, no matter what its wattage, is deficient in blue wavelengths and has a dominance in the orange-red part of the spectrum; this is because the filament responsible for the bulb's light emits white light whose spectrum—although continuous—does not match that of sunlight, but is weighted toward the longer wavelengths.

The only way an incandescent light can be made to simulate daylight is if a blue coating is placed on the interior surface of the bulb or if the bulb is made of blue glass. The resulting "daylight" bulbs have a color quality that is less warm but still does not equal that of full-spectrum daylight. The warm colors, red-oranges and yellows, are greatly enhanced by incandescent lighting; the cool colors, blue-greens and blue-violets, are dulled by it.

Another source of artificial light is the fluorescent tube. Manufacturers produce a warm tube, which has a pink quality, and a cool or white tube, which appears much cooler or bluer. Neither tube is an adequate substitute for full-spectrum light. At present, Westinghouse, General Electric and Duro-Lite make full-spectrum fluorescent lighting; other companies may also have begun producing such tubes. The light from these fluorescent tubes simulates daylight quality so well that, although the light is of artificial origin, color assessment and control in the studio are quite accurate.

Another way of approximating full-spectrum light is to combine light from an incandescent bulb with light from a cool fluorescent tube or any combination of warm and cool light. Fixtures that accomodate this arrangement can be purchased in large art supply stores.

Two other common types of artificial light are the sodium-vapor lamp, and the mercury-discharge lamp. The sodium-vapor lamp, most often used for highway and street lighting, gives low-level lighting that is yellow in character. Sodium-vapor light consists entirely of wavelengths contained in a narrow yellow band of the spectrum, representing the light emitted when sodium is vaporized. The light therefore shows a discontinuous spectrum, and—although it has the property of cutting through fog and mist—it is entirely unsuitable for color rendering or identification.

The mercury-discharge lamp is also used for highway and street lighting. This light produces a discontinuous spectrum of yellow, green, and blue-violet; thus, even though the light level is considerably higher than in the case of sodium-vapor lamps, color distortion is a problem. Reds and oranges are very difficult to see accurately (if at all), and blues become unusually intense, acquiring an almost luminescent quality. Sometimes these lamps are used for general illumination in public places and office buildings. The level of illumination is good, but the effect on people is poor: color evaluation is impossible, and by the end of the day most people suffer from headaches and irritability.

The Color Temperature of Light

When a piece of metal is heated, its atoms and molecules become very active. As the heat rises, they strike each other with more and more force and produce an electromagnetic emission that is first sensed as heat or infrared radiation. If the heat is increased, the wavelength distribution shifts from the infrared parts of the great spectrum to the red area of the visible spectrum, and a faint glow is perceptible. As the object gets hotter and hotter, the energy output becomes greater, the wavelengths shorten, and the perceived color moves from red through the visible spectrum colors to blue and eventually to white.

The color quality of such light (that is, its wavelength distribution) is measured by its color temperature, which is expressed in degrees Kelvin, or kelvins. The Kelvin scale begins at absolute zero (0° K, equivalent to -273° C), the temperature at which theoretically, neither molecular motion nor light exists. Color temperature is used as a color index to describe light emitted from a specific source; it is not necessarily the same as the actual temperature of the source. For example, the color temperature of a daylight fluorescent tube may be rated at 5,500° K, meaning that the color quality of the light emitted by the tube imitates the color quality from a superheated blue-white source whose temperature is 5,500° K. The actual heat generated by the tube itself, however, is much less.

Light sources such as fluorescent tubing are often described in advertising according to their Kelvin temperatures. Since the Kelvin rating is an index of color, the consumer can use this rating to predict how surface color will be affected by a particular light; thus, accurate or distorted color rendering becomes possible. Color temperatures for various types of light are given in figure 1-11.

Light source	Temperature (° K)
Glowing hot plate—dark red	800°
Glowing hot plate—orange	1,200°
40-watt incandescent (tungsten) light bulb	2,650°
75-watt incandescent (tungsten) light bulb	2,800°
100-watt incandescent (tungsten) light bulb	2,900°
Sunrise and/or sunset	3,100°
Photographic (quartz) floodlights	3,200°
Photographic tungsten lights	3,400°
Daylight (b1/b2) Incandescent	3,500°
Photoflood	3,800°
(Vary with use)	
One hour before sunset	3,600°
One hour after sunrise	3,600°
Two hours before sunset	3,900°
Two hours after sunrise	3,900°
Northlight and sunlight mixed, called daylight	5,500°
Color temperature of full-spectrum	5,300-5,700°
daylight fluorescent tubes	
(also photographic daylight)	
Overcast sky	7,000°
Bright, clear open sky	10,000°

1-11. **Color temperatures in degrees Kelvin (approximate), showing color shifts from dark red to high-value blue.**

Lighting and Perception

The color quality and intensity levels of light change repeatedly in our daily lives, but we nevertheless see colors in a remarkably consistent way. This phenomenon, called color constancy, is due in great part to our sense of recall: we tend to remember colors as we have seen them in daylight. Other factors, such as space discrimination, movement, and association, also play a part in color constancy, however, so the total impression we form of a color is a combination of conscious and unconscious elements. If we lacked color constancy, our visual world would become a jumble of altered colors every time a light source changed.

A red apple shows little apparent color change when seen separately under daylight, incandescent lighting, and fluorescent lighting. The color shifts become easily recognizable when simultaneous comparisons are made, however, having a subtle influence on emotional response in the viewer. A red illuminated by cool fluorescent lighting may appear red when viewed in isolation, but the red effect is dulled considerably and lacks the emotional impact it has when seen under a warm light.

When illumination is reduced, no matter what the light source, warm colors tend to be cooled. Reds appear more violet or gray, oranges move toward grays and browns, and yellows shift to greens and grays. This visual adaptation to low light levels occurs as the result of a specific response by light-sensitive nerve cells in the eye and is known as the Purkinje shift. The human eye possesses two types of light-sensitive nerve cells (or photoreceptors), known because of their shapes as rods and cones. These cells are found in the retina—the netlike membrane at the back of the eye, which acts as a screen and transmitting device for sending electrical impulses (stimulated by light and color) to the brain. The cones enable us to see color and fine detail; they operate when the level of light is moderate to high. The rods make colorless and low-light vision possible and are sensitive to blues, greens, and violets. The Purkinje shift is a change from vision based on the cone photoreceptors to vision based on the rod photoreceptors.

The fiber artist can augment or diminish the color effect of a work by accommodating or ignoring the type and level of illumination used in producing and exhibiting it. Ideally, a work should be produced and exhibited in the same kind of light, so as to avoid unplanned color distortions. Unfortunately, that is not always possible, and problems often arise because of drastic changes in lighting conditions. The fiber artist who creates a work in the studio under daylight conditions and then exhibits the piece under fluorescent light will notice marked differences; and even though the casual viewer may not be aware of these differences, the work's expressive impact will be changed to some extent.

The phenomenon of varying illumination and its effects on color cannot safely be dismissed as unimportant or too technical. Understanding these matters is an essential ingredient in esthetic color control.

Chapter 2

Reflected Color

Reflected color can be discussed in terms of four characteristics: *hue, value, intensity,* and *temperature.* These properties of color are not isolated phenomena, but appear simultaneously in every color.

This chapter analyzes each of the four characteristics separately and then considers them in combination, to reinforce the point that they work together and can be carefully orchestrated. In fact, working with color is strikingly similar to making music, where tonalties, harmonies, and texture are woven together to produce a desired effect.

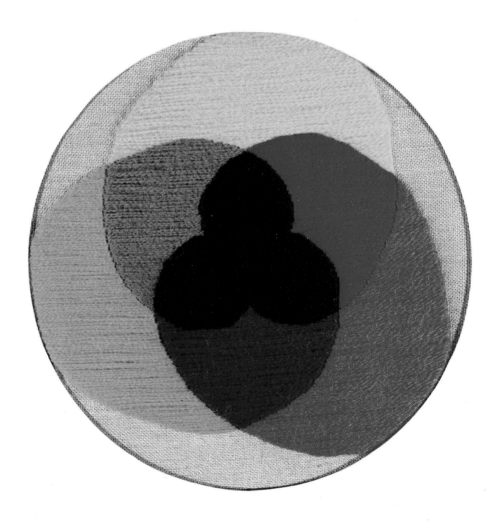

2-1. Light secondaries (magenta, yellow, and cyan) as pigment primaries.
Design Execution: Mary Fry
Photo: Patricia Lambert

Hue

Although the words *color* and *hue* are often used as synonyms, this is not entirely accurate. *Color* is a broad term referring to any color sensation. *Hue* is more specific and has two definitions: first, the quality of a color that identifies it by family or color quality, such as a color *with* a blue hue or a color with a yellow hue; second, a totally pure color to which nothing has been added that would alter its purity. By this second definition, a colorant *is* a red hue and theoretically reflects only red wavelengths of light, absorbing other wavelengths that would adulterate the purity of the red.

When reference is made to a color *with* a red-violet hue, a classification by color quality has been made, but nothing more precise about the nature of the color has been established. To say a color *is* a red-violet hue not only classifies it by color quality but also asserts that it is a pure color—that it is as close to a spectral hue as is possible in a reflected color.

Modern technology has enabled physicists to isolate, amplify, and project single wavelengths of light by means of a laser (an acronym for Light Amplification of Stimulated Emission of Radiation). The color produced by a laser is totally pure and unbelievably brilliant. Colorants and surfaces can only approximate this dazzling purity.

All colorants contain some degree of impurity, the amount of which depends on source and manufacturer. All such impurities reflect light from parts of the spectrum other than that of the dominant wavelength seen, tending to dull the hue somewhat. For their intended purposes, however, colorant hues are completely satisfactory and can be considered pure.

The traditional method of teaching basic color theory to people who use colorants begins with the premise that the primary hues are red, blue, and yellow. The identification of these colors as primaries is not based on light hues but on the fact that people discovered centuries ago that red, blue, and yellow could not be made by mixing other hues or colors together. Because orange, green, and violet could be made with mixtures of red/yellow, blue/yellow, and red/blue, respectively, they were called the colorant secondaries.

This traditional colorant hue circle is only an approximation of the spectral hue circle, however. Consequently using red, blue, and yellow as complements to green, orange, and violet does not produce true subtractive complementary mixes; that is, a mixture of any of these complementary pairs does not yield a true black. The results of such complementary combinations are better described as chromatic neutrals—neutrals that, when compared to black-and-white mixtures, appear still to have a trace of color.

Red/green, blue/orange, and yellow/violet are quite beautiful color pairs, and we do not suggest dismissing the traditional hue circle altogether. The relationship of light hue to colorant hue is more readily understandable, however, if the two types of hue are seen as mirror images. A colorant hue circle based on the light (or additive) secondaries—yellow, magenta, and cyan—as colorant (or subtractive) primaries provides this kind of image (see Figure 2-1). The colorant secondaries are then the light primaries: red-orange, green, and blue-violet. The true complements for colorants are thus the same as those for light: magenta/green, cyan/red-orange, and yellow/blue-violet. When all three subtractive primaries, (additive secondaries) are mixed, they produce a true black. For purposes of mixing, the hue circle based on the subtractive primaries gives a more accurate and consistent result in producing color than any other.

2-2. Twenty-four-hue circle based on R (red), Y (yellow), and B (blue) (the RYB system).

Dyer: Antonia Kormos
Photo: Patricia Lambert)

The illustration of the traditional hue circle in Figure 2-2 includes twenty-four hues, of which three are primary, red, yellow and blue (R, Y, B), three are secondary, orange, green and violet (O, G, V), and eighteen are intermediaries. There are three intermediaries between each primary and secondary hue. The decision to represent twenty-four hues is arbitrary, and the total might well be reduced to eighteen hues or fewer.

Figure 2-3 illustrates an eighteen-hue circle based on the MYC system. The circle consists of three primaries, magenta, yellow and cyan (M, Y, C), three secondaries, red, blue and green (R, B, G), and twelve intermediaries. The advantages of making hue circles as reference tools are numerous. A hue circle establishes a consistent measure of the variations of hue within a single family or across a group of hues having one hue in common (for example, BG, GBG, G,

2-3. **Eighteen-hue circle based on M (magenta), Y (yellow), and C (cyan) (the MYC system).**

Dyer: Antonia Kormos
Photo: Patricia Lambert

GYG, and so on). The reminder a hue circle provides of subtle color shifts encourages maximum use of the expressive qualities of hue by the artist/designer. For dyers especially, frequent reference to the MYC hue circle is extremely useful.

Contiguous hues on the circle and hues closely related to one another—such as a green, green-blue-green, and yellow-green—are referred to as *analogs* or *analogous hues.* Hues that lie directly across the circle from one another are called *complements* or *complementary hues.* The traditional pigment complements are violet/yellow, red/green, and blue/orange. A pigment primary lies opposite a pigment secondary, just as a light primary lies opposite a light secondary. Any pair of hues lying opposite one another (in either system) contains all three primaries; in the additive system of colored lights they combine to create white while in the subtractive system of colorants they combine to create black.

Two definitions of the term *tertiary color* are in use today. The first and most widely used of these defines a tertiary as a combination of the three primary hues (either RYB or MYC) produced by adding two secondary hues. In the RYB system, combinations of orange and green yield a series of tertiary colors that vary based on the amount of each secondary hue used; combinations of violet and orange or of violet and green yield comparable series (see Figure 2-4). In the MYC system, the shifts produce slight variations from the RYB mixes—for example, combinations of red-orange and green or of green and blue-violet in place of combinations of orange and green or of green and violet. Even though these shifts are slight, the color variations that result are subtly and quite beautifully different.

The second (and less accurate) definition of a tertiary is the hue that lies between a primary and a secondary on the hue circle. Yellow-orange, which falls halfway between yellow and orange on the RYB circle, is a tertiary of this sort. More commonly, however, these hues are called *intermediaries,* and in this text, the term *tertiary* is only used to mean a mix of two secondaries or all three primaries.

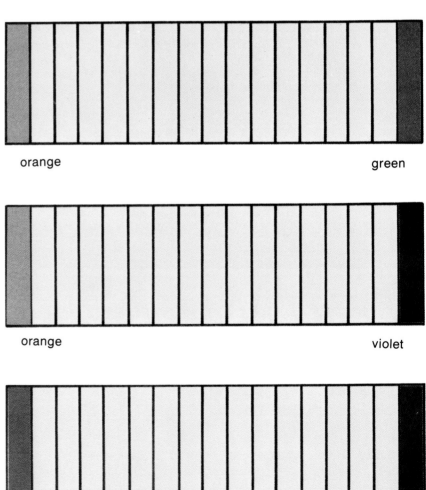

orange   green

orange   violet

2-4. **a. Step scales of tertiary colors mixed from secondaries in the RYB system.**

green   violet

28

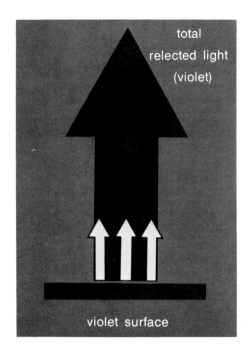

violet surface

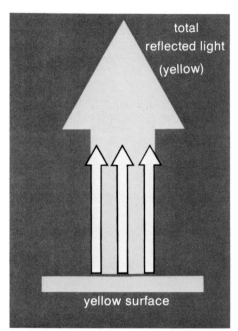

yellow surface

2-5. **Reflected light: a. violet surface; b. yellow surface.**

Value

In addition to selectively reflecting wavelengths of light, colors have the property of reflecting light nonselectively. For example, yellow as a surface color has a high degree of reflectance (or low absorption); the surface not only selectively reflects wavelengths of light which produce a yellow sensation, it also reflects a high percentage of the total light hitting the surface, absorbing very little of it (see Figure 2-5). The hue perceived is yellow, but if the hue (or selective reflection) is removed, what remains is a very light gray, representing only the total level of light actually reflected (or absorbed). The gray that has the same light reflectance as the yellow is known as the *relative value* of yellow.

Every hue has a relative value, or specific degree of lightness or darkness, described as a gray that falls between the limits of white and black. Value is therefore, the degree of lightness or darkness possessed by a color. Black, white, and all grays are values that contain no hue (see Figure 2-6).

2-6. **Value scale of rug samples.**
Weaver/Dyer: Antonia Kormos
Photo: Patricia Lambert

Many other words in the literature of color are used as synonyms of value: *tone, shade, luminosity, brightness, lightness,* and *grayness.* Unfortunately, these words have confusing alternate meanings and moreover, are often used incorrectly. *Tone* is commonly used in a very general way, but in colorant usage its precise meaning is a hue mixed with its relative value. When a person speaks of a tone, the reference is often to a color that has been grayed; but this speaks to the purity of the color, rather than to its value. *Shade* means a hue or color mixed with black. This makes specific reference to a color's being changed by getting darker, so in part it is accurate, but it does not include the case of a color that becomes lighter. *Luminosity* and *brightness* are also general descriptive terms that can be easily misunderstood. They usually refer not to lightness and darkness but to purity.

The importance of value as a color characteristic cannot be overemphasized. In design, the aesthetic effect of a value is relative rather than absolute. Values change their apparent quality of lightness and darkness depending on the other values that surround them (see Figure 2-7). When a gray is placed on white it looks darker than when it is placed on black. A dark gray and a light gray can be made to look almost the same if the former is placed on a value that makes it appear lighter and the latter is placed on a value that makes it appear darker.

2-7. Four values look like six (black work).
Artist: Mary Fry
Photo: Patricia Lambert

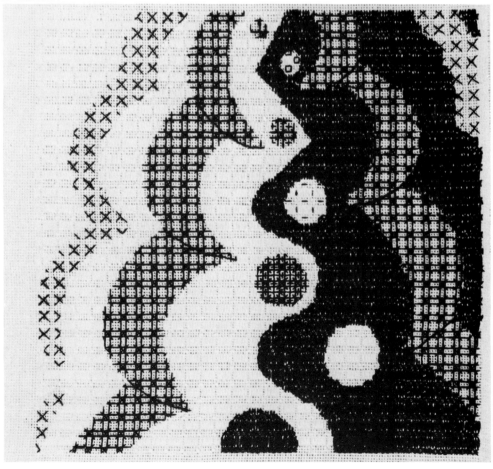

An effective beginning to a complete understanding of value is an acquaintance with the value scale—a gradation of grays from black to white (also known as a gray or achromatic scale) that constitutes a vital tool in designing with color. People who use pigments, inks, and dyes usually refer to the scale in terms of absorption rather than of reflection. White has 0 percent absorption; it represents the case in which no light is absorbed and all light is reflected. White is therefore a 0 percent value, while black is a 100 percent value. If a small amount of black pigment or dye is added to white, a light gray is produced because a small amount of total light is absorbed. This gray may then be described as a 5 or 10 percent value. Through close comparison to a calibrated value scale, the description of the value becomes quite accurate.

Percentages refer to the amount of black added to produce a value change from white toward black. An 80 percent value is a dark gray, and a 10 percent value is a light gray. The descriptive terms *high/light* and *low/dark* refer to the overall feeling of light that the value represents. The greater the percentage of dark (proportion of black) the lower the light effect; the smaller the percentage of dark, the higher the light effect. The following percentages are approximations only: Values ranging from white (0 percent) to 25 percent are called high or light values; those from 25 to 50 percent are referred to as high-middle; those from 50 to 75 percent are called low-middle; and those from 75 percent to black (100 percent) are referred to as low or dark values (see Figure 2-8).

In order to control values with the greatest ease and understanding, it is helpful to think of the value scale as a gauge of the quantity of light present in a design and of the psychological changes these light levels produce. Changes in light levels cause changes in mood. Sunlight or bright artificial light often stimulates a feeling of well-being. The light on a gray overcast day—or even at dusk or twilight—calms, quiets, and perhaps depresses. The darkness of night can be mysterious, frightening, depressing, or comforting, depending on the individual. These various light levels can be represented by values organized according to the subliminal effect they have on the viewer. Value relationships that produce specific light-level effects are termed *value keys;* they may also be expressed as types of mood or tonality.

The value key of a work describes the first impression of the relationship between lightness and darkness in an artwork; it thus refers to an emotional response evoked independently of the hues or colors used. The response of the viewer is to light level, and then to hue. For this reason, understanding values and their relationships is an extremely valuable tool in producing work that is fully controlled, both intellectually and intuitively.

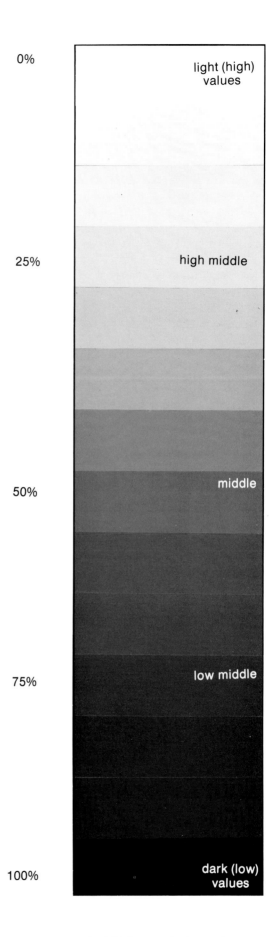

0%

25%

50%

75%

100%

light (high) values

high middle

middle

low middle

dark (low) values

2-8. **Value scale (paper).**

Value keys fall into two categories, major and minor, akin to the major and minor tonalities in music. In the visual arts, a major key shows great contrast or large intervals between values. The full range of values from black to white is represented, even if only a few specific values are used (see Figure 2-9). Major keys, as in music, tend to be *bold, dramatic,* and *stable.* The major keys also show a dominance or greater proportion of one particular value or group of values.

The three major keys are classified as high major, middle major, and low major. A high major key shows a dominance of light or high values; works done in this key tend to be luminous and happy. The middle major key shows a dominance of values falling into the middle range of the value scale, and its overall feeling is strong and well-balanced. The low major key shows a dominance of values in the low or dark end of the value scale; as a result, it tends to produce mysterious, somber, and dramatic effects.

2-9. **Schematic illustration of major keys.**

high major: high-value dominance

middle major: middle-value dominance

low major: low-value dominance

32

The minor keys, unlike the majors, do not cover the full value scale. Instead, they consist of organizations of closely related values within a specific limited range. Consequently, less value contrast is present in the minor keys (see Figure 2-10), and their emotional impact is more subdued.

The four groups of minor keys are: high minor, middle minor, extended middle minor, and low minor (see Figure 2-11). The high minor takes its values exclusively from the high or light end of the value scale; the effect of this key in design is *delicate, atmospheric,* and *serene.* The middle minor takes values from the midrange of the value scale, and its feeling too is atmospheric but with a quality more reminiscent of twilight or an unreal dreamlike condition. Words such as *slumber, peace, fog,* and *calm* describe this midrange minor key. The low minor feeling has been called sinister, evil, depressed, gloomy, and funereal. The fourth minor key, extended middle minor, is a middle minor that has been pulled out to some degree in the direction of black-and-white. It is a middle minor key with slightly greater contrast than the middle minor; as a result, it loses some of its serenity but does not become as visually strong as a middle major. A questioning ambiguity premeates the sense of light it evokes, suggesting a feeling of fantasy, mystery, or surrealism.

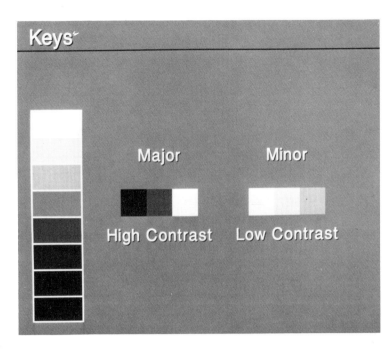

2-10. **Keys.**

high minor: closely related high values

low minor: closely related low values

middle minor: closely related middle values

extended middle minor

2-11. **Schematic illustration of minor keys.**

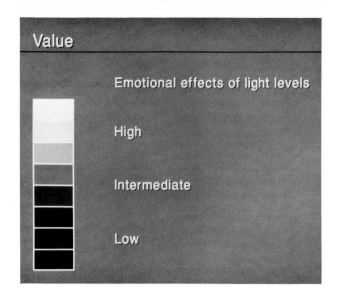

Value

Emotional effects of light levels

High

Intermediate

Low

2-12. **Value, light level, and mood.**

a. **Major Keys**

High	=	Positive, Stimulating, Happy
Middle	=	Strong, Posteresque, Rich, Open, Direct
Low	=	Dignified, Theatrical, Dramatic, Ponderous

b. **Minor Keys**

High	=	Delicate, Atmospheric
Middle	=	Surreal, Dreamlike
Low	=	Funereal, Somber, Depressed

2-13. **Keys and subliminal messages: a. major; b. minor.**

Human beings react to light and light contrasts on both a conscious level and an unconscious level. A viewer responds to the value organization of a visual work in the same way, seeing the value contrasts immediately and translating them into mood. As might be expected, the sense of key or light level is highly individual. Some people respond most strongly to major keys; others, to minor keys. There is no right or wrong response.

Frequently, people try to correct color design problems by dealing with hue alone without considering value. But problems that arise in planning a design are often solvable through early and careful consideration of the value relationships; color problems are often value problems.

a.

b.

34

c.

f.

d.

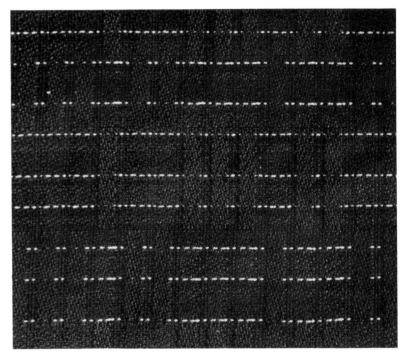

g

e.

2-14. **Weaving samples illustrating keys: a. high minor; b. middle minor; c. low minor; d. extended middle minor; e. high major; f. middle major; g. low major.**

Weaver: Melissa Seligman
Photos: Patricia Lambert

Intensity relates to the purity of a color. By definition, a hue is a fully intense or pure color. No black, white, gray, or complementary color has been added to the hue to "break it" or make it duller. If anything is added, the intensity of the hue changes, and the intensity is said to be lowered or broken. Common synonyms for *intensity* are *purity, saturation, strength, brightness,* and *chroma.*

The comparison of pure-and-impure or of bright-and-dull is a relative one; the only absolutes are 100 percent (a fully intense hue) and 0 percent (its relative value) (see Figure 2-15).

Because relative intensity is a subtle characteristic, it is most easily seen in a comparison of one color with another color having the same hue but having a different degree of intensity. A color that appears quite intense next to a gray may appear very dull next to a hue (see Figure 2-16).

The intensity of a hue can be lowered or broken in any of five ways:

2-15. **Intensity gradation, from hue at 100 percent to relative value at 0 percent.**

Weaver/Dyer: Antonia Kormos
Photo: Patricia Lambert

2-16. **The relativity of intensity.**

Dyer: Antonia Kormos
Photo: Patricia Lambert

2-17.Tinting to white.

Dyer: Antonia Kormos
Photo: Patricia Lambert

2-18. Shading to black.

Dyer: Antonia Kormos
Photo: Patricia Lambert

1. Tinting, or the addition of white to a color (see Figure 2-17). In dyeing, the dilution needed to achieve a color lighter than the original color of the dye.
2. Shading, or the addition of black to a color (see Figure 2-18). In dyeing, the addition of black is used to achieve a color effect darker than the original hue or color.
3. Direct modulating, or the addition of the complement to a color (see Figure 2-19). When this is done according to a scale showing the progression of the mix, it is called a direct complementary modulation.

2-19. Direct modulation of complements, showing tints of mid-range.

Dyer: Antonia Kormos
Photo: Patricia Lambert

4. Indirect modulating, or the mixture of two hues in the course of which a temperature change occurs (see Figure 2-10). Such mixtures exist when two hues containing hue complements—or when combinations of two hues that together contain all three pigment primaries—are present. This may seem to be no more than an extension or embellishment of 3., but actually it is a more subtle way of changing intensity.

5. Toning, or the addition of grays or the relative value of the color (see Figure 2-21). Fiber-blending a hue and its relative value is an excellent way of reducing the intensity of a color without changing its value. Other methods of toning include overdying yarn with a dilute solution of black, and selecting a color of yarn that has a definite gray quality to use with the hue of the same value (this also gives a tonal range).

Figure 2-21 demonstrates a tonal scale of red, starting at 100 percent intensity (on the left) and moving toward its relative value of pure gray, through decreasing intensities of the red, until no hue remains. By squinting at the tonal scale and the woven example of intensity gradation, the reader can see that all the values are the same. A tonal gradation of a hue to its relative value is the only way of lowering intensity (and thereby producing new color effects) without changing value or hue. It is neither necessary nor advisable to restrict the use of lowered intensities to tones of a hue or color—although these can be very beautiful.

2-20. Indirect modulation: yellow to red-violet.
Dyer: Antonia Kormos
Photo: Patricia Lambert

2-21. Toning, from hue to relative value.
Dyer: Antonia Kormos
Photo: Patricia Lambert

38

Temperature

The term *color temperature* is used to describe color produced either by light or by colorants. The color temperature of light is an important tool for the fiber artist because the appearance of a color under a given light can be adjusted to satisfy specific requirements. The color temperature of a colorant is a different phenomenon, one to which we respond intuitively or by association. This can be controlled consciously to broaden aesthetic effects.

The temperature of a reflected color is defined as its apparent *warmth* or *coolness* in relation to another color. Traditionally, warm and cool colors have been defined in absolute terms—yellow, orange, and red representing warmth, and green, blue, and violet representing coolness. Typically, the red-to-violet and yellow-to-green segments of the RYB hue circle were either ignored or described as temperate colors,

neither warm nor cool. These segments of the hue circle do contain elements of both warm and cool colors. The quality of a red-violet-red (RVR) becomes less red and more blue as the hues migrate toward violet; the quality of the yellow-green-yellow (YGY) becomes less yellow and more blue as the hue becomes more green.

The relativity of the hues in the red-to-violet segment is illustrated in figure 2-22. There, the two red-violets shown are of exactly the same hue, but their appearance seems altered because one modulates to orange and the other to blue. Is red-violet a warm hue or a cool one? The same exercise can be done with any other hues, but those exhibiting the greatest degree of change will be hues combining primaries and secondaries. This is an important point to consider when dealing with the quality of color temperature in fiber design. It can be misleading and costly to assume that a color will always give the same feeling of warmth or coolness, regardless of its physical context.

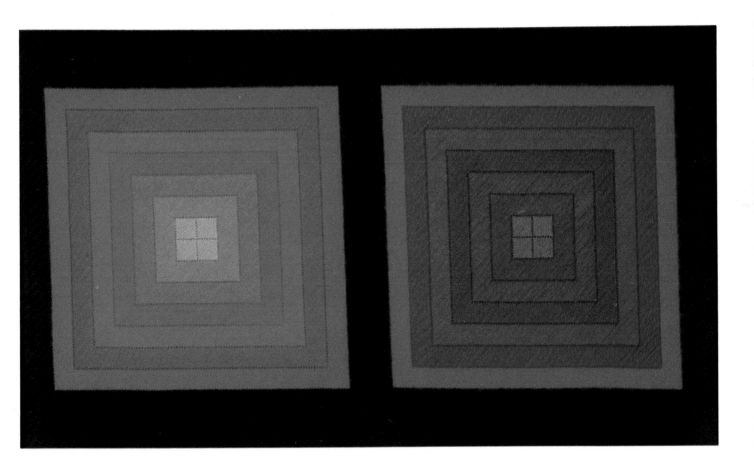

2-22. **The relativity of temperature: red-violet changes in apparent temperature, depending on its relation to other colors.**
Design: Liz Gordon
Photo: Patricia Lambert

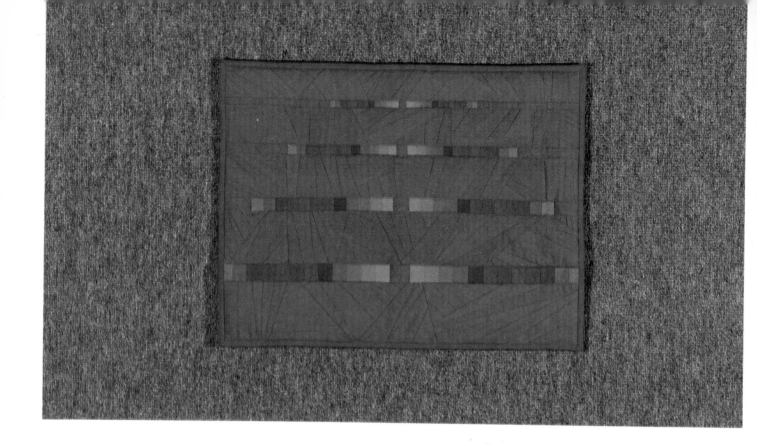

2-23. **Advancing-warm / receding-cool colors:** *Gray Space* **(quilt, 1981).**

Artist: Jan Myers
Photo: Mark Karell
Courtesy of Mr. and Mrs. Ralph Doran; Atlanta, Georgia

One area of dramatic temperature polarity is located in the yellow-to-red segment; where no truly cool hue exists, orange becomes the hottest hue. The other warm hues can only be considered cool in comparison to orange. In the violet-to-green segment, blue assumes the position of coolest hue because no trace of a truly warm hue is present. The other cool hues in that segment can only be considered warm in comparison to blue. These examples show that blue and orange are the only colors that possess absolute qualities of coolness (blue) or warmth (orange); consequently, these colors are thought be provide the greatest sense of polarity in association with temperature and hue.

Warm and cool colors also possess the illusory qualities of advancing or receding in relation to the surface plane of a work (see Figure 2-23). Warm colors seem to advance or come forward from the surface; cool colors tend to recede, falling back from the surface and into the space within it.

It may seem strange to identify a sensation of temperature with the visual realm of color. After all, heat is an invisible phenomenon of the electromagnetic spectrum, perceived through nerve endings scattered across the surface of the skin. In contrast, color sensation is produced by visible wavelengths of light reacting with the eye and brain. Is there a relationship between the tactile and the visual? And further, is there a mental or psychological connection linking color, temperature, and emotion? Evidence suggests that a strong connection exists.

In *The Art of Color,* Johannes Itten reports on experiments demonstrating differences of five to seven Fahrenheit degrees in the subjective feeling of warmth or coolness between a workroom painted blue-green and one painted red-orange. In the blue-green room, occupants felt cold at 59° F, whereas in the red-orange room they did not feel cold until the temperature fell to 52-54° F. Itten concluded that the blue-green surfaces slowed down the occupants' physiological circulation and that the red-orange stimulated it. It is an interesting experiment to ponder. Do we associate warm things with warm colors, and hence are we simply reacting to prior conditioning when our tactile senses are stimulated by a color?

In a second experiment cited by Itten, a riding stable was divided into two sections. One of the sections was painted an intense red, and the other was painted blue. The horses in both sides were given the same amount of exercise. It was found that the horses in the blue side of the stable quieted down (that is, their respiration returned to normal after exercise) faster than did the horses in the red side of the stable. It was also found that more flies congregated in the red side of the stable than in the blue side. These results, like those of the preceding experiment, might be attributable to other variables within the experiment than the longer and shorter wavelengths of reflected light, but they nonetheless present an interesting case for the relationship between color and physiological temperature.

As an informal experiment undertaken in many of our classes, we have blindfolded students and asked them to hold their hands out, palms down, over a table. The hands are placed two inches or so above the table's surface to minimize reflected body heat. Then, while the student's eyes remain closed, a 6" x 9" piece of intensely red paper is placed under one hand, and a piece of blue paper of the same size is placed under the other hand. After a few moments of concentration with eyes closed, most students remark that one palm feels slightly warmer; it is consistently the hand over the sheet of red paper. Not every student given this test can differentiate between the two surfaces, and in no way are we claiming that our test constitutes any kind of controlled experiment, but it is thought-provoking.

One reasonable conclusion might be that human skin is sufficiently sensitive to distinguish the longer wavelengths of radiant energy reflected by the red paper from the shorter wavelengths reflected by the blue paper, so that we feel the difference between the red and blue paper as a difference in warmth. Tactile sensations are even more complex than those of sight because they are mixtures of five stimuli, including contact, pressure, cold, heat, and pain. Reflected radiant energy that our sight perceives as color may indeed affect our skin's nerve endings, producing a subliminal awareness of relative warmth or coolness.

HUE/VALUE

If it is true that we react to light and dark before we respond to hue, then knowing the approximate relative values of fibers can only improve a fiber artist's color expression. The ability to translate hue into value and value into hue therefore becomes essential.

The first step in correlating hue and value is to learn how to match a hue with its relative value. Although several techniques for finding the relative values of hues are available, the following is perhaps the most direct method for work with fiber. First, a value scale is made. The scale should consist of at least fifteen steps, each represented by a 1" x 3" strip of a different gray. Glue the steps down on a piece of paper or cardboard (for ease in handling) to form a continuous gradation with no separations. After the scale is glued down and set, make a hole in the center of each step with a paper punch.

2-24. **The relative value of the moiré is found with the aid of a value scale with holes. Squinting makes the value disappear at the correct gray level.**

Photo: Patricia Lambert

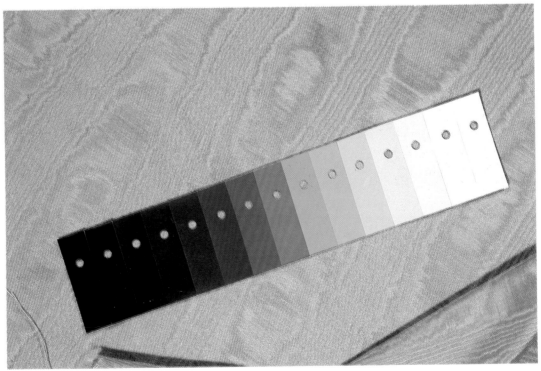

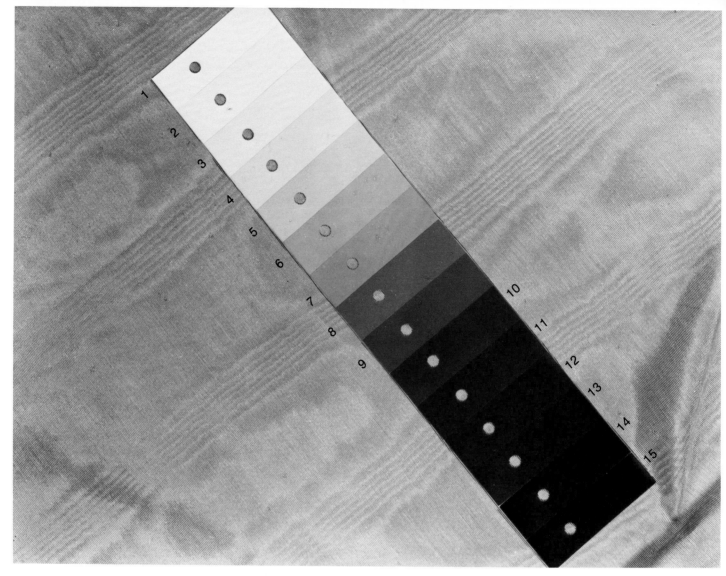

2-25. **The preceding figure becomes simple in black-and-white.**

The gray scale is then held over the yarn or fabric whose relative value is being sought (see Figures 2-24 and 2-25). Make a conscious effort to squint at the material that is visible though the holes. Squinting is essential because it helps to decrease color vision and increase colorless vision. If the value of the fiber is darker than the value of the step placed over it, the hole in the center of the gray will appear darker than the rest of the strip. If the value of the fiber is lighter than the value of the step placed over it, the hole in the center of the gray will appear lighter than the rest of the strip. If the hole seems to disappear, the value and the hue are the same.

When matching hue and value make certain that the ratio of hue to value is small; that is, a relatively large amount of value and a relatively small amount of hue or color should be involved. A small fiber sample on a gray background, for example, is appropriate. If instead a small amount of gray is set against a large amount of hue, the results may be misleading because of simultaneous contrast (see pages 53-56). Another

important rule to observe is to avoid matching a hue or color to a value in very bright light. Strong sunlight or artificial light of a high wattage invites incorrect results. At high light levels, it is impossible for a person to squint sufficiently to reduce the level of light entering the eye below the point at which strong hue perception interferes with value appraisal. A medium, comfortable light level at which squinting can be effective should be chosen. Low light levels should be avoided, too, because in excessively weak light it becomes difficult to distinguish small differences in value.

Warmer, lighter hues such as orange and yellow-orange are relatively difficult to deal with in the early stages of learning this technique, because of the advancing nature of the hues, but with a little practice the whole procedure becomes easier. Eventually, finding the relative value of different colors as part of matching tints, shades, and tones in creating designs becomes extremely simple.

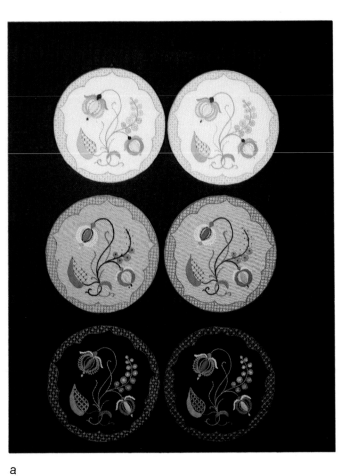

a

b

2-26. **Matching hue/value pairs of keys in traditional crewel embroidery designs: a. major (high, middle, low); b. minor (high, middle, low); c. a comparison of (1) middle major, (2) extended middle minor, and (3) middle minor.**

Artist: Mary Fry
Photo: Patricia Lambert

1   2   3

c

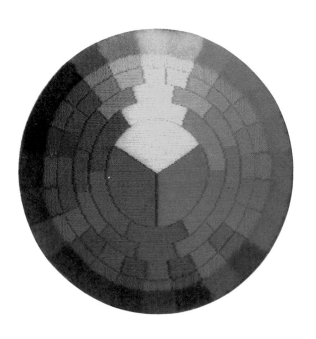

a.1

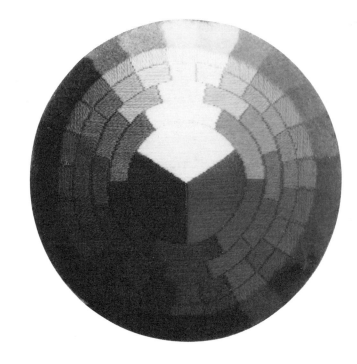

b.1

a.2

b.2

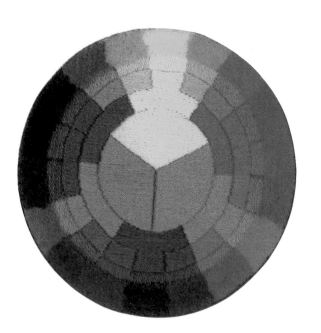

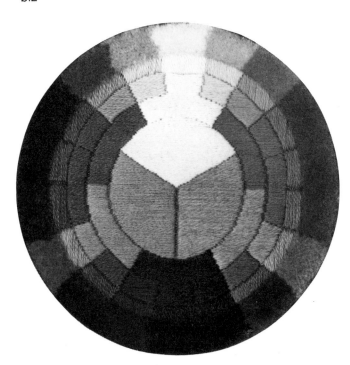

2-27. **The hue circles and their relative values: a.1. The red / yellow / blue hue circle; a.2. the magenta / yellow / cyan hue circle; b.1. the RYB hue circle in values; b.2. the MYC hue circle in values.**

Designs: Mary Fry
Photos: Patricia Lambert

When the RYB hue circle is translated into a value circle, a gradation appears that goes from a high value at yellow to a middle value in the reds and red-violets to the lowest or darkest values in the region of the violets and blue-violets (see Figure 2-27a). The values become noticeably lighter or higher in the greens, culminating again in the high value at yellow. In the MYC circle, value changes dramatically at cyan (see Figure 2-27b). This contrasts markedly with the RYB circle, in which value changes little from violet through blue-green.

The greatest polarity or distance in value between the hues lies between yellow and violet in the RYB system and between yellow and blue-violet in the MYC system. The value difference lessens between orange/blue (RYB) and cyan/red (MYC), and decreases further between red/green (RYB) and green/magenta (MYC)—so much so, in fact, that for all practical purposes the complementary pairs of red/green and magenta/green have virtually identical values.

Hue/value relationships are deceptively important in designing. In order to control the color balance in a design between contrasting or complementary hues, the designer must take into account the relative value of each hue involved. The impact or expressiveness of a hue is determined by its quantity (or proportion) and its value. The hues with relatively high values have a stronger visual impact in the same quantity of surface than do the lower-value hues. This aspect of hue/value relationships is sometimes described as contrast of extension or proportion.

For example, yellow has a very high reflectance and violet has a low reflectance. In order to equalize or balance the visual reflectances of the two hues, it is necessary to establish a larger area of violet than of yellow. A ratio of the hues can be found that will give a visually balanced proportion of the two in terms of value, impact, and expressive power.

In his treatise *On the Theory of Colors* (published in 1810), Goethe developed a set of numbers representing the approximate value of each of the primary and secondary hues of the RYB system. They are: yellow, 9; orange, 8; red, 6; violet, 3; blue, 4; and green, 6. These numbers are based on light reflectance, which corresponds to and can be interpreted visually as value. Expressed as a ratio, the relationship of yellow to violet is 9:3, or 3:1, meaning that (according to Goethe's system) yellow has a value three times greater in reflectance than the value of violet. In order to balance a design using this pair of complementary colors, then, a designer must use yellow in an area one-third as large as the area occupied by violet.

Because Goethe's numbers are expressed in terms of light reflectance, ratios among them have to be inverted in order to express relative values. His scale can be restated, however, in numbers appropriate for work with relative values. The balanced or harmonious relationships are: yellow, 3; orange, 4; red, 6; violet, 9; blue, 8; and green, 6. The yellow-to-violet ratio becomes 1:3, the orange-to-blue ratio becomes 1:2, and the red-to-green ratio becomes 1:1 (see Figure 2-28). These harmonious proportions give designs static, comfortable effects, and any change in these proportions produces unsettling expressive qualities. Consequently, disproportionate amounts of contrasting hues can be used deliberately to create visually disturbing, dynamic designs.

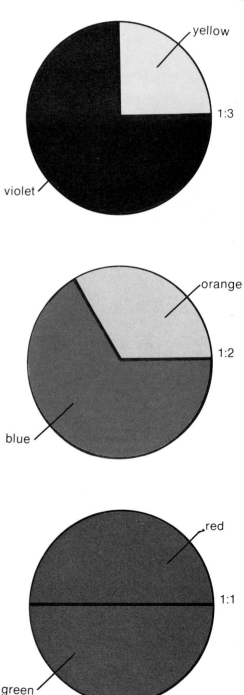

2-28. **Goethe's proportions of light reflectance.**

Within the circle, the following labels appear: **primary arc** (upper left), **primary arc** (upper right), and **primary arc** (lower center).

HUE/INTENSITY/TEMPERATURE

One method of lowering the intensity of a hue is to mix it with a second, not directly complementary hue, but one that nonetheless produces a mixture containing all three primaries. For example, a mixture of the hues red and yellow-green lowers the intensity of each. This can be demonstrated in terms of temperature.

Every hue circle consists of three segments or arcs bordered on each side by a primary hue. In the RYB system, the arcs extend from yellow to red, from red to blue, and from blue to yellow. In the MYC system, the arcs extend from yellow to magenta, from magenta to cyan, and from cyan to yellow. The area between any two primaries is called a primary arc (see Figure 2-29). Each primary arc defines a secondary hue consisting of a mixture of the two primary hues by which it is bordered. The order of hues in the RYB system shows the differences between primary arcs with more clarity than does the order of hues in the MYC system.

2-29. **Division of primary arcs (RYB system).**

Whenever a hue is made by a mixture of the two bordering primaries, no matter what their proportion, the result is still a hue and still falls into that arc; moreover, the temperature feeling within the arc remains the same. But when a hue composed of primaries from one arc is mixed with a hue composed of primaries from another arc, so that all three primaries are present to some degree, a color of lower intensity is produced. For example, mixtures of hues bounded by yellow and red can only yield hues related within the yellow-to-red arc, with no decrease in intensity. As soon as a hue from the yellow-to-red primary arc is mixed with a hue outside that arc, however—that is, as soon as it is mixed with a hue containing blue—the intensity of the resulting color is lowered; and although these mixtures can be beautiful and useful, they no longer qualify as hues. The extent to which the new color's intensity is lowered (and the extent to which its temperature feeling changes) depends on the proportion of the third primary used in the mixture.

HUE/TEMPERATURE: UNDERTONES

The *undertone* of a hue is the color effect seen when a hue is diluted with white or with the equivalent of white (such as water), or when a paint film is made transparent. These color effects can be described most easily in terms of temperature, when comparison is between similar hues (see Figure 2-30).

Two factors must be considered in dealing with undertones for color effect in designing: the undertone contrast between tints of two hues belonging to the same family; and the undertone contrast between a hue or color and its tint if a temperature shift exists (this becomes critical when specific mixes are desired).

Not every hue has a contrasting undertone in the tint; some show the same basic color effect in both hue and tint. More often, however, the undertones of hues usually swing toward one or another of the colorant primaries. For example, one blue, when tinted, may have a quality of violet (indicating that the undertone is of a red nature), while another blue, when tinted, may have a quality of green (suggesting a yellow undertone). These undertones mark temperature shifts rather than actual hue shifts; knowledge of them can be used very effectively in developing the color design potential and relationship of two reds, two blues, or some other pair of closely matched hues.

2-30. **Undertones: tinted comparisons of reds and blues showing undertones of red, yellow, or blue.**

The second application of undertones plays a part in mixing. The fact that an apparent temperature change may occur in the hue or body color as a result of tinting means that undertone contrast can be responsible for preventing successful mixtures from taking place. For example, shading gives color effects related to the undertone of black that commonly is blue but in paint sometimes appears as violet because of furnacing (mars black). This explains why when yellow is mixed with black, a variety of greens or browns is produced.

Mixing secondaries can also create problems if it is done without prior awareness of undertones. For example, if a dyer wishes to produce a violet but selects for this purpose a red and blue that have yellow undertones, a successful violet cannot be achieved. Instead the resultant color will be muddy. In the language of color, the explanation for this result is that the blue and red have complementary rather than analogous qualities. If, however, the red has an undertone of blue and the blue has an undertone of red, the resultant mixture will appear a truer violet.

When a hue is mixed with its complement—producing a scale of color that moves from one hue, through an area of low-intensity, lower-value colors, to the complementary hue (see Figures 2-31 and 2-32)—a new and beautiful range of colors is produced. This procedure is called *complementary modulation.* If the colors that are too dark in value to be seen easily are tinted to a 25 percent value, the colors that result are soft, subtle, and atmospheric. In no other way can these colors be mixed with such ease and simplicity.

2-31. **Complementary modulation with tints of midrange.**
Dyer: Antonia Kormos
Photo: Patricia Lambert

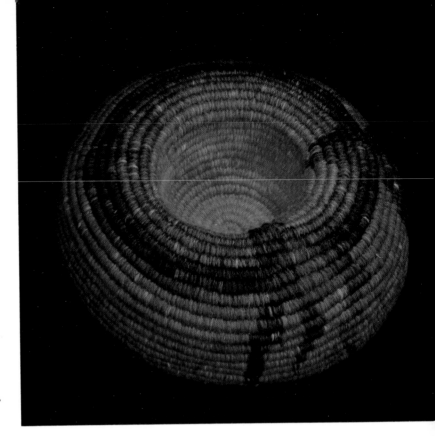

2-32. **Complementary modulation:** *Volcano* **(basket).**
Artist: Ellen Clague
Photo: Patricia Lambert

Theoretically, the mixture of any complementary pair of hues produces a neutral gray. In the RYB system, the nature of the impurities in the colorants and the inaccurcy of the complementary pairs disallow this result. Neutrals can be mixed from any two primaries, but the character of each of the three possible neutrals varies slightly from the others; each of the three is in fact a faintly chromatic neutral. Primaries of the MYC system produces more truly neutral grays.

If the midrange of a complementary modulation is tinted, each color to the same value (approximately 25 percent), one color will appear that has neither a warm nor a cool quality when compared with its neighboring colors and that resembles neither of its parent hues in temperature. In work involving colors of such low intensity, it is helpful to compare the colors' relative temperatures. These midrange colors are often called neutrals because they are so low in intensity, but actually there is only one true neutral in a complementary modulation.

Pigment and dye hues can only approximate the spectral hues; hence, several different reds (for example) can be produced by different companies and still be called hues, i.e. pure colors. The results that will be obtained when hues having different undertones are used in complementary modulation are always dubious unless preliminary testing is done. In paint and dye mixing, complementary modulations of different reds and greens (or other groups of complementary pairs) can be used to make different sets of low-intensity colors.

In paint mixing, a cadmium red/permanent green modulation and an alizarin/viridian modulation yield different low-intensity colors. The reason lies in the undertones of the original hues. The undertone of both cadmium red and permanent green is yellow, whereas the undertone of both alizarin and viridian is blue. This means that the quality of the low-intensity colors produced is warmer in the first modulation and cooler in the second. The same concept is true in dye mixing.

Natural dyes are not high-intensity colors to begin with, but are beautiful and soft in their "pure" (hue) state; as a result, modulations of these colors produce extremely low-intensity colors. In commercial dyes, a much greater range of color is possible and the range of intensities is wider and much more controllable. This is not to say that commercial dyes are better, only that they are different.

The number of low-intensity colors that can be produced by complementary modulation is breathtaking. Paint and paint mixtures, while seeming superfluous to some, can serve as an excellent reference glossary of new color for fiber work. As a first step, at least, paint mixtures seem to offer a simpler, more direct way of understanding and illustrating color scales. In addition, color samples of paints may be seen on flat surfaces, without raising problems of texture and irregular light reflectance.

Although value changes are produced when complementary hues are mixed, the most dramatic changes take place in the areas of hue and intensity. Sometimes, lowering the intensity of a hue or color by adding black or white is inappropriate for a particular design

2-33. Small changes in intensity, producing minimal value shifts.

Dyer: Antonia Kormos
Photo: Patricia Lambert

because the color shift or change in value involved, may be undesirable. The most direct way of making small changes in the intensity of a hue is to add very small amounts of the complementary hue (see Figure 2-33). When a hue is broken to a very small degree, the value remains unchanged. Even when a small amount of violet is added to yellow, only the "glow" of the saturated hue is removed. If this first step in a yellow-violet modulation were taken and isolated, the color would still be identified as yellow. The only visible difference lies in the slight decrease in intensity as compared to the intensity of the pure hue. Shadows in flowers, the undersides of leaves, and other areas of color that the artist wants the viewer to identify as "body color" despite their being less intense can be produced in this way.

Another technique for creating low-intensity colors is *secondary modulation*. Mixing two secondary hues in a scale produces moderate value changes and creates colors known as tertiaries (see Figure 2-34). The term *tertiary* refers to a mixture of red, yellow, and blue—or of magenta, cyan, and yellow—in proportions that differ from those of complementary pairs. Mixtures of secondaries are not quite as simple as mixtures of complementary pairs.

If orange and green are mixed, for example, the mixture contains red + yellow + blue + yellow. The red in the orange and the blue in the green yield violet, and violet and yellow are complements; however, because both the green and the orange contain yellow, a dominance of yellow exists. In this mixture, therefore, the low-intensity colors all have a yellow quality, and no true neutral can be produced. Values do change across the series, but when the darker values are tinted out for the sake of visibility, the colors show consistent hue characteristics throughout the modulation.

The two other possible sets of secondary hue mixtures are violet/orange and violet/green. The violet/orange combination is equal to red + blue + red + yellow. The complementary pair in this union is red and green, with a dominance of red; the tertiary colors are all warm. The violet/green combination is equal to blue + red + blue + yellow. Here the complementary pair is blue and orange, with a dominance of blue; the resulting low-intensity tertiary colors are all cool. Neutrals cannot appear in any of these situations because of the dominance of a different primary in each secondary modulation. Again, as with complementary modulations, the nature of the colorants leads to slightly different chromatic results.

2-34. **Secondary modulations, showing tints.**

Dyer: Antonia Kormos
Photo: Patricia Lambert

VALUE/HUE/INTENSITY/TEMPERATURE

Tinting produces colors of lower intensity and higher value. The word *tint* is technically defined as a hue mixed with white, but commercially the term may refer to any light value of any color. In the case of certain dyes, the dyebath can simply be exhausted, effectively creating a tint as though by increasing the water concentation (which lightens the value and lowers the intensity). If the yarn or fabric being prepared for dyeing is white, the process becomes clear, and a step-by-step progression showing an ever-ascending value scale of tints is created by exhausting the dye concentration. Another method of "tinting" that raises the value and lowers the intensity is to produce an optically blended tint by carding or spinning colored fibers and white fibers together.

A color that lowers the value and intensity of a hue when mixed with it is often referred to as a *shade*. This term is unfortunate because it is misleading; *shade* technically means a color that results when a hue is mixed with black. Depending on the amount of black added to the hue, the value and intensity of the color is lowered to a greater or lesser extent, but the resulting value is always darker than the original hue. As more and more black is added, the value of the shade becomes lower and lower—as does the intensity—until the value is so dark that no color is discernible. At this point, it is advisable to mix the shade with white in order to help ascertain the presence of any hue.

The process of *tinting shades* can yield color mixtures of different values and very low intensities that form a completely new vocabulary of subtle, delicate colors. The most sensitive neutrals are colors made in this manner. The intensity of these colors is almost 0 percent, but when they are compared to one another their subtle differences in temperature make them surprisingly expressive and atmospheric.

Students sometimes ask why they should not just add a gray or a sequence of grays? Of course, that option is available, but much more control is maintained by producing a shade or tint first, and beautiful combinations and color effects can be missed if too much territory is covered at one time. A hue, therefore, can be tinted or shaded; and the shades themselves can be tinted, or the tints shaded, to form new color glossaries. Shades of tints and tints of shades may sound like two ways of saying exactly the same thing, but the basic approach to the mixture and the proportions involved are different, and therefore, the results are a different range of colors.

Although colors achieved by tinting and shading both have lowered intensities, they have very different color effects from the low-intensity colors obtained by other methods such as complementary modulation.

2-35. Tints, shades, and tints of shades of orange.
Dyer: Antonia Kormos
Photo: Patricia Lambert

Colors are dynamic. A light-value color appears even lighter when placed next to a dark-value color. A hue changes its expressive quality when juxtaposed with an analogous or complementary hue. Intensity seems to increase in a color when it is set against a gray or another color of lower intensity. A cool color appears warmer when placed next to a pure, distinctly cool hue, such as a balanced blue that has neither a red nor a yellow undertone; the same color appears cooler when compared to a warmer color. This kind of relativity can be frustrating, but it can also make color an exciting medium of expression with endless possibilities for manipulation and control.

In 1824, the Royal Manufacturers of Tapestries at Gobelins, France, were experiencing some perplexing color phenomena. The problems centered on the fact that the color of certain yarns seemed to change when the yarns were woven into a design. Black, in particular, took on qualities of shades of hues, at the same time losing its dense richness. King Louis XVIII asked the preeminent chemist, Michel-Eugène Chevreul (1786-1889), to become director of dyes at Gobelins, in the hope that he could put an end to these color shifts. After a long period of close observation, Chevreul concluded that certain color combinations fostered illusions of hue, value, and intensity in human beings, altering their color perception. Chevreul's assumptions and observations were correct. These color shifts are subjective and are caused by afterimages—compensatory visual responses of the eye/brain system upon exposure to certain visual stimuli.

Some kinds of afterimages relate to pattern, line, and movement; others involve value and color. The two types of afterimages that influence color design are designated as negative and complementary. Negative afterimages affect perception of value, creating dark/light shifts of a color or value; complementary afterimages affect perception of hue, producing color changes.

The mechanism of afterimage induction is not entirely understood, but it is thought to be related to a chemical change that takes place in the rods and cones of the retina as a result of prolonged exposure to a visual stimulus that reduces sensitivity.

The eye/brain normally maintains a balance or equilibrium in which afterimages are not produced. Equilibrium is achieved when the eye/brain system is exposed to all wavelengths in the visible spectrum that have an absorption halfway between white and black. When a portion of the visible spectrum is missing—as it is when the visual stimulus is a color—the visual response is to manufacture the missing wavelength or complement based on light, and this manufactured wavelength is seen as an afterimage, completeing the spectrum to produce the sensation of white light and a sense of balance in the eye/brain of the viewer (see Figure 2-36a). The same thing happens when a dark, light, black, or white value is seen. The eye/brain induces the opposite value to restore a visual equilibrium to a middle gray (see Figure 2-36b).

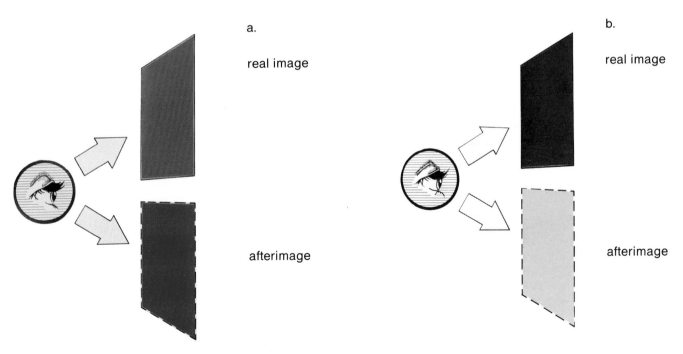

a. real image
afterimage

b. real image
afterimage

2-36. **Production of afterimages: a. complementary afterimage; b. negative afterimage.**

The eye/brain system constantly makes afterimages, although our awareness of them is usually negligible. Most of the time, the level of the stimulus is so low that we do not consciously see them, or our field of vision includes all wavelengths of the visible spectrum and no afterimages are induced. Only when intense colors are seen in relation to one another, as in a design or a random collection of pieces of fiber or fabric, do afterimages affect our color perception and produce color shifts. Fortunately, these color shifts can be controlled and used to advantage. Four basic rules of afterimages are:

High-intensity colors induce high-intensity afterimages.

Low-intensity colors induce low-intensity afterimages.

Dark values induce light afterimages.

Light values induce dark afterimages.

Afterimage and contrast of color combinations are the primary subjects of Chevreul's work on what he called simultaneous contrast. In 1839, he published his definitive work, *On the Laws of Simultaneous Contrast*. In it, he notes fourteen conditions that relate to contrast of color and afterimage:

1. Colors are modified in appearance by their proximity to other colors.
2. All colors seem lighter and more dramatic against black.
3. All colors seem cooler and more subdued against white.
4. Dark colors look darker against light colors than against dark colors.
5. Light colors look lighter against dark colors than against light colors.
6. Colors are influenced in hue by adjacent colors, each coloring its neighbor with its own complement.
7. If two complementary colors lie side-by-side, the contrast makes each seem more intense than it looks by itself.
8. Dark hues on a dark background that is not complementary appear weaker, or less intense, than they do on a complementary background.
9. Light colors on a light background that is not complementary appear weaker, or less intense, than they do on a complementary background.
10. A bright color set against a dull color of the same hue further deadens the dull color.
11. When a bright color is set against a dull color, the contrast is strongest when the latter is complementary.
12. Light colors on light backgrounds that are not complementary can be greatly strengthened if bounded by narrow bands of black or of complementary colors.
13. Dark colors on dark backgrounds that are not complementary can be greatly strengthened if bounded by narrow bands of white or of light colors.
14. The greatest afterimage appears when figure and background relationships have the same value, and when a large background is set behind a small foreground figure.

By definition, *simultaneous contrast* describes a color and an induced afterimage of its complement that are seen at the same time. This phenomenon can be observed in the following simple way. First, a 1" square is cut from the center of a 6" x 9" piece of paper of a primary or secondary hue (see Figure 2-37). Any colored paper system such as Color-aid or Chromarama, has good colors for this purpose. The sheet is then placed over a piece of gray paper that has approximately the same value as the hue, to eliminate the possibility of inducing a negative afterimage and to allow the complementary hue to be seen more effectively. Another piece of the gray paper is placed off to one side. As the viewer stares at the gray square at the center of the colored sheet (this should be done for at least 15 seconds), the gray gradually takes on the color of the complement to the hue of the surrounding colored sheet. The center square acts as a screen upon which the afterimage is projected, mixing with the gray to produce a chromatic neutral. When any small area of color (the figure) is surrounded by a larger area of color (the ground), the color of the figure is shifted toward the color of the afterimage of the ground.

Afterimages can also be demonstrated by the use of successive contrast. Illusory colors and/or values are induced by this means, but the viewer must look at a piece of white paper or board to see the complementary afterimage. Successive contrast is a particularly useful technique if there is any question about the hue quality of an afterimage.

The procedure for testing successive contrast begins with cutting a 4" square of red-orange paper, and gluing it down on the left half of a 6" x 12" piece of white board or heavy paper; the right half of the board remains blank. A dot is then marked in pencil at the center of the red-orange square and a matching dot is marked at the center of the blank right half of the board. Under a good strong light, the viewer stares at the dot in the middle of the red-orange square (for at least 20 seconds), and then shifts focus to the dot on the right half of the board, staring at it until another image appears. For a few seconds, a blue-green afterimage will be visible (see Figure 2-38).

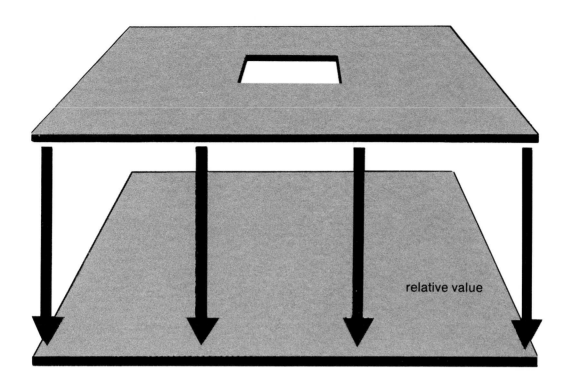

2-37. **Simultaneous contrast.**

2-38. **Successive contrast.**

A negative afterimage can be visualized by means of a similar procedure. A piece of gray paper or board, at least 12" x 12", is divided with light pencil lines into quarters. A 1" square of black paper and a 1" square of white paper are then cut and placed in the center of the upper left quadrant of the gray board and in the center of the upper right quadrant, respectively. A dot is marked in pencil midway between the two squares on the vertical dividing line. A second dot is similarly marked between the two empty lower quarters. The viewer stares at the upper dot for 15 to 30 seconds, and then looks at the lower dot. Two illusory squares will appear on the lower half of the gray board, in reverse order from the upper squares; that is, a light square will appear below the black square, and a dark square will appear below the white square (see Figure 2-39).

The presence, intensity, and longevity of afterimage can vary, depending on the age, general health, and eye physiology of the individual.

2-39. **von Bezold effect: note the change in color effect when black is substituted for white.**

Design Execution: Mary Fry
Photo: Patricia Lambert

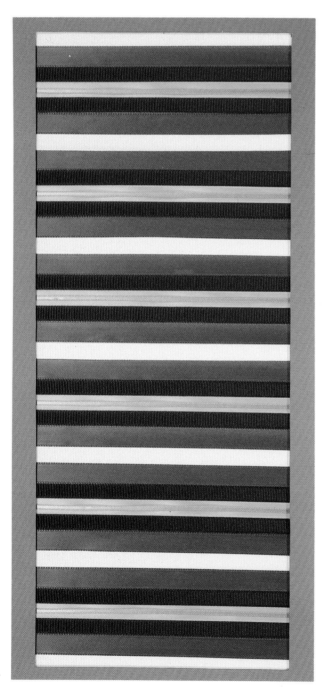

a.

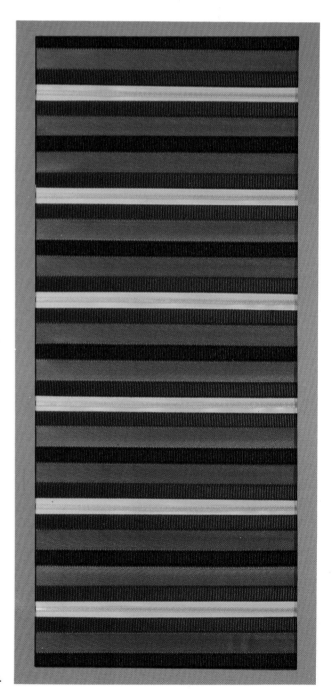

b.

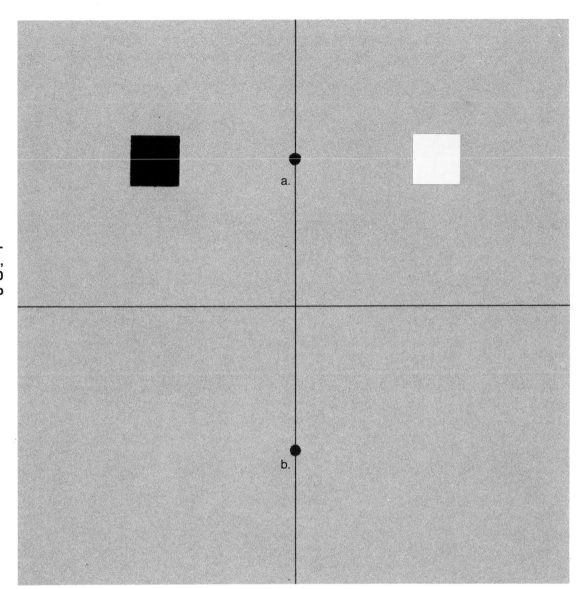

2-40. **Negative after-image: in strong light, stare at a for 10-20 seconds; then look at b for 5-10 seconds.**

OPTICAL COLOR MIXTURES

Optical color mixtures are produced by eye/brain responses to the placement of colorants rather than to actual physical mixtures of either light or colorants. The term *optical mixture* itself can be somewhat misleading; and even though *optical* means relating to vision and *optics* refers to the science that deals with light, the phrase *perceptual mixture* may be more accurate.

Pointillism

As the nineteenth century came to a close in Europe, an incredible amount of new information about color—including results of research in the new disciplines of psychology and perception—was being made available to the public. During the 1870s, advances in color photography began to influence avant garde painters in France. They wanted to emulate natural qualities of light with pigment. A specific group of painters (later known as the Impressionists and the Neo-impressionists) had come to the realization that objects, especially those seen out of doors, did not actually have one true color. Color, they reasoned, was the effect of changing light and atmospheric conditions. As such, an object reflected many nuances of changing color, and the artist must depict its color in this way to reproduce the true quality of light.

Contained in Chevreul's work on simultaneous contrast were observations on the juxtaposition of tiny points or lines of color as a means of creating color mixtures. He felt that these mixtures behaved more like mixtures of light than like mixtures of pigment. Chevreul also noted that dark points of color, such as blues and violets, lost their apparent hue at a distance and were perceived simply as low values or as black, while light points of color (yellows or tints) also lost their hue at the same distance and were seen as high values or as white.

During the same year that Chevreul's observations were published (1839), another French scientist, Jean Mile, attempted to simulate light by placing large quantities of small dots composed of different pure pigments side-by-side. When viewed at the proper distance, these dots of color yielded the same color effects, he thought, as mixtures made from the projected beams of colored lights. In a strange way, both mixtures appeared to be additive.

The Impressionists were excited by these new ideas and techniques, and they sought to replicate in pigment mixtures the appearance of light mixtures. They were convinced that ordinary subtractive paint mixing reduced the brilliance and power of color, so they turned to the ideas of Chevreul and Mile in an attempt to give their canvases a luminosity they thought impossible to achieve with traditional mixing methods.

The term *pointillism* was probably first used to describe a system of painting based on dots of color by the nineteenth century French critic Felix Fénéon, who in 1886 began writing a series of essays on the work of the Neo-impressionists, most notably that of the young French painter Georges Seurat (1859-91). In 1886, Fénéon wrote a careful and thoughtful analysis of Seurat's painting *Sunday Afternoon on the Island of the Grande Jatte,* explaining to the general public the optical theories Seurat had learned from Chevreul, Mile, and the master-works of Joseph Turner and Eugène Delacroix.

The optical mixing of small dots of pure pigment produced canvases that were neither as lustrous nor as beautifully filled with light as the Neo-impressionists had hoped; instead, these works have a grayed quality. Studies have shown that optical mixtures act as average value mixtures rather than as additive light mixtures as was originally believed. It was only partly true that the technique of pointillism simulated a blend of colored light. If forty units of blue light and forty units of yellow light are added to one another, the result is eighty units of white light. In pointillism and other optical methods of color mixing, however, such a mix yields forty units of gray whose value is the average of the values of the blue surface and the yellow surface. This result occurs because of surface absorption; the mixtures are not strictly additive, but *partitive.*

Successful results in optical mixing, no matter what the medium, depend on four factors: the size or scale of the dot; the *distance* from which the work is viewed; the *angle* at which the work is viewed; and the *relative value* of the dots of pure pigment used. If the scale is too small or the distance is too long, everything grays; if the scale is too large or the distance is too short, optical mixtures do not occur. The dots must be in proper scale, in order to be seen and yet fused; the mixtures are then at their most exciting. In general, it is good to remember that color perception of very small areas of color is unreliable, since all colors tend to

become achromatic in general. At certain distances, when dot size is too small for maximum color effectiveness but not small enough to turn gray, the colors blue, blue-green, and green tend to appear green, while orange-reds and violets tend to appear pink. Dark colors tend to appear black and light colors tend to appear white or light gray, as Chevreul demonstrated.

The closer the relative values of the two or three pigments being juxtaposed are, the more successful the optical mix will be. If blue dots and red dots of similar value are used in quantity, the result is a violet that can easily be perceived as violet at the right distance. If a dark blue and a yellow are put together, the result is a gray (when seen at the proper distance or scale). However, if the blue dots are a lighter value approaching cyan in hue, the resultant optical mix appears distinctly green. A similar effect is evident in the making of an orange optical mix: the resultant mix will look oranger if the yellow and red used are close to each other in value. A hue change is most dramatic when the values are similar.

Optical color mixtures tend to appear duller or grayer as the viewing distance increases, and they convey vibrancy and luminosity only when blended in the proper scale or size of dots to enable the viewer to see the dots and the mixtures almost simultaneously. It is our physiological nature to limit color production by optical mixing.

THE VON BEZOLD EFFECT

The von Bezold effect, named after its originator, Wilhelm von Bezold (1837-1907), is a unique form of optical mixing. A German rug designer and meteorologist, von Bezold was looking for a way to introduce pronounced changes in the color effects of his rug designs by adding or changing only one color. He found that when intense colors or values such as black and white were evenly distributed throughout a design, the color effect was changed. The von Bezold effect is sometimes known as the spreading effect because the color effect seems to spread over the entire design. The black or white elements seem to produce a more noticeable effect on the background color when presented as a pattern than they would have if the same amount of black or white were interspersed randomly in the design (see Figure 2-39).

White lines or patterns superimposed on a hue tend to make the whole area appear lighter, the white seeming to spread over all the color. Conversely, black lines or patterns superimposed on a hue seem to spread over the entire color area, darkening the effect. The effect is subtle and seems most applicable to borders or to designs in which a pattern is repeated. In general, light areas tend to look larger than dark areas; this seems to be due to the greater stimulation lightness offers the retina. The optical effect is closely related to simultaneous contrast and afterimage.

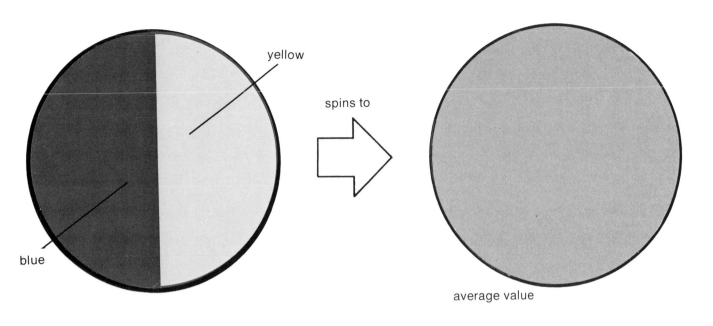

yellow

blue

spins to

average value

2-41. **Maxwell's disks.**

MAXWELL'S DISKS

James Clerk Maxwell (1831-79), a Scottish physicist and mathematician, is probably best known for his work in discovering the electromagnetic nature of light, but he was also vitally interested in color perception and sensation. In particular, Maxwell was concerned with the perception of surface color.

Maxwell devised disks or wheels on which he placed two or more colors. He then spun the disks rapidly, creating new color mixtures whose appearance depended on the proportions of the different colors that were placed on the wheel's surface (see Figure 2-41). Maxwell suggested that these spun colors represented another way of mixing light. The mixing of the colors seemed to be occuring in the eye of the observer, since the spinning disk continued to consist of two or three flat, distinct surface areas of color. Maxwell hypothesized that the new color was produced by a mixture of wavelengths of light that were being reflected from the surface very rapidly. The most troubling question was why, when a disk showing the correct proportions of yellow and blue was spun, the resultant color was a gray with an approximate value of 35 percent instead of white. After all, the mixture of blue and yellow light in proper proportions creates white light!

In Maxwell's disks, as in pointillism, the optical mixing of pigments differs fundamentally from the additive mixing of projected light. Where the two lights of a projection are overlapped, the new color formed is lighter in value than either parent color. This is a basic law of additive mixing. The offspring in true light mixtures is the sum of the light levels of the two parent colors.

With Maxwell's disks, the surface colors do not present themselves simultaneously, as happens in a purely additive or purely subtractive mix. They present themselves alternately, although so rapidly that they cannot be seen consciously as separate colors. The value of the mixture, therefore, is not the sum but the average of the values of the two component colors, as in pointillism. The color that appears optically has the averaged value of the two colors and has a hue similar to an additive mix although modifiable to appear more subtractive when the color proportions on the wheel are changed. For example, yellow and blue in the right proportion will spin to gray, not green; but if cyan and yellow are used, the spun mix has a greenish appearance.

If a disk that is approximately one-half magenta and one-half green is spun rapidly, the resultant color is gray. This effect is caused by a mixture of wavelengths of light reflected from each half of the disk. The retina is affected by the rapidly alternating wavelengths produced by the spinning disk, but it does not perceive the alternations subliminally, and as a result the spinning acts as a virtually simultaneous presentation. The gray is the result of the values of the two colors. If the mix were truly additive, of course, the color should be white, but because a measurable amount of absorption exists, the mix is perceived as the average of the values (and in this case the values are just about the same).

How can these disks be applicable to the process of determining optical mixtures of color in fiber? Perhaps warp and weft colors can be predetermined more accurately in situations where tightly woven optical mixes are desired. Maxwell's disk may also offer a way of previsualizing all kinds of optical mixtures in fiber. In any case, room surely exists for experimentation and discovery.

Color Mixtures: A Summing Up

Three separate phenomena produce color mixtures: additive mixtures, which are basic to color perception involve the addition of wavelengths of light to create higher-value colors, culminating in white light (the sum of the additive or light primaries blue-violet, green, and red); subtractive mixtures, which are created by the addition of materials such as dyes, inks, and paints that remove reflecting wavelengths of light from each other, allowing us to see the result as new color and culminating in black (the sum of the subtractive or pigment primaries magenta, yellow and cyan); and optical mixtures, an elusive yet effective method of creating mixtures that appear to vibrate and glow at a particular distance when small areas of color are juxtaposed. Optical mixtures, sometimes called partitive mixtures, combine aspects of the laws governing additive and subtractive phenomena, as well as of those governing our eye/brain physiology.

Additive mixtures are basic to color perception, but subtractive mixing usually determines our aesthetic world of color. Optical mixing blends the laws governing both additive and subtractive mixing, and introduces the concept of partitive mixtures.

Part Two

Fiber Structure, Light, and Color

Yarns and fabrics are capable of a wonderful depth, brilliance, and richness of color that cannot be attained by a painted surface. The unique color properties of fiber depend on the interaction of fabric structure, dye application, and light.

Fabric is constructed from yarn, yarn from fibers, and fibers from molecules. Fabric has certain general properties—such as moisture absorbency, fiber luster, structural uniformity, and fiber resilience—that directly affect the way the fiber interacts with dye and light to create fiber's characteristic depth and richness of color.

For structural reasons, some types of fiber absorb moisture more readily than others. *Fiber absorbency* directly affects the ability of a fiber to take a dye. Highly absorbent fibers such as cotton take water (and dye molecules in water) readily into their structure; consequently, they are easy to dye. Other fibers, including some synthetic fibers, are structured in such a way that they absorb little or no moisture and are difficult or impossible to dye in the traditional manner. These fibers must be colored during their chemical manufacture, and this results in a uniformly colored fiber.

Fiber luster refers to the gloss, sheen, or shine of a fiber, and by extension to these characteristics of the yarn or fabric made from it. Fiber luster is a direct product of fiber structure in that the larger the reflecting surfaces and the more orderly and more uniformly these surfaces are arranged in the structure of a fiber (or a fabric), the more orderly the light reflectance from that fiber and the higher its luster will be. High luster increases a fiber's total reflectance and thus raises the value of its color. A high-luster fiber is thus higher in value than a low-luster fiber dyed in the same dyebath.

The *structural uniformity* of a fiber affects how the fiber responds to dye and how it reflects light. A fiber with uniform molecular and cellular structure will accept dyestuff evenly along the entire fiber; consequently, one fiber of this type accepts a dye in exactly the same way as the next. A less structurally uniform fiber may be porous in one area and non-porous in another. This type of fiber accepts dye most readily in areas where its structure is most open and porous, and it repels dye in areas where the structure is tighter, closer, and less porous. Structural variation causes variation of color from one area of the fiber to the next and from one fiber to another.

Similarly, light reflects more uniformly from a structurally regular fiber or yarn than from a fiber or yarn that possesses structural variation. A structurally uniform fabric, such as a simple flat plain weave, creates a more uniform color effect than does a fabric designed with irregularities of structure and surface texture, such as a twill or a crepe fabric.

Fiber resilience refers to the ability of a fiber to stretch or bend under pressure and then snap back to its original position when the pressure is released. Resilience in a fiber makes fabric constructed from it wrinkle-resistent; it makes a rug pile crush-resistent. Fiber resilience also affects the general drapability of a fabric.

Wrinkled fabric and smooth fabric reflect light differently. Wrinkled fabric includes large or small areas of shadow that occur because light is reflected from the surface in different directions. As a result, wrinkled fabric appears darker and less intensely colored than the same fabric, unwrinkled. Fabric drape also influences fabric color, by affecting the kinds of folds and curves the fabric takes. The drape directly affects the angle of reflectance of the fabric surface and the interplay of reflecting areas and shadow areas; these in turn change the value and intensity nuances of the fabric color. Similarly, because of changes in angle of light reflectance, a rug pile that has been crushed and flattened appears lighter and less intense in color than a more resilient rug pile that repeatedly returns to an uncrushed vertical position.

This section of the book examines how variables at each structural level—molecule, fiber, yarn, and fabric—influence our color perception of the finished fabric.

Chapter 3

Fiber Structure and Colorants

Dye and Pigment

Fibers can be colored by either dyes or pigments. Many dyers consider that the term *dye* refers to any colorant that can be fixed on a fiber more or less permanently—a definition that includes both dyes and pigments. Technically, however, fundamental differences distinguish pigments from dyes. A dye is a colorant that goes into solution (or dissolves). The dye particles break apart into single molecules in water or some other solvent that is used in the dyeing process. In contrast, a pigment is a colorant that remains insoluble when mixed with liquid. Instead of breaking apart or dissolving into single molecules in solution, pigment particles remain clustered together in suspension, floating around intact in the liquid or dyebath.

Dyes have a chemical affinity or attraction for fiber, but pigments generally do not. Their chemical attraction to fiber causes dye molecules to migrate out of the solution, be absorbed into the fiber, diffuse from the surface of the fiber toward its center, and there do one of two things. They either bond chemically with fiber molecules (which means that each dye molecule will stick to a fiber molecule, more or less firmly, depending on the type of bond) or react chemically with fiber molecules to form permanent, enlarged, colored fiber molecules. In either situation, the dye enters the fiber and becomes a permanent part of the fiber structure.

Pigment molecules, to the contrary, carry their own color. Most pigments have no affinity for fiber, which means that pigment molecules do not unite with fiber molecules chemically and so must be fixed to the fibers with adhesives, resins, or other bonding agents. In the case of man-made fibers, pigments can be mixed into the viscous fiber solution so that the fiber is already colored when it is formed. Color introduced by this means into man-made fibers is permanent, but pigments fixed to fibers with bonding agents only last

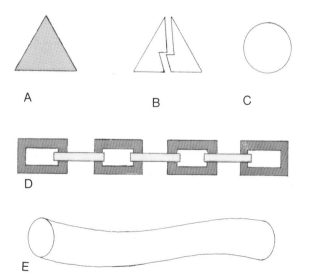

3-1. **Key: Symbols key for structure and dye illustrations: A — dye molecule; B — dye molecule divided (becomes colorless); C — free atom; D — long chain fiber molecule (polymer); E — textile fiber.**

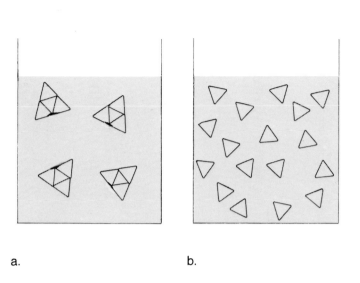

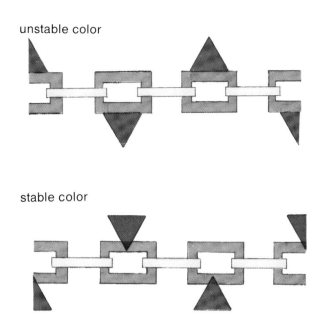

a.   b.

unstable color

stable color

3-2. Pigment and dye in liquids: a. pigment particles remain in suspension; b. dye particles go into solution.

3-3. Different types of chemical reactions, producing stable or unstable color.

until the agent wears away. Mild abrasion thus reduces color.

Some colorfast pigments present an exception to the rule. Natural dyers have used mineral pigments to color fabrics for years, and iron rust (iron oxide) is so colorfast that it has been used to dye sails. Manganese, chrome, and copper are also used as pigments. With metal oxides, depth of color is achieved by successive dipping and airing (or oxidizing) of the fabric. Metal oxide coloration is lightfast and washfast; that is, neither sunlight nor washing can fade the color.

A final point of difference is that metal oxides and other pigments tend to make fabric stiff, whereas dyes generally yield a more flexible fabric.

How Dye Works

The way dye works is directly related to the nature of light and of visual perception. Dye in a fiber absorbs some wavelengths of white light and reflects others; the latter are perceived as the color of the fiber. The ability of dye to create color comes from the presence of chemical groups called chromophores. Substances whose molecules contain chromophores in various arrangements produce the sensations of different hues. Exactly how this happens is still not known, but most theories about it focus on the electrical energy of the molecule. It has been suggested that electrons vibrating at a certain frequency within a chromophore molecule absorb color waves of the same frequency, and reflect the others.

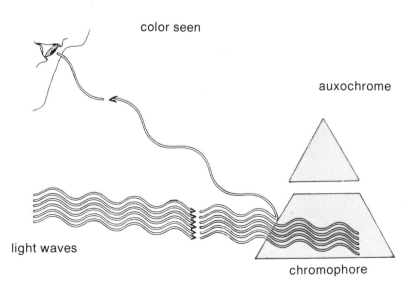

color seen

auxochrome

light waves

chromophore

3-4. Selective reflection: chromophore molecules absorb certain wavelengths of light and reflect others.

63

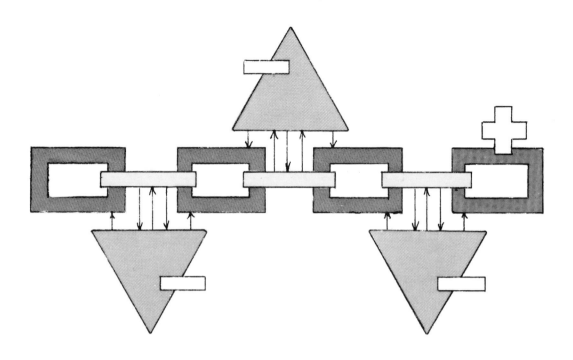

3-5. **A negative dye molecule links with a positive fiber molecule.**

While chromophores impart color to a substance, the intensity of the color depends on the presence of one or more substances called auxochromes. Auxochromes also make dyes water-soluble and provide the chemical groups that form bonds between dye and fiber. A dyebath must contain both chromophores and auxochromes, either from the dyestuff alone or from the mixture of dyestuff and other chemicals added to the dyebath.

One standard way of categorizing the thousands of different dyes available today is by their method of application to the fibers. These dye categories include direct dyes, azoic dyes, acid dyes, mordant dyes, basic dyes, disperse dyes, vat dyes, sulfer dyes, and reactive dyes. Although dyes generally have a chemical affinity for fiber, not every kind of dye has an affinity for every kind of fiber. On the molecular level, the chemical affinities between fiber and dye must be matched.

During dyeing, the assembly of dye molecules at the fiber surface is governed by three influences; electro-potential forces, sometimes called potential surface charge; temperature; and agitation. In simplified terms, a connecting site of a dye molecule having an electric potential or surface charge of + or – must meet a connecting site on a fiber having the opposite electric potential. When this occurs, the + and – charges attract

one another, and the two molecules adhere to one another. Proper temperature and agitation aid in this process.

When soaked in water, all fibers acquire an electric potential or surface charge. Cotton and other plant (or cellulosic) fibers acquire – charges. The charge of protein fibers varies, depending on the acidity or alkalinity (pH) of the water. Wool has both + and – charge sites.

A mild acid solution helps break down protein fibers so that wool and silk dye sites are available to the dye. Cellulosic fibers such as cotton and linen must be soaked in alkaline washing soda to activate the dye sites so that they can accept color. With cotton, salt is used to set up an electrical movement that initiates the movement of dye molecules in search of a resting place or dye site on the fiber. Salt continues to be added over the period of dyeing to maintain an even rate of movement.

Different fibers have different numbers of dye sites, and this causes them to take the dye molecules more or less readily. A wool fiber has about 1,000 dye sites, while a piece of silk fiber of similar length has 100, and cotton and nylon have fewer than 10. As a result, wool and silk take dye more readily than cotton and nylon do.

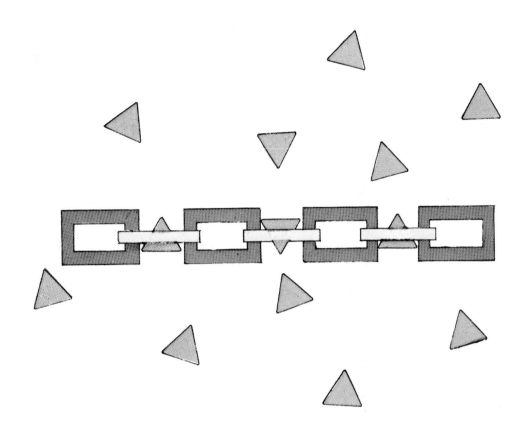

3-6. **Absorption of direct dyes into fiber structure.**

DIRECT OR SUBSTANTIVE DYES

Direct dyes are a group of dyes that are absorbed directly from the water solution into the fiber structure without aid of complicated application procedures or chemical assistants. Direct dyes are also sometimes called substantive dyes; substantive means that the dye does not require a mordant—a chemical that combines with the dye in the fiber to form insoluble dyestuff.

Direct dyes are used most commonly on natural cellulosic fibers such as cotton or linen and on the man-made cellulosic fiber, rayon. Less often, they are used on protein fibers such as wool or silk and on the synthetic fiber, nylon. Chemically, animal fibers and nylon are much alike, and this is why they can be dyed with the same substance.

Since they require no mordants, direct dyes are easy to apply. In addition, they are normally the least expensive dyes available and are relatively lightfast. Their chief drawback is that laundering tends to dissolve part of the dye and wash it back out again. Direct dyes owe their fiber affinity to a type of chemical bonding called hydrogen bonding, which creates only a moderately strong bond between dye and fiber molecules. No chemical reaction permanently unites direct dye molecules and fiber molecules, and the chemical attraction of the hydrogen bonding is insufficient to render them completely washfast. Direct dyes are therefore most suitable for uses in which lightfastness is necessary and the fabric will not be laundered very often—such as for draperies or for a tapestry.

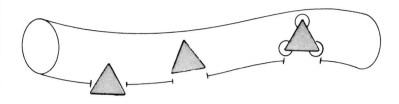

3-7. **Once the dye molecule enters the fiber, it is developed preventing its exit.**

The colorfastness of direct dyes in laundering can be improved somewhat through the use of finishes such as formaldehyde or one of the resins used for wash-and-wear and wrinkle-resistent finishes. Direct dyes can also be made more washfast by being developed after application to the fabric. The term develop means to treat with an agent to cause color to appear; commonly, it refers to the process of sticking molecules of a dye together inside a fiber. When a dye molecule is developed after passing into the structure of the fiber, one of three things occurs: extra atoms are added to the dye molecule, making it too big to get back out of the fiber; the dye molecule's attraction to fiber is improved; or the dye molecule unites through chemical reaction with the structure of the fiber.

Unfortunately, developing a direct dye usually changes its color; and although developed dyes launder better, many are less lightfast. Like many things in fiber technology, the process of developing involves trading off one quality against another.

Both developed and nondeveloped direct dyes produce brightly colored fabrics at medium to low cost. Turmeric, safflower, lichens of some kinds, and walnut hulls are among the natural dyes that are members of the direct-dye group. Snythetic direct dyes are a large and commercially important group of dyestuffs. They are one of the types of dye combined in all-purpose union dyes such as Rit and Tintex, available in supermarkets. Some of these contain benzidine, which is considered carcinogenic and has been linked to bladder cancer. Dyers should handle these dyes carefully, following the directions on the package.

AZOIC OR NAPHTHOL DYES

Azoic dyes are used on cellulosic fibers, including cotton and rayon, and to some extent on synthetic fibers such as nylon, acrylic, acetate, triacetate, and polyester. Azoic dyes work in much the same way as developed direct dyes do. The dye molecule is enlarged and its color is developed after it is inside the fiber.

Azoic dyes consist of two chemically reactive colorless compounds: a diazonium compound, from which the name *azoic dye* comes; and a phenolic compound (or basic naphthol coupling agent), from which the name *naphthol dye* comes. After these two compounds are applied to the fiber, the fabric is treated in a hot detergent solution to develop the color. Color is produced as a result of a chemical reaction that unites the diazonium compound and the phenolic compound. When chemically united, these two compounds create an azo chromophore.

Azoic dyes used to be called ice colors because originally the dye bath had to be cooled with ice to keep the chemical reaction of the ingredients from becoming explosively hot. The azoic dye ingredients

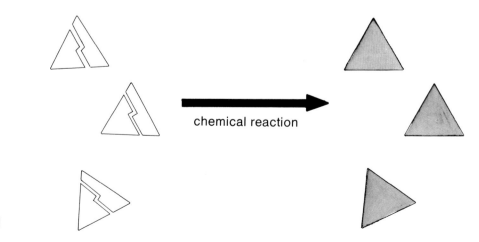

chemical reaction

3-8. **Color is produced when a divided molecule is united.**

are highly reactive chemical compounds that will react with the chemicals in human tissue and skin as well as with each other. Azoic dyes are not safe for use by the artist or craftsperson and should be used with care in industry.

Azoic dyes are cheap and produce bright color. They are colorfast to washing, bleaching, alkalies, and light. But they tend to crock (or rub off) on other fabrics.

ACID DYES

Acid dyes are a large group of chemical dyes. In hand dyeing, they are used mainly on wool and silk (protein or animal fibers) and on nylon. In industry, acid dyes are used on some modified polyester fibers, acrylic, spandex, and olefin fibers, as well as on wool, silk, and nylon. Although nylon resembles protein fibers chemically, it is structurally less absorbent and dyes less readily than wool or silk. Extra acid and a more concentrated dyebath can help compensate for this.

Acid dyes have no affinity at all to cellulosic fibers such as cotton, linen, ramie, or jute, and they cannot be used on any fibers that are sensitive to weak acid solution, such as rayon and acetate. These dyes vary in their fastness to light, laundering, dry cleaning, and perspiration, so they must be selected carefully according to the proposed use of the fiber.

An acid chemical group is present in the dye molecule of any acid dye. Many acid dyes must be applied with an acid dyebath in order for the dye to react chemically with the fiber and produce permanent color.

Dyeing with acid dyes involves acid, salt, heat, agitation, and time. The acid in the dyebath gives the dye an affinity for protein fibers and causes the dye molecule to react chemically with the fiber molecules. The amount of acid added to the dye affects the rate at which the dye bonds to the fiber. For level or even dyeing, small amounts of acid must be added slowly over a period of time. If too little acid is added, the dye remains in solution rather than bonding with the fiber; if too much is added, the bonding of the dye happens too rapidly and causes uneven color distribution. This latter situation can be corrected by carefully adding a base such as baking soda to the solution until the proper level of acidity is achieved.

Salt works as a leveling agent. The salt in the dye solution slows the bonding process of the dye on the fiber, helping the dye color the fiber evenly. The salt attaches to the fiber first, occupying the dye site and preventing the dye from attaching to the fiber. Gradually, the dye bumps the salt off the dye site and occupies the site, bonding with the fiber. If too much salt is added, it can prevent the dye reaction from taking place; more acid, to speed up the bonding

3-9. **Dye replaces the salt and bonds with the fiber.**

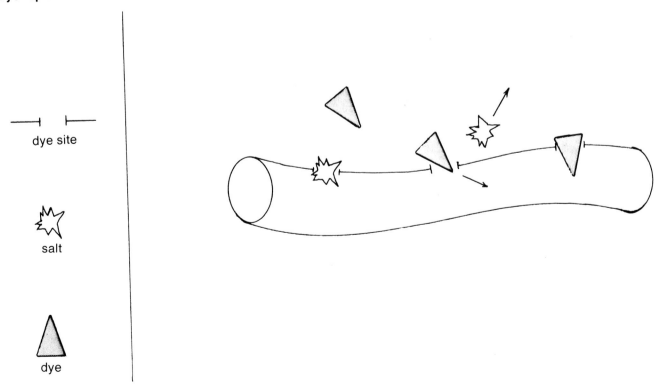

dye site

salt

dye

reaction, can help compensate for too much salt. Glauber's salt works best in a strong acid dyebath using hydrochloric, sulfuric, or nitric acid. Table salt works better in a weak acid dyebath using acetic acid (vinegar) or formic acid.

Heat affects the leveling of the dyebath by speeding up the chemical reaction. It should therefore be increased gradually to prevent the dye from grabbing the fiber too quickly and unevenly. Some variation exists, depending on particular fibers and dyes, but generally the dye bonds with the fibers slowly until the dyebath reaches about 160°F, at which point the rate of bonding increases until the dye is exhausted. Most bonding has occurred by the time the dyebath temperature reaches 180°F; however, the dyebath must continue to be heated a little further to ensure colorfastness.

Wool and silk respond differently to heat. Silk reacts to dye at a lower temperature than wool does and it will not take the dye if placed into too hot a dyebath. This is just as well because, if silk is subjected to near-boiling temperatures in a dyebath, it loses its tensile strength and luster and its fibers can rupture—a condition known as lousy silk. Wool, on the other hand, dyes more deeply at a higher temperature. Spinners and dyers can take advantage of the temperature differential by spinning a silk-and-wool blend yarn that, in the dyebath, exhibits a two-tone effect.

Agitation or stirring helps keep both chemicals and heat evenly distributed, encouraging level dye distribution. Stirring is important during the entire dyeing process, but especially during the period of most rapid dye reaction (160°-180°F).

Optimum immersion time helps determine the success of the dyeing process. A fiber may look the right color before the full immersion time has elapsed, but if the dyebath is stopped early, the color may not be lightfast and washfast.

3-10. **Acid dyes.**

Some acid dyes, called leveling acid dyes, require a strong acid assistant—such as hydrochloric, sulfuric, or nitric acid—in the dyebath. Home dyers can use large amounts of acetic acid (vinegar) in place of these if they want to avoid handling the stronger acids. Leveling acid dyes owe their fiber affinity to chemical bonds that are easily broken and reformed. This chemical characteristic allows the dye to adjust and spread evenly over the fibers if they are left simmering in the dyebath long enough. Unfortunately, the same weak bonds that foster good leveling properties in these dyes also lead to poor washfastness: the bonds can be broken and some of the dye washed out in subsequent launderings. To correct this tendency, the dyebath must be made more acidic, giving the fiber greater attraction to the dye. In general, leveling acid dyes produce rich color with good lightfastness and only fair washfastness. The dyes mix well to form a wide variety of colors.

Another group of acid dyes requires a weak acid, such as acetic or formic acid, in the dyebath. These weak acid dyes have a stronger natural affinity to the fiber, form a stronger bond with it, and therefore do not need as strong an acid to assist in the process.

Hand dyers more commonly use weak acid dyes than strong ones because they give rich colors, because they have generally good fastness characteristics and fairly good leveling properties, and because the acids involved are safer to handle and store. The lightfastness of this group is as good as that of the strong acid dyes, and the washfastness is better. Washfastness and leveling tend to work in opposite directions, however, and the leveling properties of weak acid dyes are not quite as good as the corresponding properties of some strong acid dyes.

Members of the third acid dye group, the fast acid dyes, do not need acid in the dyebath in order to react with the fiber. The attitional fiber affinity of these dyes allows them to be dyed in a neutral bath that is neither

Acid Dyes						
Type	Special Characteristics	Leveling	Washfastness	Lightfastness	Brightness of Color	Colors Mix to Form Palette
Strong Acid (or Leveling Acid) Dyes	Poor fiber affinity and weak chemical bonds with fiber. Bonds easily broken and reformed. Requires strong acid assistant (hydrochloric, sulfuric, nitric, or large amounts of acetic acid) in dyebath to bond with fiber.	Excellent	Fair	Good	Good	Well
Weak Acid Dyes	Stronger fiber affinity. Requires only weak acid (acetic or formic acid) in dyebath to bond with fiber.	Moderate	Good	Good	Good	Well.
Fast Acid Dyes	Strong fiber affinity. Requires no acid assistant. Dyed from a neutral dyebath.	Poor; tends to streak	Excellent	Good	Good	Poorly

acid nor alkaline. They bond rapidly and permanently with the fiber, are washfast and (predictably) do not level well. Indeed, the color tends to streak. Fast acid dyes are sometimes called milling dyes; milling is a fulling (or felting) process similar to laundering that many wool fabrics go through after they are woven. During milling, the milling dye colors do not level or move from one area of the fabric to another—especially if the fabric contains several colors of yarn, as in a plaid fabric. Like all acid dyes, members of this group give rich colors. In addition to their excellent wash-fastness, they have good lightfastness, but they do not mix well to form a range of colors because dyes of different colors bond with the fiber at different rates of speed in the dyebath, yielding uneven and unpredictable color results.

Acid dyes are among the safest dyes for home use by the craftsperson. In fact, most food colorings are mild acid dyes not readily absorbed by the body. Special care should be taken in handling and storing strong acids to be used with acid dyes, in addition to the basic hygienic precautions appropriate in handling all dyes.

MORDANT DYES

Mordant dyes, sometimes called metallized or pre-metallized dyes, cannot be fixed on the fiber without the use of metallic salts (or mordants) as chemical assistants. The mordant—a salt of some metal such as aluminum, chromium, iron, tin, copper, cobalt, or nickel—combines with the dye molecules within the fiber to form multiple bonds between fibers and dyes that otherwise have no affinity for one another. This creates a relatively insoluble dyestuff with good light-fastness and colorfastness in laundering and dry cleaning. Most natural dyes and some synthetic dyes belong to the mordant dye group.

Although their chemical compositions differ, mordant dyes and acid dyes have some things in common. Both require assistants in bonding with fiber, and both are used on the same fibers. The main difference is that, in mordant dyes, metal is added to the dye molecule. Mordant dyes are more washfast than acid dyes but do not level or spread their color evenly over the fiber, which makes them tend to steak. These dyes do not mix well to create a good range of colors. They are especially suited for printing because they give a hard edge, and they are used on yarns that are expected to be washed or dry cleaned often. Mordant dyes give duller colors than acid dyes do.

Metal salts, especially those containing chromium, are corrosive and are thought to be carcinogenic. For the natural dyes used by many craftspeople, the preferred mordants are alum (potassium aluminum sulfate) and salts of tin or iron. The more corrosive chromium salts are primarily used in the textile industry.

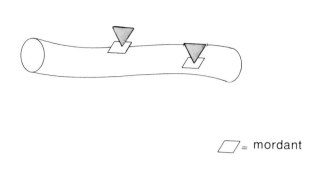

= mordant

3-11. **A mordant helps a dye to bond with a fiber.**

As a group, however, mordant dyes are not used extensively in industry. Workers should wear respirators and other protective clothing when handling and processing them.

BASIC (OR CATIONIC) DYES

In basic (or cationic) dyes, the chromophore is positively charged (cationic), so it attracts a negative group to form the molecules of dyestuff. This is the opposite situation from the one prevailing with acid dyes. The basic dye group includes mauviene (the first synthetic dye), as well as many other snythetic and some natural dyes.

All of these dyes are dyed from a neutral bath. They are very good on acrylic fibers, where the dye molecule unites in a chemical reaction with the acrylic fiber molecule to produce a colorfast result. They also work well on modified nylon fibers, modified polyester fibers, and some plant fibers: reed, raffia, grasses, barks, and so on. Basic dyes were at one time used on cotton, linen, and wool, but their colors are not permanent with these fibers. They can be used on cotton that has been previously mordanted with tannic acid, or they can be used over direct dyes, enlisting the direct dye as a mordant.

Basic dyes produce brilliant colors and sometimes are used as topping colors in overdyeing to increase the brilliance of a fabric; the fluorescent or Day-Glo dyes are in this category. These dyes are relatively safe to use because they are not easily absorbed by the body, but some allergic reactions have been reported. Basic dyes are often found as components in the union dyes (all-purpose dyes found in supermarkets), as are direct and acid dyes.

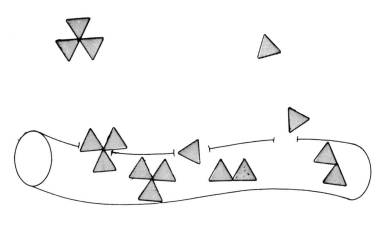

3-12. **Disperse dyes: dyeing occurs when more dye is in the fiber than is in the dyebath.**

DISPERSE DYES

Disperse dyes are synthetic dyes developed by industry for use on man-made fibers such as acetate that are often nonabsorbent and nonreactive to water-based dye. Disperse dyes were originally developed specifically for acetate fibers and were called acetate dyes, but they are used now on polyester, acrylic, nylon, and rayon, too. As new synthetic fibers are developed, new synthetic dyes are developed to color them. Today, because we use so many synthetic fibers, disperse dyes constitute one of the largest dye groups (both in amount used and in choice of brands and colors).

Disperse dyes are named for the way they behave in water and in the fiber. Unlike most dyes, which dissolve into single molecules in the dyebath, disperse dyes have very little attraction for water and do not dissolve in the dyebath; instead, they remain in suspension (or dispersion) in the dyebath, in the form of floating groups of molecules. Sometimes a few drops of detergent must be added to the dyebath to help them remain in suspension. During dyeing, the groups of disperse dye molecules leave the water and enter the fibers, for which they have more attraction. They first affix to the surface of the fiber, and then disperse into the structure of the fiber and go into suspension among the fiber molecules. The small size of individual disperse dye molecules makes it easy for the dye to enter the synthetic fiber structure.

Disperse dye molecules do not necessarily remain in suspension in the fiber molecule; some molecules leave the fiber and go back into the dyebath. Dyeing takes place when more dye molecules leave the dyebath and enter the fiber than vice versa. Eventually this happens, because overall the dye molecules have considerably less attraction to the water than to the fiber. Not every disperse dye is attracted to every type of fiber commonly dyed with disperse dyes, however, so fiber and dye must be matched. When an attraction between dye and fiber does exist, it may differ from dye to dye and from fiber to fiber, causing different dyebaths to exhaust at different rates, depending on which fiber and dye were used.

Some synthetic fibers are difficult to dye, even with disperse dyes. Polyester, for example, is extremely dense and unreactive. Dyeing it used to require many hours of boiling in a dyebath to produce even pale colors. In current practice, a carrier—a chemical that, when added to a dyebath, swells the fiber, making it less dense and allowing the dye molecules to penetrate it—is used in a dyebath for polyester. Carriers increase the affinity of fiber and dye, helping to concentrate the dye molecules on the surface of the fiber, from which position they penetrate the fiber. In industry, special high-pressure methods enable companies to dye polyester without using carriers.

The characteristic mobility of disperse dye molecules leads to two of this group's principal disadvantages: gas (or fume) fading, and sublimation. Some disperse dye molecules are capable of moving from suspension in a fiber into suspension in the air, particularly if the air contains nitrous oxide. Fabric colored with these dyes changes hue when exposed to polluted air for long periods—as can sometimes be seen in umbrellas or coat linings. Fume fading may also occur in fabric enclosed for a long time in a display case; oxygen and nitrogen in the stagnant air, aided by heat from the display lights, combine to form nitrous oxide, establishing the conditions requisite for fume fading. Newer disperse dyes have been improved to resist nitrous oxide and to eliminate the problem of fume fading.

Disperse dye molecules sometimes move into the air from dyed fibers and migrate to adjacent undyed fibers. This process, called sublimation, most often happens if the dyed and undyed fibers are stored next to one another for an extended period of time and if heat and humidity are present to aid in dye movement; sublimation can also be caused by ironing. Different disperse dyes vary in their ability to sublimate.

The ability of disperse dyes to sublimate into a vaporous state and then to transfer into an adjacent fiber led to the development of transfer (or contact) printing, also called dry dyeing. In transfer printing, disperse dyes possessing high sublimation ability are painted or printed on a paper. When a printed fabric is desired, the paper is pressed onto a synthetic fabric (such as polyester) in the presence of heat; the print then transfers from the paper to the fabric through sublimation.

Disperse dyeing involves water, detergent, heat, fiber, and dye. The amount of water is important in that too little water (or crowded fiber) in the dyebath leads to streaking, and too dilute a dyebath leads to weak color. Detergent helps the dye remain in suspension in the water and acts as a leveling agent to slow the migration of dye to the fiber. Heat causes the molecules to move: the hotter the dyebath, the more quickly the molecules move. Slow, gradual heating leads to even dyeing. The maximum acceptable temperature of the dyebath depends on the type of dye, the type of fiber, and the fiber's tolerance to heat.

Disperse dyes have the advantage of being able to dye nonabsorbent synthetic fibers, providing an alternative to dope dyeing (predyeing synthetic material before it is formed into fiber). In addition, they have excellent lightfastness and good washfastness, and they are colorfast to dry cleaning. They are quick and easy to use, can be transfer-printed with a hot iron, level well, and produce strong colors on most synthetics. Their chief drawback is that some people develop a rash from wearing polyester clothing or nylon hosiery dyed with disperse dyes.

VAT DYES

Vat dyes include synthetic dyes and some natural dyes. Natural indigo was one of the first vat dyes to be produced. Vat dye molecules are manipulated in an interesting way to get them into the fiber and make them stay there. In their original or crude state, the molecules are insoluble in water and have no affinity for fibers. Consequently, they must be converted or reduced chemically—either by bacteria or by chemicals—and formed into a product that is soluble in alkaline solution and has a molecular attraction to the fiber. This was originally done in a large vat, hence the name *vat dyes.*

The process of reducing the dye molecule breaks apart the colorbearing chromophore and produces a colorless solution of dye and alkaline substance called a leuco bath. The dye is applied to the fiber while in this leuco state. Once inside the fiber, the dye is reoxidized (put back into its original colored form) through the addition of oxygen. The reoxidized color is insoluble in water, as was the original molecule,

making it colorfast in laundering. The term *vat-dyed* has come to be synonymous with colorfast. Vat dyes are not ony incredibly washfast, they are also resistant to fading from sunlight, chlorine bleach, and seawater. In order for vat dyes to produce colorfast results, the dyeing process must be carefully controlled; if the dyeing is not done properly, the color may fade quickly.

Vat dyes are used mostly on natural and man-made cellulosic fibers—cotton, linen, and rayon. Some are suitable for wool, acetate, and some of the newer man-made fibers, but usually dyers avoid using vat dyes on protein fibers such as wool and silk because the amino acid composition of proteins can be damaged by the alkaline dye solution. Some of the newer dyeing techniques involve briefer exposure of the fibers to the alkaline solution, decreasing the likelihood of damage to protein fibers and making use of vat dyes on a wider selection of fibers possible.

The chemicals used to reduce vat dyes can cause ulcerative burns on the skin. Prereduced dye powders are also caustic and can irritate the respiratory tract; and the acid used for dye development can cause acid burns. Plain water should be kept close at hand in case the need arises for flushing eyes and skin. Goggles and protective clothing should be worn to protect eyes and skin from splashes. Some vat dyes produce allergic reactions.

SULFUR DYES

Sulfur dyes are one of the less important groups of synthetic dyes. They produce adequate brown, black, and navy colors and are used mainly on cellulosic fibers such as cotton and linen. If improperly applied, they can decompose and weaken the fabric. Sulfur dyes are first dissolved in alkaline solution, and the fabric is then immersed in the alkaline dyebath. When the fabric is washed, the dye remains on the fiber in a water-insoluble form. Besides being washfast, sulfur dyes have the advantage of being inexpensive.

3-13. **The vat dye molecule must be broken before it can enter the fiber; it is then recombined to produce the color.**

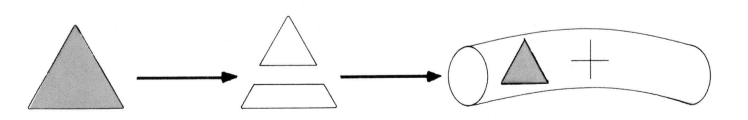

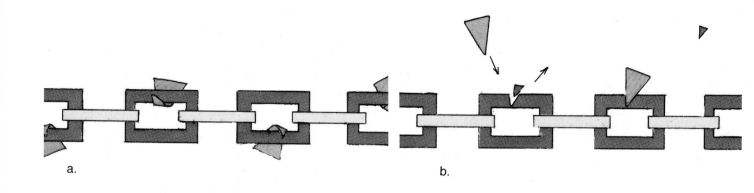

3-14. **Fiber reactive dyes: a. the addition method; b. the substitution method.**

REACTIVE DYES

Reactive dyes are synthetic dyes that were developed by the textile industry in 1956. They were named for their ability to react chemically with fibers, which enables them to form permanent chemical bonds that cannot be broken by heat, light, or water. The dye molecule unites with the fiber molecule either by addition or by substitution. In the addition method, the dye molecule simply hooks onto the fiber molecule. In the substitution method an atom is removed from the fiber molecule, providing a site for the new dye molecule to attach itself to.

Reactive dyes are used mainly on cellulosic fibers such as cotton, linen, jute, and rayon. Some reactive dyes can also be used on wool and silk. In order for reactive dyes to react with a cellulosic fiber in a dyebath, table salt (sodium chloride), soda ash (anhydrous sodium carbonate, sometimes called wash soda), water, heat, and time are required. On protein fibers, the alkaline wash soda is replaced by acetic or formic acid, which is more compatable with the protein fiber.

The salt works as a leveling agent and promotes the migration of dye molecules out of solution and onto the fiber. The soda ash causes the dye molecules to react, either with the fiber molecule or with the water molecule (whichever happens to be closer). For this reason, the soda ash is added thirty minutes into the dyebath so that the dye molecules have had time to move evenly onto the fibers for better exhaustion and leveling of the dyebath. As with disperse dyes, enough water must be present to allow the fibers uncrowded, even exposure to the dye solution; again, too much water will severely hamper the dye's ability to reach the fiber, and it will simply react with the water around it when the soda ash is added to the dyebath.

Like the soda ash, heat helps the dye react, whether with the water or with the fiber. Therefore, heat must be carefully applied. Chemical reactions at too low a temperature yield low washfastness, while too rapid an increase in temperature causes the dye to react in the water and be lost.

Time is a crucial factor in successful use of reactive dyes. Before the soda ash is added, the dye molecules move from the water solution to the fiber but do not yet bond. Allowing enough time before the soda ash is added gives the molecules time to get to the fiber and improves dyebath exhaustion. Addition of the soda ash initiates the dye molecules' bonding with the fibers onto which they have presumably moved by this time. If a dark color is desired, the dyebath should run longer after the alkali addition.

Reactive dyes are among the best dyes for cotton and are suitable for such other cellulosic fibers as linen, rayon, and jute. Sometimes in industry they are used for nylon, wool, silk, acrylics, and blends through adaptation in the dye process. Reactive dyes have many advantages (see Figure 3-15). They yield bright colors and mix easily to produce a color palette. They are simple to use. They dissolve readily in water and work quickly, dyeing in forty-five minutes in a warm dyebath, and needing only salt and soda ash as dye assistants to help them enter the fiber. Because of their speed and ease of application, reactive dyes are used extensively by craftspeople for tie-dye and batik work. They are colorfast to light, washing, perspiration, and dry cleaning, and they will not fume-fade as disperse dyes do. They are, however, damaged by chlorine.

As in the case of disperse dyes, some of the dye molecules in reactive dyes leave the fiber while others are entering it during the dyeing process. This trading-off process makes complete exhaustion of the dyebath difficult, and some dye is inevitably wasted; it is therefore necesary to start with a stronger solution at the beginning of the dyebath in order to get well-saturated color. Reactive dyes cannot be stored in solution as acid dyes can because they decompose quickly.

Reactive dyes are extremely reactive chemical compounds that will react harmfully with body tissues—especially in the respiratory tract. Crafts-people should avoid breathing dye dust; respirators (or dust masks) and protective clothing are essential. These dyes can also cause allergies.

REVIEW OF CHEMICAL DYES

Few dyes are absolutely colorfast under all circumstances—to light, to washing, to perspiration, to acid fumes, to steam and ironing, and to crocking (or rubbing off)—but most are permanent to one or more of these when used on the proper fibers. Successful dyeing depends on the selection of a dye that possesses affinity for the particular fiber being dyed and that will be colorfast for the proposed use of the fiber. Figure 3-16 identifies and compares specific properties of the various dye groups discussed in this chapter.

In general, wool and silk (the animal protein fibers) combine chemically with acid dyes. Silk is more delicate and easier to damage than wool because of its fineness, and it must be handled more carefully. The acid dyes show excellent washfastness with wool but lower washfastness with silk. Wool can also be dyed with chrome mordant dyes, with direct dyes, and with vat dyes that have been processed for minimum alkali damage. Some direct dyes can be used to dye silk; these work best on silk in an acid dyebath. Some natural dyes also work well with silk, but some do not; they should be tested individually. When using a mordant, the dyer should be careful not to overweight the silk. (*Weighting* silk means adding metallic salts to the silk dyebath, which makes the silk fiber stiffer but at the same time weakens it.)

Basic dyes are good on acrylic fibers and show brilliant colors. They can be used on wool and silk, but they require special equipment and are not as safe for the home dyer to use as are acid dyes applicable to the same fibers.

Cotton, rayon, linen, and other cellulosic fibers dye well with direct, developed direct, reactive, sulfur, vat, and azoic (naphthol) dyes. If mordants are used first, basic dyes can also be used for dyeing these cellulosic fibers.

Acetate fibers are commonly dyed with disperse (acetate) dyes, azoic (naphthol) dyes, acid dyes, and vat dyes; alternatively, they may be colored by pigments added to the spinning solution before the fiber is formed (dope dyeing). Many synthetic fibers besides acetate can be dyed with disperse dyes, azoic dyes, acid dyes, and some direct dyes (if acid is added to the dyebath), and they can be dyed with vat dyes if a mordant is used.

Structural Orientation

Structural orientation is the arrangement of parts relative to one another within a fiber piece—for example, the arrangement of molecules in a fiber, or fibers in a piece of yarn, or of yarn in a piece of fabric. Structural orientation is an important factor in dyeing results at every level of fabric structure, but most particularly at the molecular and fiber levels because it strongly affects moisture and dye absorption.

The characteristic constituent molecules of fibers of all kinds are called polymers. Polymers are large, compound, and long chain molecules that form through the linking of smaller molecules (called monomers) together in a chain. The textile polymer can be thought of as a chain with each of whose links is a monomer. As a result of this linear hookup, the polymers that make up fibers have the same long thin shape that the actual fibers do.

The structural orientation of the polymers within the fiber varies greatly from one type of fiber to another, and this arrangement pattern partially determines the dyeing results of the fiber. Structural orientation also affects other fiber properties, including elongation, recovery, resilience, and fiber luster, which in turn affect our color perception of the fiber.

Fiber polymers can be highly oriented (meaning that they are parallel to one another and aligned parallel with the length of the fiber), or they can have a more random or amorphous arrangement in which the polymers lie criss-crossed at various angles to one another, or they can lie in crystalline groupings, with the polymers parallel to each other within the group but not necessarily parallel to the length of the fiber or to other groupings of polymers within the fiber. Highly oriented polymers are also crystalline, but crystalline polymers are not necessarily highly oriented (see Figure 3-17).

Highly oriented, crystalline, and amorphous areas commonly coexist within the same fiber. Although patterns of crystalline, highly oriented, and amorphous

Name	Craft Uses	Light Fastness	Wash Fastness	Advantages	Disadvantages	Miscellaneous
Direct dyes (Substantive)	(Most often:) cotton, linen, rayon, jute, hemp, sisal, (Ocassionally:) wool, silk, nylon	Moderate to good	Fair to moderate; requires finishes or chemical developing for fastness	Easy to apply; inexpensive; bright colors	Moderate wash-fastness; contains benz-idine (linked with bladder cancer)	
Azoic Dyes (Naphthol Dyes)	Cotton, rayon, nylon, acrylic, acetate, triacetate, polyester	Moderate	Excellent	Good reds	Unsafe for crafts-person; may crock; bleeds in dry cleaning	Used mainly in industry
Acid Dyes	Wool, silk, nylon, polyester, acrylic, spandex, olefin	Varies with type of dye	Varies	Easy to apply; good bright colors; safe		Gives blurry edge when used in printing
Mordant Dyes	Wool, silk, nylon, some modacrylics	Very good	Excellent	Fastness	Duller colors than acid dyes; dyes do not mix well to create palette; tendency to streak	Gives hard edge when used in printing
Basic Dyes	Acrylic, modified nylon, modified polyester, reed, raffia, grasses, cotton with tannic acid mordant	Excellent on acrylic; good with reed, raffia, and grasses; poor on others	Excellent on acrylics; poor on others	Bright colors; good for grasses, reeds, and raffia; rela-tively safe	Poor fastness; stains sinks, floors, and work area	Day glow colors in this category
Disperse Dyes	Acetate, triacetate, acrylic, nylon, rayon, polyester with a carrier, plastics	Very good	Very good	Bright colors; easy to use; levels well; can dye non-absorbent materials (polyesters and plastics)	Fume fading; fades to nearby materials; can cause skin rash	Can be used for transfer printing; gives hard edge in printing
Vat Dyes	Cotton, linen, rayon, sometimes wool, acetate, and new synthetics	Excellent	Excellent	Fastness	Alkaline dye solution can damage protein fibers; burns skin; irritates respira-tory tract; causes allergies	Dye process must be per-formed accurate-ly or color will fade; user must wear goggles and protective clothing to pro-tect from splashes
Sulfur Dyes	Cotton, linen, rayon	Very good	Very good	Inexpensive	Limited to dark colors (navy, black, brown); can weaken fiber if applied improperly	
Dyes-reactive	Cotton, linen, hemp, jute, ramie, rayon, wool, silk	Excellent	Excellent	Bright colors; mixes well to create palette; fastness; easy to use and works quickly	Some dye wasted in dye-bath, increasing cost; cannot be stored, due to decomposition; requires much rinsing; causes allergies	One of the best dyes for cotton; user must wear protective cloth-ing and respira-tor

Credit: Fiber Arts Magazine

3-16. **Dye chart.**

areas vary widely from one kind of fiber to another, certain patterns are typical of each kind of fiber, and these patterns affect dyeing results of the fiber in a predictable manner. Highly oriented polymers and crystalline polymers are tightly packed and do not provide many spaces in the fiber through which moisture and dye can penetrate the fiber. Randomly arranged or amorphous polymers, on the other hand, do create empty spaces in the fiber structure that allow water molecules and dye molecules to move in and out.

Traditional dyeing problems involve variables in the amount and size of the amorphous spaces in the fiber and in the sizes of the dye molecules. In the case of developed direct dyes and azoic dyes, for example, once the dye molecules have entered the fiber structure, extra atoms attach to the dye molecule, either making it too big to get back out again or rendering it capable of reacting with the fiber and becoming a permanent part of the fiber structure. Vat dyes, too, assemble a larger molecule once the dye is inside the fiber, thus making it colorfast.

Since amorphous areas of a fiber take more dye than do highly oriented or crystalline areas, they will dye a darker and more intense color in the dyebath. Different patterns of crystalline and amorphous molecular orientation therefore cause variations in color intensity and uniformity in different fibers. Much of a fiber's typical character depends on the subtleties of the almost imperceptible color changes that take place from the dyeable amorphous areas to the nondyeable crystalline and highly oriented areas. This kind of subtle variation is more frequently encountered in the natural fibers than in the man-made ones. The molecular structure of natural fibers is a product of natural forces—the way the fibers grew in response to their natural environment—and the circumstances of nature are rarely precisely uniform. The properties of man-made fibers, however, can be totally controlled and engineered into standardized fibers, starting at the molecular level and continuing through the levels of fiber, yarn, and fabric.

Like natural fibers, man-made fibers consist of threadlike compound molecules (or polymers) whose

3-17. **Different patterns of molecular orientation.**

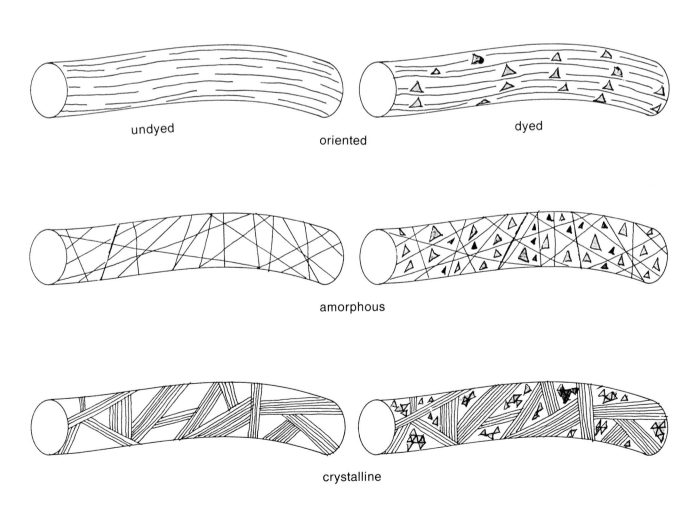

undyed   dyed

oriented

amorphous

crystalline

75

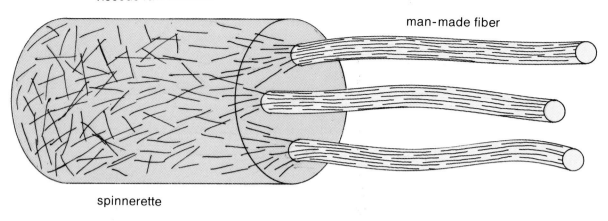

viscous raw material

man-made fiber

spinnerette

3-18. **Polymers are aligned along the length of the fiber, creating high orientation.**

smaller, constituent molecules (or monomers) are arranged to form a long chain. The properties of the fibers are derived from the chemical construction and internal arrangement of these polymers, which in turn can be managed by the chemist. All man-made fibers are produced in essentially the same way. The material from which the fiber is to be made is manufactured in bulk, with the molecules lying at random in the material. The substance is then dissolved into a viscous state and extruded through the fine holes in a spinerette, a device resembling a shower head. During the extrusion process, the polymers within the viscous raw material are aligned along the length of the fiber, which hardens into a filament (see Figure 3-18). The result is a highly oriented molecular structure in the man-made fibers. The polymers align themselves parallel to the length of the fiber and parallel to each other during the drawing out process, as the filament emerges from the spinerette. The fiber can be further stretched to bring the polymers closer together, allowing the molecules to bond together more firmly and making the fiber stronger.

This dense, highly oriented molecular arrangement is one of the reasons why man-made fibers are more difficult to dye than natural fibers: fewer spaces lie between the polymers and serve as sites for the dye molecules to enter into the fiber structure. Some synthetic fibers are so highly oriented that dye cannot penetrate easily. Such fibers must be solution (or dope) dyed; that is, the dye or pigment must be added to the viscous solution before it is forced through the spinerette, so the colorant becomes an integral part of the fiber structure. This kind of dyeing creates extreme uniformity of color as well as good colorfastness. Color uniformity may be desirable in some cases, but the extremely even dyeing of dope-dyed fibers tends

to give the yarn or fabric produced from these fibers a flat, uninteresting color quality.

The same relationships among structural orientation, dye penetration, and color uniformity that exist at the molecular level also exist at the fiber level. Just as the amorphous molecular arrangement in a fiber allows space for moisture and dye molecules to enter the fiber, a loose, random arrangement of fibers in the dyebath allows good dye penetration in the fibers. A tighter, more oriented arrangement of fibers (as can be found in a carded, combed, and tightly twisted yarn) does not allow the sort of easy and complete dye penetration possible with loose, unspun fibers. For this reason natural textile fibers such as wool and cotton are often dyed before they are spun into yarn. This is called stock dyeing or (in the case of wool fibers) dyeing in the fleece. Besides promoting dye penetration and colorfastness, stock dyeing gives the spinner the option of blending different colored fibers into a yarn to produce optically mixed color.

In wool and other hair fibers dyed in this way, a color difference from one end of the fiber to the other is sometimes noticeable, the outer end being darker. This happens because the outer end of the fiber has been on the animal the longest time and consequently has had more exposure to damaging natural elements than any other part of the fiber has; and the damaged portion absorbs dye more readily than the rest of the fiber. Fiber artists may consider this color variation an interesting element of the finished yarn—one that adds character and color variation to the yarn—but dyers who do not want variations due to natural fiber damage can avoid it by snipping the damaged ends off each lock of fiber before it is spun.

In the industrial spinning process, loose fibers are carded and sometimes combed; then they are formed

76

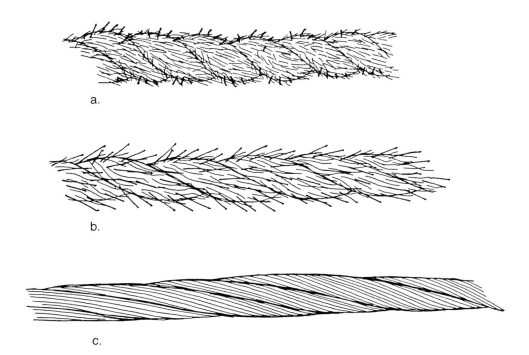

3-19. **Yarn staples: a. lightly carded short staple yarn (excellent dye penetration); b. carded and combed long staple yarn (fair to good dye penetration); c. tightly packed filament yarn (poor dye penetration).**

into a loose, untwisted, continuous ropelike roll that is suitable for spinning and is called a sliver, a top, or a roving. Fibers carded only and then formed into a soft, loose rope yield what is called *a carder sliver.* When fibers are combed and attenuated into a finer, untwisted, ribbonlike form ready for spinning, the product is called a *top.* If the sliver is further drawn out to about 1/4" in diameter, it is called a *roving.* Commercially processed textile fibers are often dyed at the sliver or roving stage of production, an operation sometimes called *top dyeing* or *dyeing in the roving.* This form of dyeing is similar to stock dyeing in that the loose arrangement of the fibers allows good dye penetration.

Yarn is a general term for a continuous strand of textile fibers, filaments, or other material whose form is suitable for intertwining to produce a textile fabric. The results of dyeing a yarn are affected by factors including the origin, size, and texture of the fiber, the method used in dyeing the yarn, the timing of the dye process, and the type of yarn construction involved.

Yarn can be divided into two categories: staple and filament. *Staple yarn* is composed of short fibers held together with a twist. Short staple yarn is carded lightly so that the staple fibers are somewhat organized for spinning, but lie more or less criss-crossed in the yarn held together with a light twist. This kind of yarn is more loosely organized, softer, and loftier (fluffier to the touch) than long staple yarn; its yarn structure resembles the amorphous type of molecular structure in fiber (see Figure 3-19a). Long staple yarn is made from longer fibers that have been carded and combed

so that the fibers lie lengthwise in the yarn, parallel to one another and to the length of the yarn, in a structure similar to the highly oriented molecular structure (see Figure 3-19b).

Short staple yarns are loftier and warmer than long staple yarns, and pull apart more easily. For these reasons, they are used as weft yarns in fabric construction. Long staple yarns are smoother, denser, and stronger, and are suitable for both warp and weft yarns. Different terms are used to distinguish between yarns made from short fibers in amorphous arrangement and yarns made from long fibers in a more orderly arrangement. In wool yarns, the term *woolen* refers to short staple, low-twist yarn, while *worsted* designates long staple, combed yarn. *Tow linen* identifies short staple linen, and *line linen* refers to long staple linen. *Combed cotton* is used for longer staple cotton yarns and threads that are more oriented and (therefore) stronger.

Space for dye to circulate and move into the fibers is necessary for good dyeing results. The structural orientation of the fibers in the yarn affects yarn density and dye results, just as the structural orientation of the molecules in the fiber does. In addition, dye penetration can be influenced by other structural factors, such as the amount of twist imparted to the yarn and the yarn's overall thickness. If a yarn is tightly twisted, its fibers are packed together, and dye will have difficulty penetrating all the way to the yarn's center. Similarly, if a yarn is very thick, dye will have difficulty penetrating to the yarn's center (see Figure 3-19c).

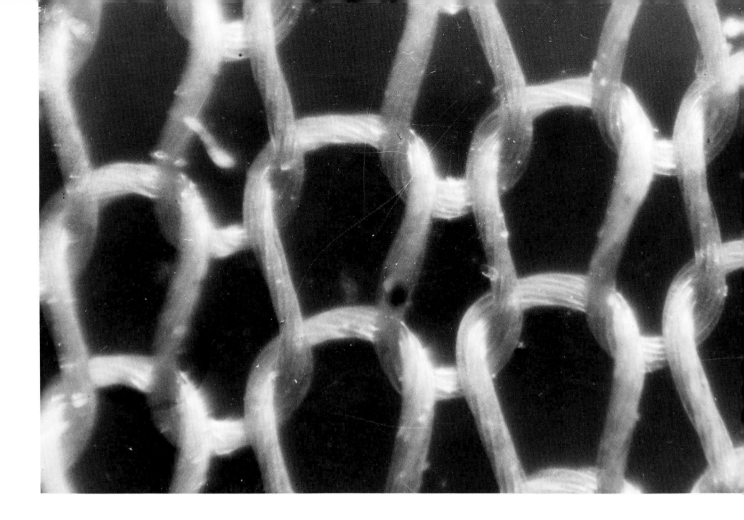

3-20. **Nylon stocking enlarged 250X.**

Photo: Dr. Maximillan Toch

Filament yarn is made from continous fibers such as reeled silk or man-made fibers extruded from a spinerette in continuous form. Like staple yarns, filament yarns are held together with a twist. The filaments lie parallel to one another and parallel to the length of the fiber, in a highly oriented structure (see Figure 3-20).

Optical Mixing

Optical mixing is a special color mixing technique that creates a new color by placing small areas, dots, or particles of two different colors side by side so that the viewer's eye perceives a third color that appears to be a mixture of the first two. Optically mixed colors can be either more intense or less intense than the parent colors, depending on the hue and value contrasts of the two parent colors.

An optical mixture of two colors closely related in hue and value—as for example, two blues with a barely perceptible difference—does not appear to create a third color, but rather a richer, livelier, or more intense version of the basic color (here, blue). An optical mixture of two colors that obviously differ in hue and value—as, for example, yellow and blue—results in a third color that is different from either of the

parent colors. The resulting color also has a softer, less intense, or more grayed quality than either of the parent colors.

Other factors that influence the intensity of the color created from an optical mixture are the intimacy of the fiber blend (the size or scale of the dots) and the intensity of the original colors used to create the optical mixture. Smaller, more intimately blended particles of color yield a mixture that blends more easily in the viewer's eye and is easier to see as a single, integrated color than as areas of separate color. Other things being equal, relatively intense analogous parent colors produce a mixture that is relatively intense in color.

Optical mixes are created in yarns by spinning together fibers of two or more colors. The fibers are stock dyed in one or another color, and then fibers of different colors are spun together. Optically mixed yarns give us the heathers and the soft tints and shades that present very appealing color variations. Any colored fiber mixed with the white fiber in yarn yields an optically mixed tint, while any colored fiber blended with black fiber in a yarn yields an optically mixed shade. Lovely soft grays are often blended optically from black and white fibers; and a little color may be included with these grays to add a slight hint of a hue to what is essentially a gray yarn. Rich chromatic grays can be optically blended from combinations of all three primary hues or from pairs of complementary hues.

Both natural and man-made fibers can be blended in this way. In fact, optical mixing is used to correct the flat, overly uniform, mechanical color that occurs in dope dyed snythetics. In this case, two very similar colors of fiber (such as two close reds) are combined in a yarn to make an optical blend that appears to be the same red color but has a livelier more interesting quality—more like the color quality of natural fibers.

Once the colors and their proportions have been decided upon, they can still be blended in different ways to create different color effects. If different-colored fibers are blended early in the spinning process, the blending is more intimate and produces the effect of a single color. Colored fibers blended when in a loose fiber state produce the most uniform blends, with less variation in color and more visible hue.

Slivers of different colors can be blended before being drawn out and spun, in which case the intimacy of the blend depends on how many times the slivers are doubled and redrawn before being spun. Yarns spun directly from different colored rovings are called marl yarns; their limited color blending causes them to resemble ply yarn made of single strands of different-colored yarn twisted together. Melange yarns are produced from slivers dyed in bands of differnt colors so that the subsequent drawing of the slivers causes the colors to become more or less intermingled. Another variation introduces small patches of dyed fibers into slivers of another color, resulting in a yarn spotted with color. The largest scale in optically blended yarns is produced by plying (or twisting together) two single strands of different-colored yarn to create a two-ply yarn (see Figure 3-21).

Optical mixtures can be created in fabric structure in a number of ways. Any time predyed yarns or threads of different colors are combined in the structure of a fabric at a scale small enough to permit perception of a new color by the viewer, an optical mixture is created. When several colors of thread are combined in an embroiderer's needle or a weaver's shuttle, for example, an optically mixed color results. When a red warp crosses a blue weft in a piece of plaid fabric, the violet color that appears at the junction of the two is an optically mixed violet. Even the colors of a small print in a piece of fabric used by a quilter for patchwork may blend at the proper distance into a single optically mixed color. Quilters should be aware of this pheno-menon when working with print fabrics because the emotional and visual impact of the print's optically blended color is often markedly different from that of the print's individual colors when viewed close up.

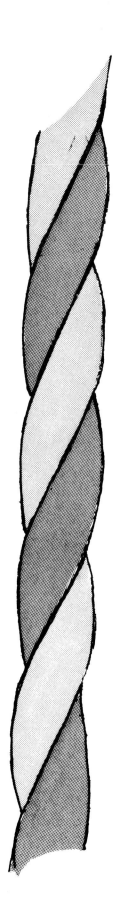

3-21. **In optical mixing, the largest scale at the yarn level is made by plying two colors into a single strand.**

YARN TECHNIQUES

There are many methods of dyeing yarns after they have been spun. Yarns can be dyed in the skein or rolled on special tubes—a process often called *package dyeing.* Recently a system for dyeing yarns after they have been rolled on the warp beam (beam dyeing) has been developed in the textile industry. Yarn dyeing in general provides good color absorption and in most cases adequate penetration, although obviously these are not as good as in stock or fiber-level dyeing. Penetration in dyeing at the yarn level depends on the dye type, the method of application, and the yarn's density, twist, and thickness.

Space dyeing is an interesting variation on this process, in which selected areas of the yarn are dyed different colors to produce a pattern in the fabric. This technique, like most fiber techniques, has a wide range of application in finished fiber pieces—from the abominations crocheted out of cheap, commercially space-printed yarns to the subtle, exquisite beauty and juicy color effects of well-designed and carefully executed Ikat (see Figure 3-22).

Ikat is a hand-dyeing technique in which certain areas of the yarn are bound off to resist the dye and produce a pattern that is developed later in the weave. It may be applied to warp, weft, or both; warp is the most common. In this technique, bundles of yarn are partially covered and tied with impenetrable material such as bast fiber, paper, rubber, or plastic, and then they are dyed. Later the dyer removes the protective material, revealing the undyed parts.

This process can be repeated for a many-colored yarn, with areas of new color introduced on the undyed areas or overdyed on the already-colored ones. The finished Ikat pattern can be the result of one color set off with undyed spaces or of a combination of as many colors as the artist is prepared to fool with. Ikat patterns can be developed in the warp only, in either a warp-faced weave or a balanced weave, giving two entirely different effects. They can also be developed with space-dyed yarns in the weft only, again with a weft-faced or a balanced weave; or the Ikat motif can be developed with space-dyed yarns in both the warp and the weft (see Figure 6-26), or by compound arrangements of any of the above.

This is pure manipulation of color through the interrelated operation of yarn-level dye patterning and fabric technique. The trick is that the yarn must be handled as it will appear on the warp, so that the intended pattern can be controlled and realized as successive layers of dye are applied to the yarn. In the case of weft Ikat, the back-and-forth sequence of the weft must be taken into account. All parts of the patterned yarn must be kept firmly in place while being dyed (so that they will not slip or shift) and must be mounted on the loom in precisely that position (so that the pattern does not become indistinct). If an indistinct pattern is desired, fine; but it should be a consequence of deliberate choice in that case and not of sloppy craft.

3-22. **Ikat:** *Color Progressions II* **(wool, 25" x 48").**
Artist: Joan Hausrath
Photo: Joan Hausrath
Courtesy of Josephine Hausrath

FABRIC TECHNIQUES

Most commercial solid-color fabrics are dyed after the fabric is completed because this is the easiest and cheapest method. Manufacturers can color fabrics as ordered and keep a smaller stock of fabric on hand, avoiding obsolete colors if fashion changes. This approach, called piece dyeing, is sometimes simply a matter of matching the proper dye with a particular fabric; however, a much different situation is posed if the fabric is made of a blend of fibers that do not have the same reaction to dyes. Such a situation can be approached in either of two ways, depending on the result the dyer wants.

Union dyeing is the first approach to dyeing a fabric containing two or more fibers. The goal of union dyeing is to achieve a single uniform color in all of the fibers. Since different dyes are appropriate for different fibers, the dyestuffs must be carefully selected and applied to achieve color uniformity. Sometimes they can be applied simultaneously, and othertimes they must be applied individually; these are known as one-bath processes.

Cross dyeing is the second alternative. In this case, the fibers are dyed in such a way that each fiber accepts a different dyestuff and becomes a different color, creating optically mixed hues, heathers, tints, and shades. Cross dyeing can work with several different fibers with different dye affinities, each of which will color differently in the same dyebath (one-bath process), or each fiber can take a different dye, while remaining inert to the others (two-bath and three-bath processes). Fibers that accept color can also be combined with fibers that do not, resulting in an optically blended tint (white fibers plus colored fibers).

Cross dyeing can thus be used to enrich a single hue—each different type of fiber in the yarn blend receiving the dye, but with a very slight color variation—or to produce multicolored fabric, based on each type of fiber's requiring a different dye and being inert to the others. Another approach is to add a predyed fiber (that may or may not overdye) to the blend of fibers with different dye potentials, again increasing the possibilities for achieving varied coloration. Cross dyeing, like other forms of piece dyeing, is economical in that a fabric with a two-color (or greater) potential can be stored undyed until fashion dictates the colors.

The end result of cross dyeing can depend on the placement of the different types of fiber in the fabric. An overall blend of fibers throughout the yarn and fabric can yield muted, optically mixed color. Little flecks of one fiber spun into a yarn that is composed mostly of another fiber can yield (after weaving and dyeing) a tweed. Yarns made exclusively of fibers with different dye potentials and woven undyed in an invisible pattern can yield a check, a plaid, a stripe, or some

3-23. **Experiment using pulled-thread stitch patterns and dye (the stitches are removed after dyeing).**
Artist: Mary Fry
Photo: Patricia Lambert

82

other colored design. Even fibers within the same general type (such as several acrylics or several polyesters) can be designed to be dye selective so that fabrics of one general fiber type come from the dyebath checked or striped.

Polychromatic dyeing is a process in which streams of individually colored dyes are poured over a moving piece of fabric. The dyes are set with a mangle. In this technique, the amount of color poured, the arrangement of the color, and the movement of the cloth all determine the pattern produced.

Other dyeing techniques employed at the fabric level include resist techniques, such as Plangi tie dyeing and batik, and printing techniques, such as stencil printing, block printing, silk-screen printing, discharge printing, roller printing, and photographic printing.

Tie dyeing (or Plangi) is one of the resist methods. *Resist* refers to the fabric's resisting the dye in certain areas. In the case of tie dyeing, the material is gathered up in any of a number of ways and wrapped in certain areas with waxed string or some other impenetrable material, such as jute or plastic to protect those areas from taking dye when the fabric is immersed in the dyebath. Dozens of different kinds of patterns can be produced in this way depending on how the material is gathered up.

The material can be bunched and wrapped, intricately folded, or stitched with thread and needle and drawn up into fine little gathers; or the fabric can be twisted, knotted, or braided. Wherever the fabric layers are tightly pressed together, the dye will not penetrate, leaving different kinds of white patterned areas. The fabric can be retied and redyed to create multicolored, and overdyed effects.

The fabric can also be dip dyed, first overall in water and then in a series of dyebaths containing increasingly darker values of the same color or of a related color. As the dyebaths get darker, the part of the fabric actually dipped in the solution gets smaller and smaller, until only the bottom part is dipped in the last bath; this technique gives the fabric a graduated color effect. Alternatively, a predyed fabric can be tied and immersed in a discharge solution so that the untied part is bleached rather than dyed.

3-24. **Tie-dyed fabric: silk crepe de Chine. Contemporary adaption of** *arashi shibori*—**a Japanese tie-dye technique.**

Artist: Ana Lisa Hedstrom
Photo: Patricia Lambert
Courtesy of the artist

In *batik* techniques, hot wax is used as the resist element on the fabrics. The design created by the hot wax appears silhouetted against the colored background when it emerges from the dyebath. Batik was perfected by the Javanese, who are still known for the intricate designs and color quality of their batiks. The two basic processes of batik are known as the Javanese method and the American method. The Javanese method involves removing the wax and rewaxing before each color is added (in its own dyebath) to the design. The dyeing process proceeds from dark colors to light ones, and the second application of wax covers both the old pattern and the new pattern. It is consequently a time-consuming technique.

The American method works from light to dark and uses overdyeing to create the darker colors. The part that is to remain the color of the undyed cloth is waxed first; the cloth is then dyed, and the original wax is not removed. The second waxing consists of adding wax to the areas that are to remain the color of the first dyebath, after which the cloth is dyed again. Since overdyeing is used to create new colors, care and experience with the results of overdyeing are necessary. The dyer should avoid dyeing colors over their complements, for example. The wax can be removed by ironing the fabric between pads of newsprint, changing the newsprint often, and taking the last of the wax out with cleaning fluid—or it can be boiled out (the Javanese method). In the latter case, the dye must be boilfast.

Outlines to a pattern can be created by painting wax guidelines and then filling in the line by hand with a brush. Crackle batik can be created by dipping an entire cloth in wax and, when the wax is cold, crushing it to crackle the wax. The dye will penetrate the cracked wax and create a veined pattern.

Besides the commercial and hand-dyeing methods described above, several printing techniques are used to color textiles.

Stencil printing is also a resist process, the resist being the stencil itself. Stencil printing was first developed by the Japanese and was the precursor of modern silk-screen printing. In the present day, it is mostly done as a handcraft; used properly, the technique can result in beautiful designs. Each stencil adds one color to the design, and each stencil must be made so that it registers or fits the design exactly in order to produce a perfect print.

3-25. *Batik Series #1, #7* **(pieced hanging, 1981).**

Artist: Susan Schroeder
Photo: George S. Schroeder
Courtesy of the artist

The difficulty with stencil is that the solid, nonprinting areas of the stencil must all connect to prevent some areas of the stencil from falling out, and the design must be planned around this (see Figure 3-26). Japanese craftsmen avoided this issue by connecting areas of the stencil with silk filaments or human hair. Once the stencil is in place, the color can be applied to the fabric by brush, airbrush, or spraygun.

3-26. **b. Mulberry paper stencil used in Katazome dyeing process (used to apply rice paste resist) (15½" x 17½", 1979); heron feather pattern four-way repeat).**

Artist: Susanna Kuo
Photo: Susanna Kuo
Collection: Mr. and Mrs. C. Herald Campbell

3-26. **a.** *Square Sail* **(Katazome stencil resist dyeing on organdy in acrylic case) 18" x 18" x 3", 1979); turkey quills pattern.**

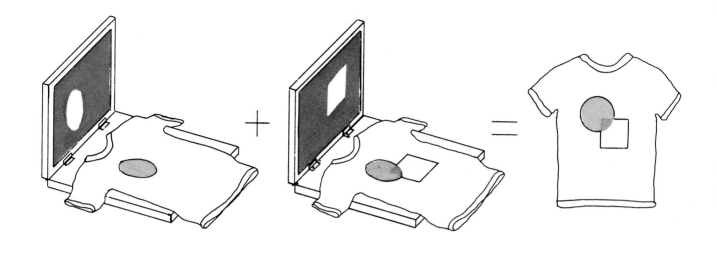

3-27. **Silk-screen printing: a separate screen is made for each color.**

Silk-screen printing is essentially a stenciling process. A screen resist is made by covering a frame with silk, metal, nylon, or polyester filament cloth. A resist film made of a film-producing substance is painted on the screen cloth over the area that the color is not to penetrate, leaving the screen cloth open where the dyestuff is to pass through and print the fabric.

In the printing process, the frame is laid on the fabric to be printed, the dye is placed along one edge of the frame, and a squeegee moves the dye across the screen, forcing the color through the open areas not covered by the resist film and thence onto the fabric. One screen is made for each color to be applied.

Direct printing is a printing category that includes some of the most common methods for applying designs to commercial fabrics. Among these are block printing, roller printing, and photographic printing.

Block printing involves carving the designs to be printed on wood blocks or making metal shapes and attaching these to a wood base. The design area remains raised, while the background is carved away. Each block prints only one color, so several blocks must be made if a design of several colors is desired. The craftsperson colors each block by dipping it directly into the printing paste or by applying it over the block with a roller. The block is pressed on the fabric and pounded with a mallet to produce clear color areas on the fabric (see Figure 3-28).

Roller printing is used to print most commercial fabrics. It is also the only method mentioned here that is not used by craftspeople. The equipment is automated and evolved out of block printing; in roller printing, though, the design is transferred onto metal rollers. The area to print on the roll is left untouched, and the nonprinting areas are coated with chemical-resistant paint. The roll is then dipped in acid, which etches away the surface of the metal at the places that will print the design (and where no resistant coating was applied to protect the metal.) After the acid etching

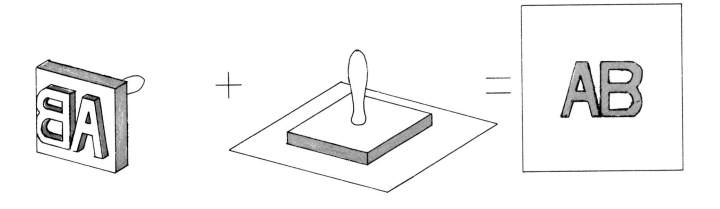

3-28. **Block printing: color is applied to the block; the block is then pressed onto the fabric.**

is complete, the coating is removed and the roller is polished. The rolls are set up around the printing cylinder, each roll equipped with a dye trough and a blade for scraping excess dye off the smooth parts of the roll. Thus the etched part of the roll picks up and holds dye to print with, while the smooth part of the roll does not.

A printing machine can carry as many as sixteen rolls around the main cylinder, each printing a different color. Electronic equipment controls the position of the rolls so that the printed design comes out matched, clear, and even. Colored backgrounds can be printed onto the fabric from an etched roller at the same time as the design is going on. A modified direct-roller printing machine can print the design on both sides of the fabric.

Photographic prints can be produced on fabric much as a photograph is printed on paper. The fabric is treated with a light-sensitive dye, a negative is placed on the fabric, light is transmitted to it, and the color is developed. The print is as permanent as any photograph. With this technique, any opaque shape can be used in place of a negative; the result resembles discharge printing in that it consists of a solid, uncolored shape on the developed or colored ground.

Discharge printing involves printing a dyed fabric with reducing bleach to achieve a white pattern on a colored ground. The white areas can then either be redyed or not. Discharging and redying can also be done in a single process, with the discharge chemical removing one color at the same time that a dye in solution is printed on in place of the original color. In some cases, the discharge chemical can be printed on a fabric before initial dying so that it counteracts the dye in those spaces—rather than simply bleaching out color from already-dyed areas. The principal difficulty with discharge printing is that the bleaching can weaken fabric in the areas where it is applied.

Chapter 4

Fiber Structure and Light Reflectance

In addition to having molecular, fiber, yarn, and fabric levels of structural arrangement, natural plant and animal fibers—such as cotton, linen, ramie, jute, and wool—have a distinguishable level of organization known as cell structure. Cell shape and arrangement significantly affects these materials' properties, at the fiber level and at all succeeding levels. Silk, despite being a natural animal fiber, does not have a cell structure because it is manufactured by the worm and does not grow, as other natural fibers do.

The study of color in textiles is inextricably linked with the study of fiber structure. Dye is absorbed into and becomes a part of the structure of the fiber. Light falls on the textile and enters the fiber, where it meets the color-bearing dye molecule. The structure of the textile (in conjunction with the chemical structure of the dye mmolecule) rearrange the light, absorbing some and reflecting the rest back for our eyes to see.

The fiber artist thus works not only with the color imparted to the fiber by the dye, but also with the structural arrangement of the molecules, fibers, and yarns involved. Kitting, weaving, embroidery, crochet, macramé, and other fiber arts provide techniques for developing these structural influences on color further.

The Effect of Structural Shape on Value

The shapes of the structural units that affect value are: the length of the molecule, the fiber, and the yarn floats; the diameter of the fiber and the yarn; the cross-sectional shape of the fiber; and the longitudinal shape of the fiber and the yarn. Each structural unit provides surfaces that reflect and absorb light, and the shape of these surfaces dictates both the total light reflectance possible from the finished fabric and the direction in which the light is reflected. The amount and direction of reflectance are in turn responsible for the perceived value of the fabric color. A high level of total light reflectance results in a high value (or light color), while a low level of total light reflectance results in a low value (or dark color). If light from a surface is organized and reflected in a single direction, as happens with light from a single large flat shape, the surface appears either very light (if it is reflecting toward the viewer), or dark (if it is reflecting away from the viewer) (see Figure 4-1). If light is scattered from a surface in many directions, as happens with light from a curved surface, a uniform value will be seen from all points of view.

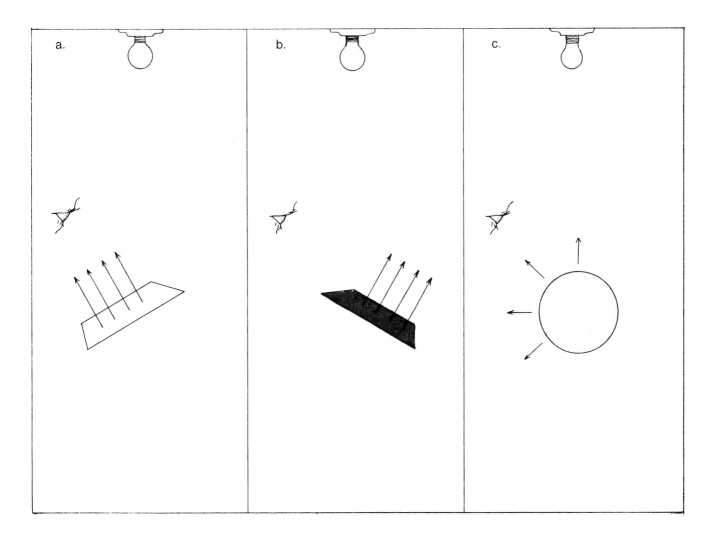

LENGTH

Imagining each structural unit as a reflecting surface makes it easier to visualize how each unit's length affects the amount of surface available to reflect light in a given direction. A longer reflecting surface reflects more light in a given direction than a shorter reflecting surface does. Fiber molecules (polymers) are long and thin, as are the fibers they compose. The principal characteristic determined by polymer length is fiber strength; however, polymer length also affects visible color. The cell structure of both plant stem and plant leaf fibers is also long and thin. The long cell structure of plant fibers such as linen and ramie contributes to their relatively high luster.

Longer fibers create larger, more organized reflecting surfaces and significantly raise the value of the yarn color. In the production of yarns from natural fibers, short staple fibers are often separated from long staple fibers, and the two are spun into different types of yarn. Short staple wool is carded and spun into warm, soft, fluffy, low-twist woolen yarns; in contrast, long staple wool fibers are combed as well as carded,

4-1. **A flat surface appears: a. lighter reflecting toward the viewer; b. darker reflecting away from the viewer; c. lower than a and more consistant in overall from a curved surface.**

and then are spun into a harder, more compact, stronger, and more tightly twisted worsted yarn. Cotton fibers are similarly divided according to staple length. Short staple cotton is simply carded and spun, while long staple cotton fibers are combed after carding and spun into a stronger, finer yarn called combed cotton. The same happens with linen fibers: the longer staple, carded, and combed linen yarns are called line linen; and the shorter staple yarns, which were carded only, are called tow linen. In silk production, perfect silk cocoons are unwound (or reeled) and spun into fine filament yarns called reeled silk. Imperfect cocoons are cut into staple lengths, carded, and spun in the same manner as any other staple fiber. Man-made fibers can be spun into filament yarns or cut into lengths as desired and spun into any kind of staple yarn.

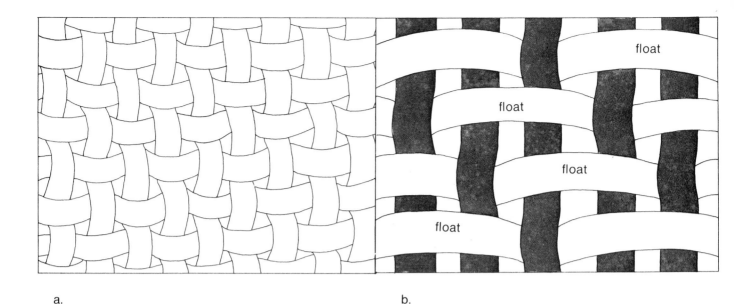

a.   b.

4-2. **Construction changes value: a. plain weave; b. showing floats (twill).**

Filament yarns, such as reeled silk and man-made filament yarns, are known for their high luster. They are much more lustrous and (therefore) lighter in color than a yarn composed of the same fibers cut into staple lengths and spun. Likewise, long staple yarns (mohair, combed cotton, line linen, ramie, and worsted wool yarns) are more lustrous and higher in value than their short staple counterparts (lamb's wool, carded cotton, tow linen, and woolen spun yarns).

At the next structural level, the length of yarn or thread floats in woven fabric construction or embroidery noticeably affects fabric luster and color value. Plain weave consists of alternate interlacing of warp and weft yarns. The weft moves at right angles to the warp, over one warp, under the next one warp,

over the next one, and so on across the fabric (see Figure 4-2).

Any deviation from the strictly consistent alternation of warp and weft yarns in plain weave necessarily produces a float—a segment of warp or weft in a woven fabric that crosses over at least two threads before again interlocking in the fabric weave. The alignment of floats can be varied to produce such float weaves as satin, sateen, and damask. In satin, the floats on the front of the fabric are vertical warp floats. In sateen fabric, the floats on the front of the fabric are horizontal weft floats. In damask fabric, patterns are created by the juxtaposition of areas of warp floats with areas of weft floats on the same face of the fabric (see Figure 4-3).

4-3. **Damask weave: the floats reflect more light than a plain alternating weave does.**

A float reflects much more light than does the simple, alternate interlacing of plain tabby weave (see Figure 4-4). Since satin, sateen, and damask use the float as a light-catching element, these fabrics appear lighter in value than a plain weave made from the same yarns. The embroidery equivalent to a float is a long straight stitch called a satin stitch. An embroidered surface done in a satin stitch appears lighter than does an embroidered surface composed of the same thread but done in a stitch that goes in and out of the fabric more often—as, for example, a needlepoint tent stitch does. The longer the satin stitch (assuming it lies smoothly on the surface of the fabric), the lighter the surface color.

4-4. **Damask, front and back: a. front, the floats are in the figure and therefore catch more light; b. back, the floats are in the background and therefore the figure is darker.**

Photo: Patricia Lambert

b.

a.

DIAMETER

The diameters of the fiber used in the yarn and of the yarn used in the fabric are a second factor in light reflectance. A yarn made of many fine fibers has more total reflecting surface (and consequently appears lighter) than a yarn of the same weight made up of fewer, coarser fibers (see Figure 4-5).

For example, an acrylic material made into fine filaments and spun into yarn for a coat fabric will produce a fabric with more total fiber surface area to reflect light than will the same acrylic material made into coarse filaments and spun into a rug yarn of the same weight or thickness. Assuming that both fabrics are woven in the same way, the coat fabric will be lighter in color than the rug fabric will be.

The extreme fineness of silk filaments is thus a significant factor contributing to the luster and the high value of colors produced in dyed reeled silk.

Yarn diameter like filament diameter, influences the value of a fabric made from it. A fabric composed of fine yarn appears lighter in value than a fabric made of coarser yarn of the same material. The fine fabric contains more warp and weft yarns per inch than a coarser yarn does, creating more total reflectance. Here, however, the surface texture of the fabric also begins to play a part in the perceived value of the fabric color. Fabric woven from coarse yarn has more surface texture than the fine fabric does and this reenforces the dark value already fostered by the coarser yarn's greater diameter.

4-5. **When combined (c), four small fibers (b) produce twice as much reflecting surface as one large fiber (a).**

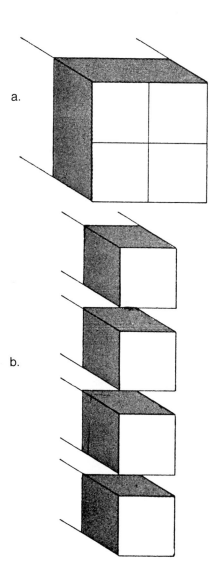

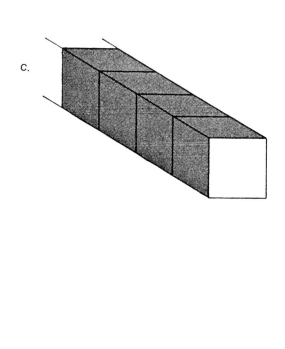

4-6. **Twist reflectance: fiber with a flat cross section shows marked value changes when twisted.**

CROSS-SECTIONAL SHAPE

The cross-sectional shape of each different fiber type determines the surface planes that are produced along the fiber. These surface planes in turn affect light reflectance, fiber luster, and the value of the fiber color. For example, a flat synthetic fiber made by extruding fluid through a dumbbell-shaped slot in a spinnerette possesses two comparatively large, flat sides that reflect light. These flat, mirrorlike surfaces switch dramatically from dark to light as the fiber twists, sending reflected light off in different directions. At the points where most of the reflected light is directed toward the viewer's eye, the fiber appears very light in value; the rest of the surface appears dark (see Figure 4-6).

A harsh, bright, mechanical kind of glittering shine and a high value are characteristic of yarns and fabrics made from fibers having flat cross-sectional shapes. Metallic threads are often made by cutting sheets of metallic material into flat strips whose shape accentuates their reflectance. Synthetics such as the acrylic fibers Orlon and Verel are often made with a light-reflecting dumbbell-shaped cross section. Crystal acetate fiber is made with flat filaments that yield a much brighter and more glittering fiber than does regular acetate, with its lobed and striated cross section (see Figure 4-7).

A triangular cross section means that only one surface in three reflects light from a given source. This creates a slightly lower total reflectance, luster, and general value than appear in two-sided, flat cross sections, where one surface in two is reflecting light. A trilobal fiber has the same dark and light value variation when twisted into yarn that a flat fiber has when twisted, but the trilobal fiber's three-sidedness makes the areas of reflectance smaller and the visual effect more subtle. Nylons and polyesters are often made with a trilobal shape. Antron, 501, Cadon, and Cumuloft are brand names of trilobal nylons; Dacron T-62 is a trilobal polyester.

4-7. **Cross sections of various fibers.**

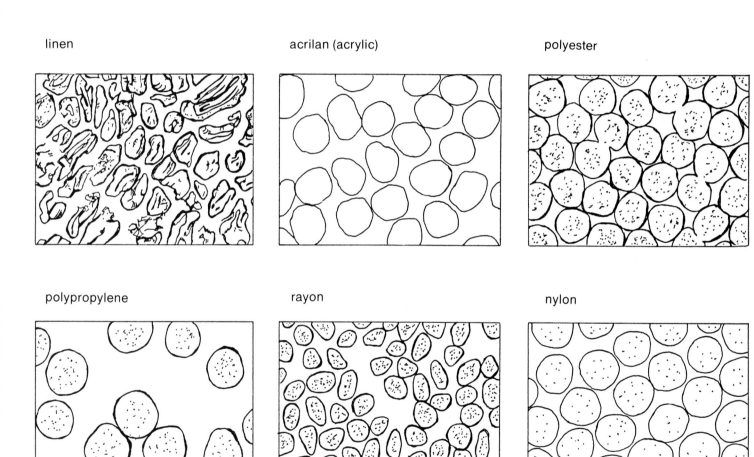

linen

acrilan (acrylic)

polyester

polypropylene

rayon

nylon

verel

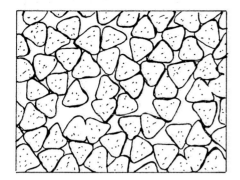

Antron

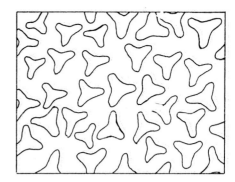

nylon T-105

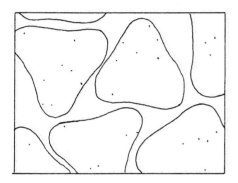

Dacron T-62

rayon

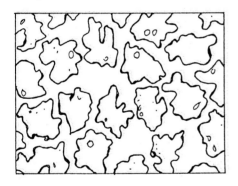

acetate

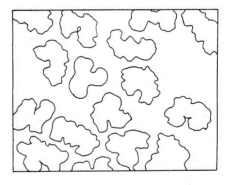

triacetate

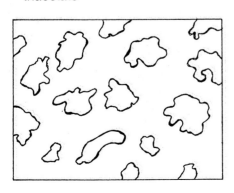

dynel

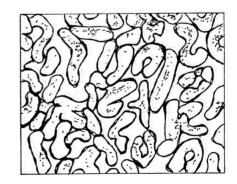

Silk is a roughly trilobal or triangular natural filament. When the silk worm spins its cocoon, it extrudes a viscous material through two holes called spinnerettes located side by side in its head. The two filaments extruded side-by-side from the spinnerettes form a single strand that is held together by a gum coating called sericin (also produced by the worm). When the silk is degummed, the strand separates into two roughly triangular filaments (see Figure 4-8)—although the cross section can vary from sharply triangular to oval with one flat side where the two strands lay against each other.

The trilobal section of the silk filament is another factor that contributes to silk's fine luster. The fact that its cross section is not an exact triangle but only roughly trilobal allows silk a subtle variation in light reflectance that makes its luster softer and more pleasing. The luster of precisely trilobal synthetic fibers such as nylons and polyesters is visually harsher and more mechanical, by comparison.

Man-made fibers can be made with any cross-sectional shape and any number of sides. They can be made round, lobed, striated, or grooved, with these features running the length of the fiber. Generally, increasing the number of sides in a fiber results in smaller reflecting surfaces and reduces the luster and value of the fiber color. Adding striations or grooves to cross-sectional shapes produces smaller, more broken reflecting surfaces and further lowers the luster and value of the fiber color. Striations also allow soil to hide in the grooves, so the fiber does not show dirt as quickly as a fiber with a smoother-shaped cross section might. Several man-made fibers—rayons, acetates, triacetates and modacrylics—are made with irregular or grooved cross secions. Linen is a roughly polygonal natural fiber; relatively immature flax (or linen) fibers are more cylindrical in cross section.

A rounded or lobed cross section translates into a rounded reflecting surface, as a result of which light moves across the fiber smoothly instead of changing abruptly from light to dark (as happens with a flat-sided fiber when twisted). This gives the fiber luster a slightly varied but fairly uniform quality.

The more perfectly cylindrical the shape of the fiber is the more mechanically uniform the luster of the fiber becomes. This uniform mechanical shine can be seen in some man-made fibers that have round cross sections, such as most acrylics, most polyesters, polypropylene (an olefin fiber), and several kinds of rayon and nylon. It can be partially overcome by fancy spinnning and yarn texturizing techniques, by use of texturized weaves like crepe weaves, or by the addition of delusterant finishes to the fiber. Wool is a natural fiber that has an oval-to-round cross section. The luster created by the round shape is partially offset, however, by the presence of scales on the outside of the fiber (which break up light reflectance) and by the crimp that runs the length of the wool fiber.

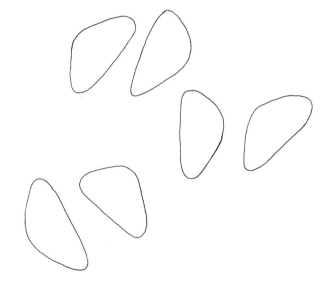

4-8. **Silk filaments after degumming.**

LONGITUDINAL SHAPE

The longitudinal shape of a fiber is the fiber's shape along its length. Longitudinally, fibers are generally straight, crimped, spiral, or twisted (see Figure 4-9). A straight longitudinal shape presents a large uninterrupted reflecting surface and lends high luster and high value to the color of the fiber. The straight longitudinal shape of silk filimants is an additional factor (besides fiber length, fiber fineness, trilobal cross section, and smooth surface) that contributes to the luster of reeled silk.

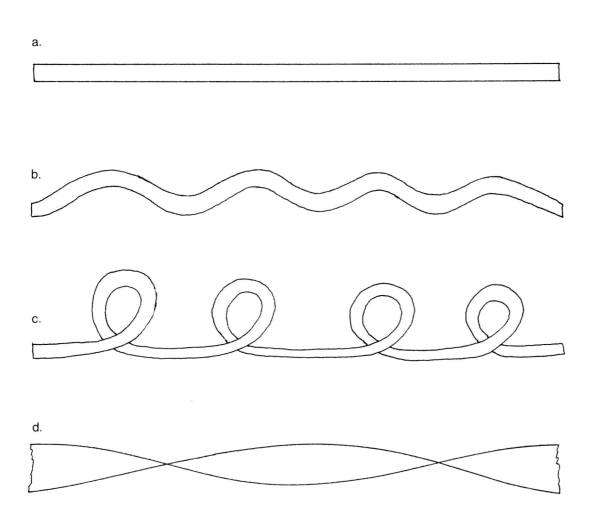

a.

b.

c.

d.

4-9. **Longitudinal shapes of fibers: a. straight; b. crimped; c. spiral; d. twisted.**

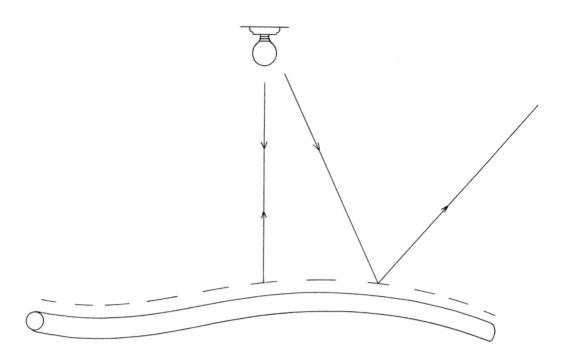

Any longitudinal shape that breaks up a straight reflecting surface—such as a crimp, spiral, or twist—reduces the value of the fiber color. The word *crimp* refers to bending or waving along the length of a fiber; crimp breaks up the longitudinal reflecting surface of a fiber into many small surfaces arranged at different angles, thereby lowering the fiber's luster and color value (see Figure 4-10). Crimp appears naturally in wool, where it tends to be a three-dimensional crimp that goes up and down as well as from side to side. Finer wools such as lamb's wool and Merino sheep's wool have a tighter crimp and make yarn of lower luster and lower color value. Longer, coarser wools such as Romney and Lincoln sheep's wool have a bigger, broader crimp that translates into a more lustrous yarn with a higher color value.

Man-made filaments are extruded from the spin-nerettes in straight filaments. If spun and used in that form, they will have a bright, uniform luster and little texture. In situations where this appearance, is not desirable, man-made fibers can be texturized—either at the fiber level or at the yarn level of construction, with similar results. The word *texturized* has come to describe the process by which man-made filaments are given longitudinal crimp, loops, coils, and crinkles to make them resemble natural fibers more closely. Most texturized yarns are made from thermoplastic fibers, in which heat can be used to set the crimp shape along the filament. The filament can then be spun as is, or cut into staple lengths and spun into a yarn whose light-reflecting characteristics closely match those of natural fibers.

4-10. Crimp lowers fiber luster and value by breaking up the reflecting surface into many small planes.

4-11. Change of reflectance in thread A = wool; B = cotton (low-luster on left, high-luster on right); C = linen; D = rayon; E = silk; F = silver).
Execution: Mary Fry

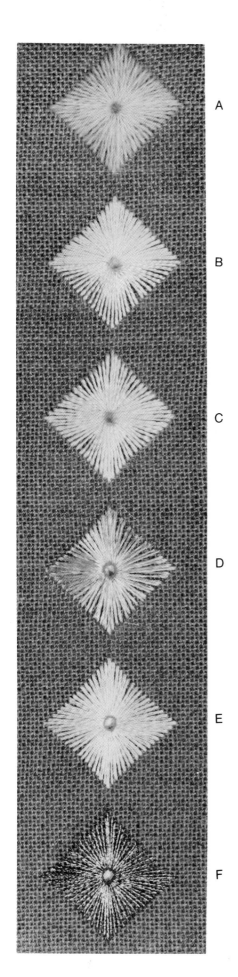

A

B

C

D

E

F

4-12. **Cotton highly magnified.**

Photo: Dr. Maximillan Toch

The word *twist* refers to a particular kind of longitudinal shape created by rotating the two ends of a fiber or piece of yarn in opposite directions; twist scatters light reflectance much as crimp, spirals, and loops do. Twist occurs naturally along some fibers. It is imparted to yarn during spinning. As with the other types of longitudinal shape, the greater the twist is, the smaller and more broken up the reflecting surfaces of the fiber or yarn, the lower the luster, and the lower the value of the fiber or yarn color will be.

Cotton is a natural fiber with twist. Raw cotton has a flat, twisted, ribbonlike shape and a crinkled, rough surface that scatters light randomly in every direction. This extremely scattered reflection creates a low-luster fiber and interferes with a viewer's perception of the *selective reflectance* from the dye molecule, thus lowering the intensity of the color. For this reason, raw cotton always appears to be a dull color. Flax fibers, from which linen is made, have some natural twist along the fiber—although considerably less than cotton fibers have.

101

4-13. **Linen highly magnified.**

Photo: Dr. Maximillan Toch

The longitudinal shape of yarn can be described according to the amount and direction of its twist and to the type of yarn construction (that is, to whether the yarn consists of a single strand, of two or more strands plied or twisted together, or of a more complex novelty yarn). Whether the yarn is staple or filament yarn, and whether it is simple or complex, the fibers are held together by the twist. Changes in the amount of twist, which may vary from high to low, along a strand of yarn create subtle changes in light reflectance from the surface of the yarn.

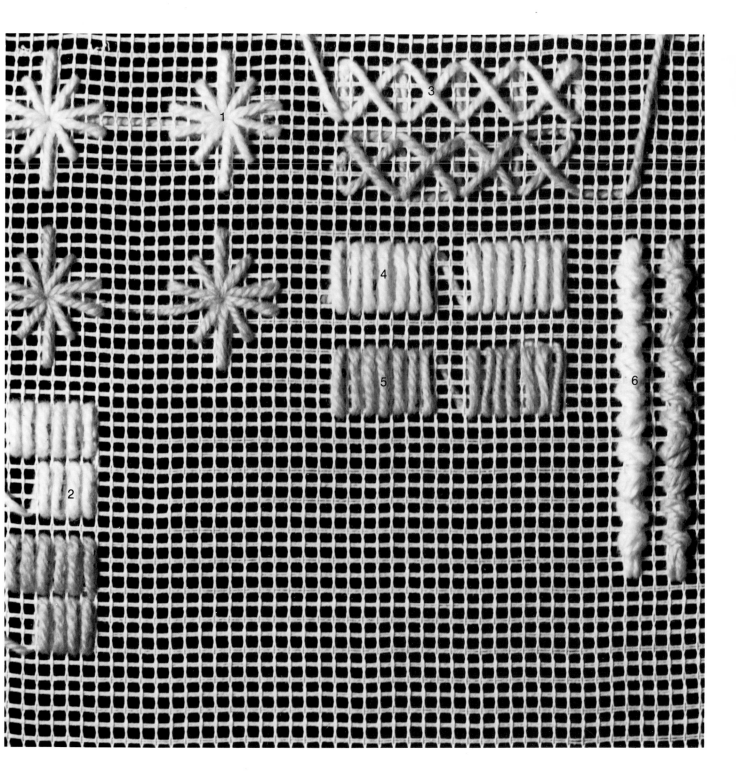

Embroiderers need to be particularly aware of the influence of yarn twist on light reflectance and color: the surface of the work will not reflect light uniformly if the twist is allowed to vary. As stitches are worked, the thread should not be twisted tighter or allowed to untwist. If the thread untwists, it forms thicker stitches that have fewer twists and higher reflectance than before; if it is twisted tighter, the stitches become thinner and the more numerous twists in each stitch produce smaller reflecting surfaces on the surface of the yarn and darker areas on the surface of the work.

4-14. **Direction of stitches (light yarn indicates correct technique; dark yarn shows poor technique): (1) angle of emergence for eyelit stitch; (2) angle of emergence for satin stitch; (3) angle of emergence and direction for cross stitch; (4) tension variance; (5) twisted thread; (6) knots.**

Artist: Mary Fry
Photo: Patricia Lambert

103

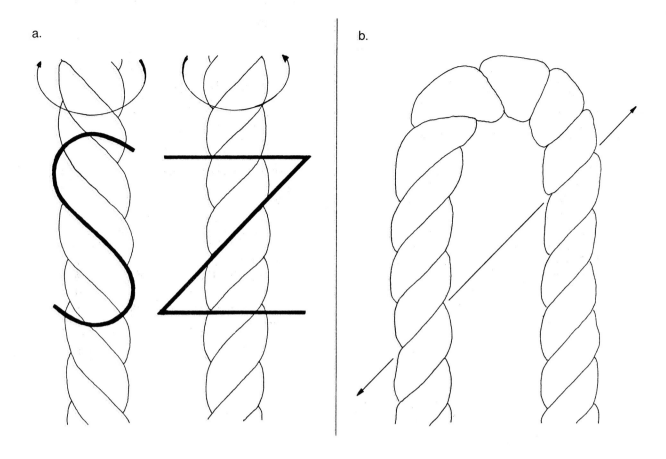

a.

b.

The direction of the twist of a strand of singles yarn can be clockwise or left-handed (an S twist), or it can be counterclockwise or right-handed (a Z twist) (see Figure 4-15). The direction of the twist conforms to the center bar of the letter. At first it might seem that the S or Z of the twist could be changed by changing the direction of the yarn or by doubling it back on itself, but reversing the direction of the yarn does not have this effect. A Z-twist yarn remains a Z-twist yarn on both halves when it is doubled back on itself.

Changes in reflectance resulting from changes in direction of yarn twist can subtly alter the colors in a work. Particularly in embroidery, such small changes in reflectance can detract from the professional appearance of the piece as a whole if they occur randomly. Because the changes in reflectance from the surface of S and Z yarns are subtle and often visible only by comparison, consistency throughout the piece is more important than the actual direction of the twist. In other words, either an S or a Z twist is fine as long as random switching back and forth between the two does not occur.

Manufacturers of yarn and embroidery thread are normally consistent in the direction and amount of twist in their products. Hand-spinners are more likely to run into changes in surface reflectance when areas are worked with both S- and Z-twist threads.

4-15. **S-Z twist: a. yarn is spun with either S or Z twist; b. the direction of the twist does not change when yarn is doubled back on itself.**

The Effect of Structural Orientation
on Value and Intensity

The interrelationship of structural orientation, fiber luster, value, and intensity begins at the molecular level. Light entering a polymer is bent much as light going through water is. Everyone is familiar with the visual effect partly immersing a pencil in a glass of water produces: the pencil appears to be bent at the point where air and water meet, not because the pencil is bent, but because the light rays are. A polymer likewise bends the light rays, and does so at either of two angles—depending on the orientation of the polymer in the fiber to the light source. Light entering at the end of the polymer is bent at one angle, whereas light entering at the side of the polymer is bent at another angle.

ORIENTATION OF MOLECULES IN FIBERS

Molecular orientation within a fiber fundamentally affects the reflectance and apparent color of that fiber. If the molecular chains are oriented or parallel within the fiber (either by natural growth or by manufacturing process), they will reflect a substantial amount of light in one direction. If the molecular chains are amorphous, however, they will reflect light diffusely.

When molecular reflecting surfaces are arranged in an orderly row, facing the same way, they make the equivalent of one large reflecting surface rather than an array of tiny reflecting surfaces pointed in many different directions. The large collective reflecting surface produces a relatively high value of the fiber color. A similar phenomenon occurs when a piece of rubber or chewing gum is stretched. Stretching aligns the molecules parallel to each other, and the stretched area gets a higher value as the molecules align and begin to reflect light in a more orderly fashion (see Figure 4-16). Thus molecular orientation increases a fiber's luster and raises its color value.

Cellulosic fibers such as linen and ramie typically have many highly oriented and crystalline areas where the molecules lie side-by-side, as well as some areas where the molecules are almost (but not quite) disordered enough to be considered truly amorphous. The many areas of oriented, crystalline arrangement give the cellulosic fiber its luster. Ramie in particular has a dense, highly crystalline molecular structure that contributes to the fiber's high luster.

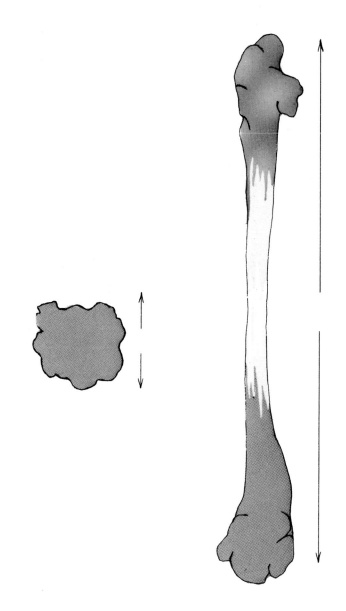

4-16. **Chewing gum: stretching aligns molecules parallel to one another, reflecting more light.**

Molecular orientation affects other fiber qualities, too, including resilience, flexibility, and draping quality, which in turn affect the play of light and shadow on the finished fabric, and the fabric's color. The same high degree of molecular orientation that gives the cellulosic fiber its luster and a higher value also gives it strength, poor elongation, and low pliability (characteristic of fabrics that can wrinkle if crushed). Wrinkled fabrics have many shadowed areas that lower both the value and the intensity of the fabric color; if the fabric is crushed and wrinkled, the wrinkles will offset the brighter color effect of the fiber luster.

Silk and man-made fibers are produced in an essentially similar way that yields similar results. Silk is made from a viscous material manufactured in the silk worm's body and extruded through its spinnerettes in such a way that the molecules in the material are aligned parallel to the length of the fiber. This high level molecular orientation contributes to the luster of silk, which in turn makes the color value of the fiber, whether dyed or natural, a little higher than it would be otherwise. In man-made fibers, the material from which the fiber is to be made is manufactured in bulk with the molecules lying at random in the material. When the substance is dissolved and extruded through the fine holes in the mechanical spinnerette, the molecules are aligned along the length of the fiber and slightly stretched—bringing them more nearly into parallel with each other and increasing fiber luster—before hardening into a filament.

ORIENTATION OF FIBERS IN YARNS

Just as the orientation of molecules within a fiber influences the light reflectance and perceived color of the fiber, the orientation of fibers within yarn influences the light reflectance and perceived color of a yarn. The longer the fibers in a yarn are, the more oriented they tend to be. A filament yarn—whether composed of natural silk or of man-made filaments—or a yarn composed of extremely long fibers, such as mohair of some bast or plant stem fibers, will be much more lustrous than a yarn composed of those same fibers cut into staple lengths and spun. This is due both to fiber length and to fiber orientation. Longer fibers reflect more light in any given direction than to shorter ones. They also tend to be arranged in more nearly parallel order in the yarn. The more highly oriented filament yarns reflect light in an even more orderly way.

In a yarn, the more randomly arranged staple fibers scatter reflected light much as an amorphous molecular arrangement does in a fiber. Similarly, worsted wool yarns whose longer wool fibers are arranged as straight as possible by means of an extra combing process take a brighter color, while woolen yarns whose shorter fibers are intermingled and crossed in a more amorphous arrangement show a softer, more mellow color intensity and a lower value, even when dyed in the same dyepot as the worsted. Combed cotton and line linen yarns likewise appear brighter than their short-fibered counterparts—carded cotton and short staple tow linen yarns.

ORIENTATION OF YARNS IN FABRICS

Yarns in a woven structure (in which warp threads are arranged parallel to one another and weft threads are arranged parallel to one another) make a lighter brighter cloth than yarns in a less highly oriented, looped structure such as knitting or crochet. Special types of weaving and embroidery depend for their effect on light reflectance that is created by fiber orientation as well as by fiber length. Satin, sateen, and damask fabrics and satin stitch embroidery use the longer float as their light-catching element. Not only do floats in weaving or in long straight satin stitches catch more light than the smaller, more broken, textured and interlacing stitches, *the direction in which they are arranged* makes a great difference in the reflectance and apparent value of the fabric, *depending on where the viewer is situated in relation to the light source and depending on the fiber direction* (see Figure 4-17).

4-17. Study in orientation (satin).

Design: Mary Fry
Photo: Patricia Lambert

107

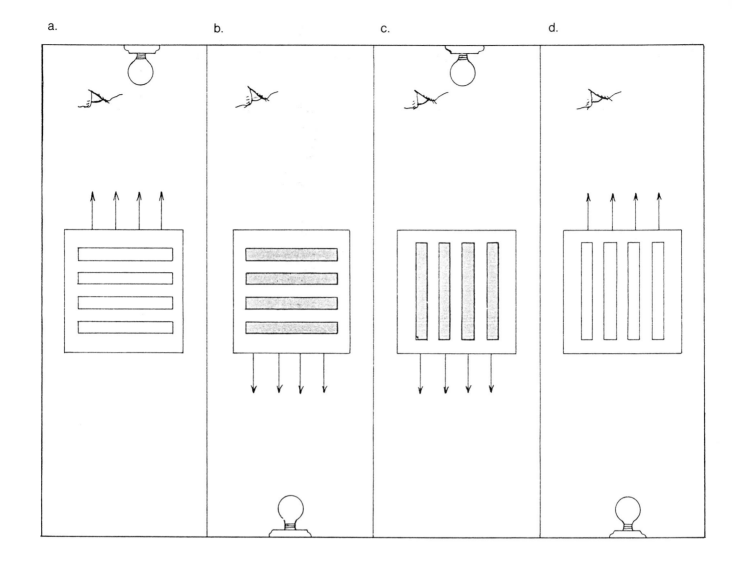

a. b. c. d.

Floats at right angles to the light source bounce light back in the direction it came from. If the surface texture from the highly oriented floats is at right angles to the eye and if the light source is coming from the same direction as the eye, the floats will appear to have high values because light is bounced back to the eye (see Figure 4-18). If the light source is opposite the eye, however, the floats will appear to have low values because light is again reflected to the direction it came from—in this case, away from the eye—by the floats. Floats parallel to the light source allow light to continue in basically the same direction, making the float appear dark (if light is coming from the direction of the viewer) or light (if light is coming toward the viewer from the other side). As the luster of the yarn used increases, so does the difference in value between two floats or stitches that lie in different directions.

4-18. **Orientation of yarns in fabric: a. floats arranged at right angles to light and viewer; b. floats appear darker when light is opposite viewer; c. floats parallel to light and viewer appear darker; d. floats parallel to light with viewer opposite appear lighter.**

4-19. Damask orientation.
Photo: Patricia Lambert

Damask weaves arrange floats at right angles in order to make a color pattern whose different value results from changes in light reflectance. When the light source, viewer position, or fiber orientation change, so do the areas of light and dark, giving a positive/negative changeability to the value pattern (see Figure 4-19).

Embroiderers need to be aware of the effects of fiber orientation in their work. Throughout the various individual embroidery styles (see Figure 4-14), aspects of technique affect fiber orientation, light reflectance, and (therefore) the color effect and overall impact of the piece of embroidered art. Small variations in the construction of stitches can alter the uniformity of thread orientation and surface reflectance, detracting from the work. Many knotted stitches can be made to lie either to the right or to the left; in order to achieve even light reflection, they should all be made the same. Changes in light reflectance can be made, either in uniform areas or alternating in a deliberate pattern, but they should not be left to chance. In any art form, the artist should make things happen, not let them happen.

109

A few other factors in stitching affect the light reflectance from the surface of embroidery work. Each stitch starts as it emerges through a hole from the back of the fabric, after which it travels across the surface and exits through a hole to the back. The thread must bend as it emerges and exits. Where it bends, it reflects light in a different direction and appears much darker than it does when it is on the surface of the fabric. This means that, when stitches meet in the same hole, an area of darker value is created. The slight differences in value that occur depend on the angle at which the stitch emerges and exits. All the stitches in an area should therefore come through at the same angle.

Another factor that affects the uniformity of embroidery stitches and the way they reflect light is the direction from which thread emerges from the back of the fabric. When the thread emerging from the back of the fabric always comes from the same direction, the stitches on the front will lie identically and parallel to each other, each reflecting identical amounts of light. If the thread comes from different directions on the back, the stitches will not lie identically on the surface and so will reflect light with subtle differences.

In some stitches, anywhere from one to sixteen (or more) stitches may emerge or exit through the same hole. All of the holes should appear identical in number of stitches per hole, in stitch order, and consequently in the direction of emergence. If they are not worked consistently throughout the area, the threads will emerge from different directions and will not reflect light in the same way; as a result, the work will look sloppy and unprofessional.

Many stitches are made by combining or building up stitches that go in different directions. With these particular stitches, consistency in the order in which they are laid is extremely important. For example, the top stitch of a cross-stitch as a rule should go in the same direction. This does not mean that the rule can never be broken: subtle effects can be planned by reversing the direction of the top stitch in selected areas, and another slight difference in value can be achieved by alternating the direction of the top stitch.

In blackwork, a counted technique characterized by a strong value contrast between thread and fabric, as little as possible of the threads on the back should be allowed to show through on the front. The best method is to have any traveling stitches on the back lie parallel to the threads of the fabic. Traveling stitches can also be hidden in places where subsequent stitches will be placed on top.

In pulled thread embroidery, a counted technique in which the values of thread and fabric are the same, the stitches are made tight in order to form holes in the fabric and force the threads of the fabric together. In this technique, the work can often be lit from behind, in which case traveling stitches on the back will show as dark lines. These lines will not be noticed if they are all planned to lie at the same angle; the eye will instead, see them as part of the pattern.

The Effect of Surface Texture on Value and Intensity

Many of us have had the experience of picking up a beautiful wet pebble on a beach or at the edge of a stream, admiring the beauty of its colors, and tucking it away to look at later, only to find that the dried pebble had lost its colors. In general wet surfaces look darker and more intensely colored. Thus, high-gloss paints have a deeper color than matte paints, and colorless looking pieces of wood often become warmer and more colorful when varnished and waxed. Conversely, dark ice on a pond becomes white when skates scratch its shiny surface, and when transparent glass or plastic is crushed the powder appears white. These phenomena are largely the result of changes in surface texture that increase the surface's ability to reflect light in an organized or unorganized way.

When light hits a smooth, uniform surface, some is transmitted through the object and the rest is reflected in an orderly way, causing the surface to appear very bright (if the viewer is standing in the line of reflectance) or quite dark (if the viewer is not.) The great value changes of shiny, smooth surfaces create a rich color effect. When the surface of the substance loses its uniformity and becomes textured or broken up by many facets, however, light is reflected in all directions from the many facets of the surface. Light that is reflected from one facet to another becomes diffused. The high degree of diffused light makes the surface appear lighter, raising its value; it also interferes with the viewer's ability to perceive the selective reflection (which creates color) from the surface, thus lowering the intensity of the surface color. The color of the object is masked by the high level of diffused light reflecting from surface facets and making the surface appear white, frosted, or matte.

The water on the surface of a richly colored wet stone fills in many of the microscopically small light-diffusing irregularities of the surface, making it appear more smooth. Polishing the stone would also eliminate surface irregularities, making the true color of the stone more accessible to the eye and lowering the overall value of the color. On some areas of a polished or wet stone, where the angle of the surface is just right in relation to the position of the light source and to the position of the viewer's eye, a large amount of light will be reflected mirror-like to the viewer's eye, creating a very high value, a shiny white area, or a highlight.

SURFACE TEXTURE OF FIBERS

The surface textures of a fiber affect the way light reacts to the fiber and the way the fiber's color is perceived. The same kind of organized reflection from a smooth shiny surface described above in the case of a wet or polished stone explains why a shiny fiber is altered in value along its length when it is worked—the changes including deeper and lighter colors and an overall richer color effect than a dull, rough-textured fiber has.

Silk filaments are a perfect example of a fiber with a smooth surface; its smoothness of texture contributes to the fiber's ability to reflect a high degree of light in an organized way. This in turn makes the color imparted to the fiber by the dye easy to see.

Hair fibers in general are covered with surface scales that catch and reflect light (see Figure 4-20a). The fiber's surface texture and luster vary according to the size of its surface scales. Hair fibers such as mohair, alpaca, and Lincoln fleece wool have large, flat outer scales. The larger scales present a relatively smooth surface that reflects light in an organized way, giving a fiber high luster, rich value changes, and relatively well-defined or intense color. The length of the fiber and the more relaxed crimp of long wool fibers also support this result.

Finer, shorter staple wools have smaller outer scales that tend to protrude at the outer edge of the scale, creating many small planes in the surface texture of the fiber. These planes disperse and diffuse light, creating lower luster and a dulled, softer, less intense color than is characteristic of the coarser, longer staple yarns, even when the two types are dyed in the same dyebath.

Raw cotton fibers have a rough, irregular surface texture (see Figure 4-20b). The high degree of light diffusion from this crinkled surface accounts for the very dull colors found in raw cotton. Mercerization—a finishing process used on cotton—rounds out the cotton fiber, creating a smooth-surfaced, rod-shaped fiber. The smooth surface and regular carved shape of mercerized cotton gives the fiber a beautiful luster not present in raw cotton. Colors are brighter and more intense in mercerized cotton fiber, and less dye is needed to achieve a specified color.

Man-made fibers can be quite lustrous if the fiber luster is not deliberately controlled. The way synthetic filaments are produced tends to yield a smooth surface and a shiny fiber. Fiber luster can be decreased by altering the shape of the spinnerette holes to form grooves or striations along the fibers by applying chemical delustrants to create a grainy or pock-marked surface (see Figure 4-20c and d).

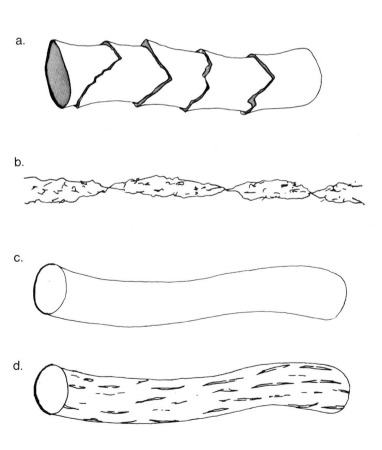

a.

b.

c.

d.

4-20. **Surface textures: a. surface scales; b. rough and irregular surface; c. shiny and lustrous surface; d. grainy surface.**

111

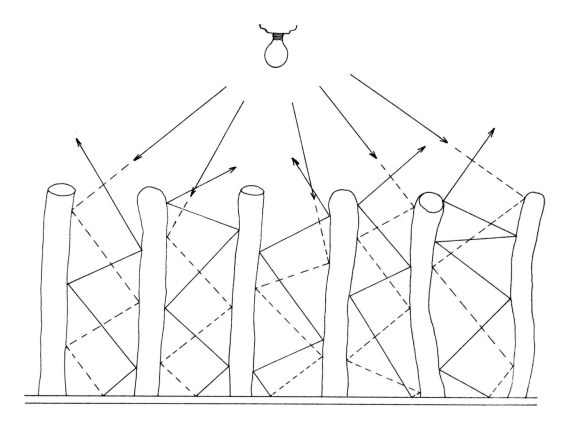

SURFACE TEXTURE OF YARNS

Interreflection

Texture in yarn behaves differently with light than does texture on the surface of a fiber. At the fiber level, surface texture diffuses or scatters light, making the color higher in value and less distinct or intense. At the yarn level, however, the dynamics are just the opposite. If a yarn has a deep surface texture light is absorbed into the texture of the yarn and there filtered, making the color of the yarn darker in value and more intense in hue. The deeper the texture, the darker and richer the color will appear. This color shift due to light absorption into a deeply textured yarn or fabric surface is called interreflection. It is most visible in a nap or pile texture, where fiber ends or yarn ends stick out from the surface (see Figure 4-21).

Interreflection occurs when white light enters the nap and is reflected back and forth among the nap's dyed fibers. Each time the light bounces off a dyed fiber surface, part of the spectrum is absorbed by the dye and the rest is selectively reflected as the color we see. Each time the selectively reflected light is bounced off another fiber of the same color, the color of the light is further filtered because light rays not of the dyed color have another chance to be absorbed by the dye surface. The particular wavelengths creating the color of the dyed fibers are thus reenforced, and the color becomes purer and more saturated each time it is bounced from one dyed fiber to another.

4-21. Interreflection lowers value and produces a feeling of greater saturation.

The light that is eventually reflected out of the nap to meet our eye looks closer to the color of the dye. It also appears lower in value because the filtering process of the nap not only makes the color more exactly that of the dye, it reduces the total amount of light that is reflected out of the nap, thereby lowering the value of the color.

112

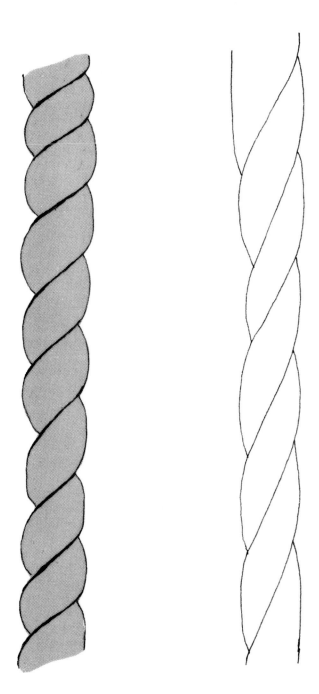

4-22. **Yarns and twist: high-twist yarns appear darker than low-twist yarns of the same material.**

Influential Aspects of Yarn Structure

Four aspects of yarn structure influence the surface texture of yarn and, through this, the yarn's color:
1. The number of fiber ends sticking out of the yarn.
2. The amount of twist imparted to the yarn in spinning.
3. The direction of the draw of the yarn in relation to the position of the viewer.
4. The type of yarn construction.

Filament yarns tend to be lustrous and high in value because of greater fiber length and greater fiber orientation. In addition, the surface texture of a filament yarn is smoother than that of a staple fiber yarn because the filament yarn has no staple ends sticking out of it. The smoother-surfaced filament yarn reflects more light than the staple yarn because it does not experience the interreflection that occurs in the nap of the staple yarn. Therefore, all other factors being equal, a filament yarn is higher in value than a staple yarn made of the same material and dyed in the same dyebath.

The amount of twist given to a yarn in the spinning process changes the yarn's surface texture. High-twist yarns have a generally rougher surface texture and smaller reflecting planes than low-twist yarns do. They also appear slightly darker in value than they would have if given less twist in spinning (see Figure 4-22).

As fibers are drawn out and twisted during spinning, the fiber ends toward the center of the yarn are caught firmly in the yarn while the fiber ends toward the outside of the yarn stick out. The direction in which the fibers are pulled out as the twist is applied (called the direction of the draw) determines the direction in which the staple ends stick out of the body of the yarn strand (see Figure 4-23). This creates a sort of directional nap—more evident in some fibers than in others—on the surface of the yarn. In many woolen threads the ends that stick out make the thread feel and look fuzzy, although some types of fiber are much fuzzier than others.

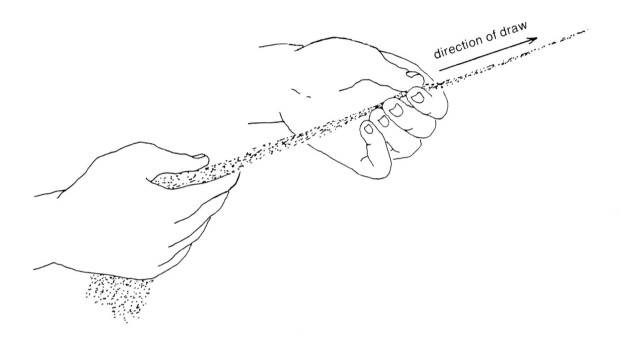

4-23. **The direction of the draw creates a directional nap on the surface of the yarn.**

The direction of the nap can often be discerned by running the thread back and forth through one's fingers: the thread feels smoother when drawn so that the nap and the ends of the fibers are made to lie against the thread; it feels rougher when drawn so that the ends are forced away from the thread. When threads are smooth and not fuzzy, the direction of the draw may be impossible to identify. Many cottons, rayons, silks, and linens have a smooth feel in both directions. In some silk threads, very small bumps can be felt when the thread is drawn through the fingers in the wrong direction.

Nap affects the way light reflects from a yarn or thread and thus helps to determine the apparent color of the yarn. Two pieces of the same yarn placed side-by-side appear slightly different in color when the direction of the draw goes in opposite directions in each (see Figure 4-24). If the yarn lies with the direction of the draw toward the viewer, so that the

ends of the fibers point away from the viewer, the yarn will appear lighter in value and less intense than it would if its position were reversed. This is because when the fiber ends, (or nap) point away from the viewer, the smooth reflecting surfaces of the sides of the fibers are presented to the viewer, giving a higher level of reflectance. If the yarn lies with the direction of the draw away from the viewer, so that the fiber ends are pointed directly at the viewer, interreflection within the nap will make the yarn appear darker and more intense in color.

Light and color changes attributable to the direction of the spinning draw are more apparent on some yarns than on others. A high-luster short staple yarn shows the greatest variation in color with the direction of the draw. The high luster makes the effect of having the nap ends toward or away from the viewer more noticeable; and the shorter length of the staple yarn's fibers means that more fiber ends are present to stick out of

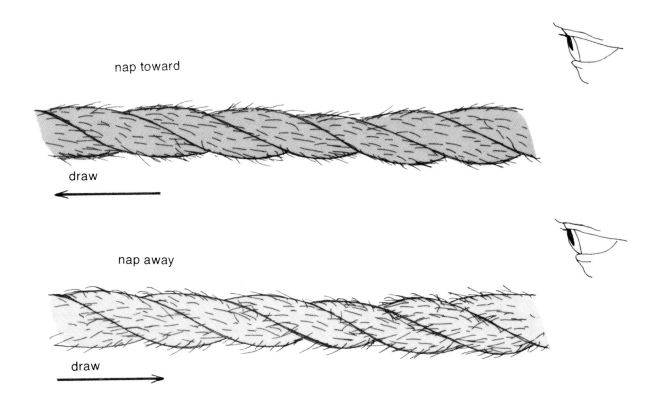

nap toward

draw

nap away

draw

4-24. **Direction of draw.**

the yarn surface and create an effective nap. As a result, it is impossible to match lustrous staple yarns for color and particularly for value unless the threads or yarns are all oriented in the same direction.

The direction of the draw is especially important in embroidery. If the thread is pulled through the fabric in the wrong direction—that is, against the nap—the ends of the fibers are forced away from the thread as the thread goes through the fabric. Light is then dispersed and reflected in many directions because the ends of the fibers lie in so many directions. Light reflects with much less dispersion when all the fibers lie parallel to each other.

When threads that have no apparent draw direction are used, the embroiderer can plan in advance to ensure that all threads are inserted in the needle in the same direction. When a new thread is to be cut from a ball or skein, for example, the needle should be threaded with the end from the previous cut, and the

thread should be knotted at the new cut. If the skein is cut at the knot through all the threads, all should be loosely knotted together at one end, and this end should be the one from which all the threads go through the needle or are knotted. Some manufacturers identify the beginning end of the skein in each package.

In Assisi embroidery—a type of work in which the entire background area is covered with small cross stitches—all threads must be used in the same direction. If some areas are worked with the draw running in opposite directions, they will reflect light slightly differently, causing an undesirable change in value. The difference in color caused by the direction of the draw is small and subtle, but attention to detail and craftsmanship in matters of this sort distinguish professional-quality work from amateurish work.

Spinning techniques to a large extent dictate the texture of given yarn. They can be used to make a simple, smooth-textured yarn or a highly textured

a.

b.

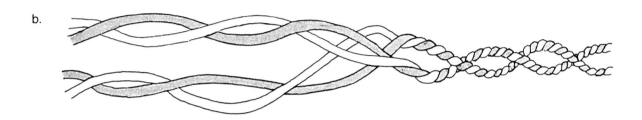

4-25. **Ply: a. plied yarn is two singles twisted together; b. a cord is two or more plied yarns twisted together.**

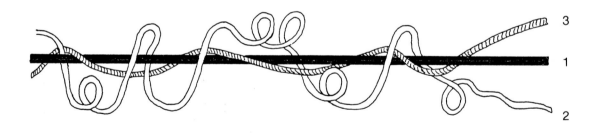

3

1

2

4-26. **Complex Yarns:**
   Most Complex Yarns Consist of: (1) a core; (2) a decorative or effect yarn, and (3) a binder.

complex (or novelty) yarn. The most basic kind of yarn (as well as the first step in a more complex yarn) is a *singles yarn*—a continuous length of fiber with a unidirectional twist (see Figure 4-25a). When two or more singles yarns are twisted together, the result is known as a *ply*. Various textural effects can be achieved by combining singles yarns into plied yarns.

The twist direction used in making a ply yarn is important. Usually, two Z-twist singles are combined by being twisted together in an S-twist direction, while two S-twist singles are plied with a Z-twist. Some of the initial twist is lost when the singles are plied in the opposite direction, allowing the fibers to loosen up to form a softer, less compact, textured yarn that exhibits a slightly softer color than appeared in either of the singles. If two or more singles are plied together in the same direction that they were spun in the result is a *cable*. Because cable formed in this way does not lose any of its twist during plying, the end result is a tighter, slightly more compact twist yarn than ordinary ply.

A *cord* yarn is one step more complicated than plied yarns. It is produced when two or more ply yarns are twisted together, with each successive twist going in the direction opposite the preceding one (see Figure 4-25b). Sometimes this process is called replying. All variations in the number of single strands and in the amount and direction of twist lead to yarns with slightly different light reflectance and color properties: lighter or darker, more or less intense.

Yarns can be classified as simple or complex. The term *simple yarn* refers to a smooth, even yarn that has an equal number of turns per inch throughout its length. Simple yarns can be singles, plies, cables, or cords. The key element of a simple yarn is its uniformity. Crepe yarn constitutes a variety of simple yarn. Although the high degree of twist in crepe yarns tends to make them kink, resulting in a rough texture, the evenness of their twist and the evenness of their size identify them as simple yarns.

By themselves, simple yarns tend to be lustrous and to produce smooth fabrics with relatively highly organized reflectance and slightly higher value than textured fabrics have. Except for the crepe yarns already mentioned, simple yarns in themselves do not create a texture; but the artist's arrangement and manipulation of combinations of yarn fibers, yarn sizes, and weaving patterns can create endless variations in texture and in visual effects.

Complex yarns (also called novelty yarns) are constructed for textural interest and appearance. They differ from simple yarns in that they are made with irregularities in size, twist, or construction. Despite their name, complex yarns need not be structurally complicated. Complex yarns may be single, plied, or occasionally a cord construction. Complex single yarns comprise various thick and thin flock or flake yarns that are spun in a single strand with textural lumps included at intervals along the length of the yarn.

Most complex ply yarns consist of a core, a decorative or effect yarn, and a binder (see Figure 4-26). In this construction, the core or base yarn controls the length and stability of the finished yarn; the effect yarn forms the design, by its color or by the way it is attached to the core yarn; and the binder yarn holds the effect yarn in position. Irregular plying of more than one strand (varying the feeding speed of one of the strands into the yarn) can produce controllable irregularities in the yarn. Complex yarns include boucles, ratine, gimp, loop, nub, seed, spiral, corkscrew, and chenille yarns, among others.

Looped and textured novelty techniques create textures that absorb light and reduce the reflectance of the yarn. Complex yarn construction can be used to control the harsh, overly mechanical luster of certain man-made fibers or to create changes in color value and color intensity in a work. Some color changes that result from changes in yarn texture alone can be fairly subtle; if used carefully and deliberately, they can give beautiful effects, whether isolated for emphasis or combined with the other elements of color design. Other color changes, in deeper-textured novelty yarns such as chenille, can be strong and very noticeable. Chenille yarn has a pilelike surface texture (see Figure 4-27). A rich, dark color is produced by the inter-reflection of light in the yarn's surface pile.

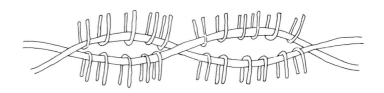

4-27. **Chenille.**

SURFACE TEXTURE OF FABRICS

Many weaves and other fiber techniques depend on the interaction of texture and light to produce light-and-shadow patterns and subtle color changes. The simplest is the effect of yarn structure alone in a plain weave. *Plain* (or tabby) *weave* is the simplest possible way of interlacing warp and weft. In it, the weft moves over one warp, under the next, over the next, and so on across the fabric. A number of changes can be made within the format of a plain weave to change fabric texture, light reflectance, and color.

Yarn Twist in Fabric Structure

The twist of yarns can be used effectively at the fabric level. A pattern can be formed by juxtaposing blocks of S-twist yarns with blocks of Z-twist yarns. The use of S (clockwise or left-handed) and Z (counterclockwise or right-handed) twists in alternating stripes an inch or so wide produces a subtle change of reflectance—a luster and matte, light and dark, striped effect—in the warp, in the weft, or in both.

Yarn twist can also create design effects in fabric structure. Yarns with a great deal of twist try to undo themselves. If a piece of fabric is woven with alternating pairs of warp and weft threads tightly twisted in opposite directions, the threads will try to undo themselves all over the piece of fabric when it is released from the loom. The S yarns will try to undo themselves to the left; the Z yarns, to the right. Since in either case the yarns are trapped by the weave, their efforts to untwist will produce the springy, crinkled, puckered effect of a crepe fabric (see Figure 4-28). Because of their springy textural surface, crepes have smaller, less highly organized, more randomly reflecting surfaces on the fabric. This effect is increased by the lower luster of the high-twist yarn itself. In general, crepe fabrics have a more matte appearance and a duller, darker color than a plain fabric woven of the same type of fiber but having a normal amount of twist and no variation in the twist direction of the yarn.

Color changes due to interreflection occur at the level of fabric structure, as well as at the level of yarn structure. Low-twist staple yarns woven into a cloth and given a brushed finish produce a napped fabric whose darker, more intense color is the result of the interreflection of light in the fabric nap.

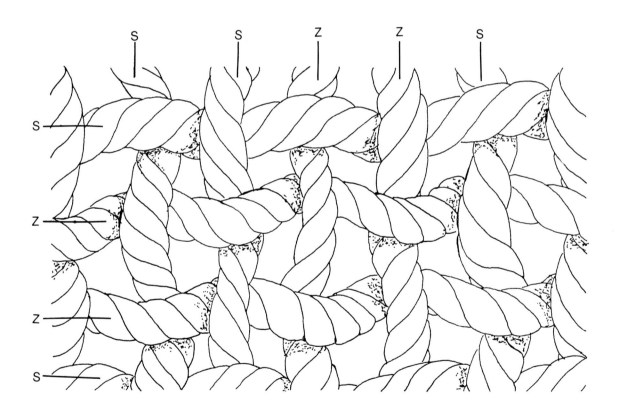

4-28. **In crepe, tightly twisted S and Z yarns try to undo within the weave, creating a springy, crinkled surface texture.**

118

4-29. **Wandering weft:** *Winter* **(Detail).**

Artist: Barbara Staepelaere
Photo: Patricia Lambert
Courtesy of the artist

Yarn Spacing in Fabric Structure

Strictly speaking, a plain weave should have the same number of warp ends as weft ends per inch. When the same number of warp ends and weft ends per inch are present in a fabric, the fabric is said to be *balanced* or *evenweave*. The yarns of warp and weft can be packed loosely or compactly. In a closely woven fabric, the warp ends should be just close enough to allow the weft thickness to show between them; when warp and weft are more spaced out than this, the result is an open fabric.

In some kinds of open weave, the weft need not be completely horizontal, but instead can cross the warp at an angle or wander along an irregular path that is pressed into place with the fingers or with a small, forklike beater (see Figure 4-29).

a.

4-30. Curtain: a. frontlit; b. backlit. From an eighteenth century Connecticut Bed Rugg.

Execution in pulled thread: Mary Fry
Photo: Patricia Lambert

Open fabric weaves can also be used to create a special light effect called the *gauze effect.* When light is reflected from the viewer's side of a light-colored open-weave fabric, the threads of the fabric appear bigger than they are and indeed appear to fill the spaces between them, creating a seemingly solid fabric. When the fabric is lit from behind, however, it reflects far less light in the direction of the viewer and takes on the more true-to-form appearance of a thin

120

b.

web (see Figure 4-30). This explains why thin white curtains at a window prevent a person who is viewing them from the bright light of a street in daylight from seeing through them and into the darker interior of the house. Instead, the viewer sees only the reflected light from the white curtain, while a person inside the darker room can look through the curtain to the daylight of the street.

The gauze effect is used in theatre work for stage backdrops and other separating technologies, taking advantage of the open-weave characteristics of a material known as scrim. When painted and lit from the front, scrim appears opaque and can be used as a backdrop or show curtain. When lit from the rear, it becomes semitransparent, allowing shadow scenes to be played behind it.

The gauze effect is a creative vehicle in the fiber arts, especially when dense areas of more colorful yarns are combined with open structures—as they are in such open techniques as leno, brocades (or inlay techniques), needle lace, bobbin lace, embroidered netting, looped or knotted netting, open-work embroidery, knitting, macramé, and sprang. The changes from color to silhouette and cast shadow produced by changes in direction of the light source can be used to create works of ephemeral beauty. The gauze effect allows fiber artists to work with lighting and to plan dynamic, changing color effects in a work.

Lace weaves all have an open effect that is created by distortion of either the warp or the weft yarns. one of the most common lace weaves is the *leno weave,* in which warp yarns are crossed at certain points and held in place by the weft shot. In single-cross leno, two adjacent warp yarns are crossed. In double leno, two warp threads are treated as one so that a total of four warps are used for each leno cross (see Figure 4-31). The warp can be twisted by hand or with the aid of extra gauze harnesses equipped with specially designed heddles.

The weft shots in the resulting leno fabric are firmly held in place by the twisted warp, so that even though the weave is open and the weft is widely spaced, the fabric is stable and makes good window curtains, where it uses light to create the same gauze effects as a scrim does in a theater. There is some confusion of terms concerning this type of weave. The terms leno weave and gauze weave are are often used interchangeably, but gauze weave can also refer to any loosely

a   b.

4-31. **Leno weaves: a. single cross leno; b. double cross leno.**

woven open mesh fabric—with or without the twisted warp of leno. Sometimes leno weave is termed *doup weave,* after the doup attachment used for changing warp position on commercial power looms.

Brocade is a double-element fabric created by adding one or more elements (often of different colors) to the basic warp and weft elements of a plain weave. These extra warp or weft elements may be continuous—running the full length of the warp or weft— or they may be discontinuous, added only in certain areas of the fabric with either the weft or the warp. Discontinuous brocades are also called inlay (see Figure 4-32).

Discontinuous weft brocade or weft inlay is simple to accomplish on a hand loom. The brocade or inlay yarn is wound on an extra shuttle and, where required, is added to the plain weave along with the regular weft yarn. The number of extra shuttles carrying different colors of inlay weft to be woven simultaneously with the regular weft yarn across the fabric is limitless. Normally, the inlay yarn is about the same weight as the regular weft yarn, and the brocade acts mainly a technique for introducing different-colored yarn to the weave. A beautiful contrast of texture can also be created with a brocade or inlay technique, however, when a fine, plain, open-weave or gauze fabric is embellished with a thicker or different-colored inlay.

4-32. **Brocade: a. front; b. back.**
Photo: Patricia Lambert

a.

b.

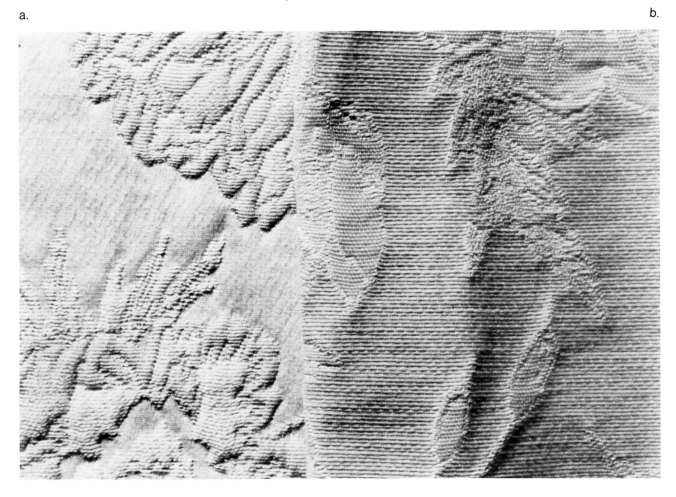

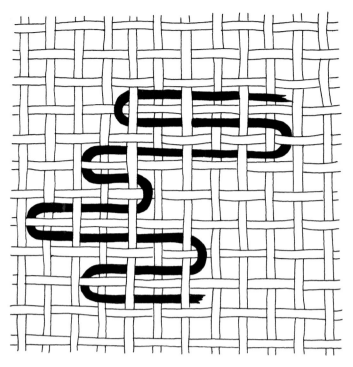

If the inlay weft is about four times heavier than the regular weft, the wider inlay weft yarns will separate the lighter weft shots so that the finer weft yarn forms a light transparent web in the midst of which the solid inlay pattern seems to float. This technique is especially attractive when hung in front of a window that is backlit in daylight—so that the inlay forms an achromatic shadow pattern in a light transparent ground—and frontlit at night, whereupon the entire weaving becomes more opaque and the colors of the inlay come to life, creating an entirely different effect (see Figure 4-33).

If either the warp or the weft has more ends per inch than the other, the fabric is said to be *unbalanced.* If the fabric has more warp ends per inch than weft ends, the warp will be more visible in the fabric, and the weft will be partially or completely hidden by the warp. For creation of a warp-faced fabric—that is, for the warp to cover the weft completely—twice as many warp ends as weft ends are needed (see Figure 4-34).

4-33. **Brocade is made by adding an extra element to either warp or weft.**

4-34. **Warp-faced weave:** *Spring Lattice* **(Detail).**
Artist: Ruth Gowell
Photo courtesy of the artist
Collection: Laura Noble/Ray Hylton

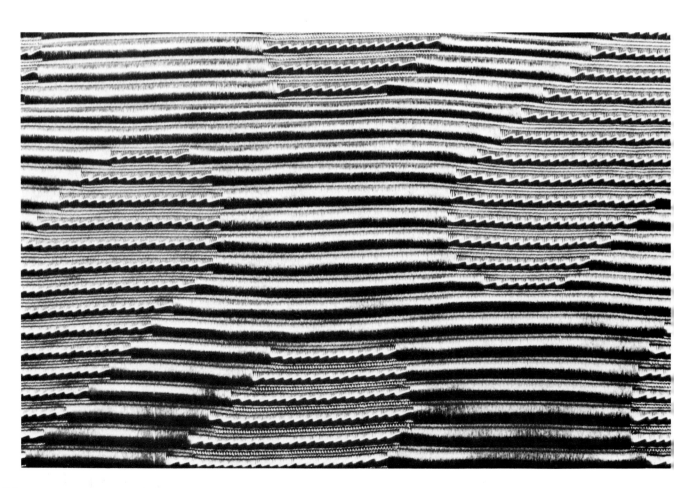

Warp-faced weaves are characterized by horizontal ridges created as the weft passes back and forth across the fabric, hidden by the close-packed warp threads. The size and height of the ridges depends on the thickness of the weft shots. For example, if the weft is a fine yarn, the horizontal ridges that result are small, creating little texture and color variation on the highly organized face of the fabric. Broadcloth is a warp-faced fabric made in this way. If the weft yarns are heavy or consist of thick groups of yarns, they create large horizontal ridges on the face of the fabric and changes in the angle of reflectance of the warp yarns as the latter bend over the bundles of weft hidden beneath them. The textural difference between fine weft and thick weft ridges in a warp-faced weave is most noticeable if the warp yarns are smooth and lustrous. Examples of warp-faced fabrics that use heavier weft yarns include poplin, faille, bengaline, and ottoman.

If a fabric has twice as many weft ends as warp ends per inch, the result is a weft-faced fabric. Tapestry is a weft-faced fabric. For a tapestry or weft-faced fabric, the warp ends should be spaced a weft's thickness apart. This allows the weft to cram down over and totally cover the warp (see Figure 4-35). In weft-faced weaves of more or less pronounced texture, depending on the thickness of the warp shots hidden under the weft threads, the surface texture shows as a series of low, vertical ribs. These vertical ribs are lower if a fine warp is hidden under the weft and more pronounced if a thicker warp is used. In general, tapestry and other weft-faced fabrics have a relatively smooth texture that by itself does little to influence the color of the yarns used.

4-35. Weft-faced weave: *Waiting* **(38" x 43", wool on cotton warp, 1985).**

Artist: Nancy Hoffman
Photo: Patricia Lambert
Courtesy of the artest

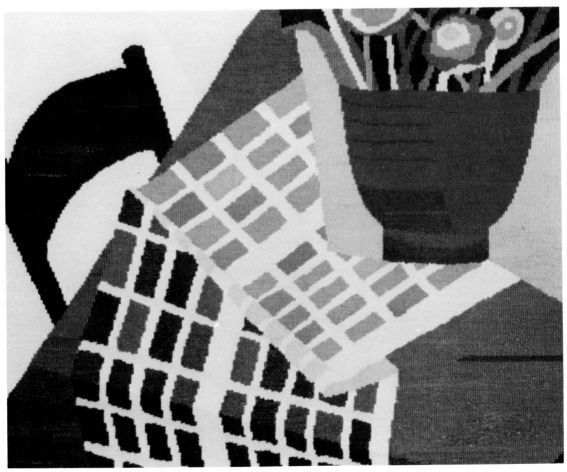

125

Weft-faced weaves rarely depend on texture for their color effect. Because the warp is covered, a weft-faced weave can produce unbroken areas of any color or combination of colors simply by changing the weft yarn. This allows a tapestry weaver to use color much as a painter does, and tapestry weaving has long been used to imitate even the painter's brushwork.

4-36. **Seersucker.**

Photo: Patricia Lambert

126

Yarn Tension in Fabric Structure

The tension on yarns as they are being woven can be used in plain weaves to create textural effects that develop after the cloth is removed from the loom. Seersucker is woven on a warp composed of alternating stripes of tight and loose tension. When the fabric is removed from the loom, the warp stripes that were woven under high tension relax more than those woven under loose tension, creating puckered stripes in the cloth (Figure 4-36).

The same effect can be achieved horizontally on the fabric by weaving alternating stripes of highly elastic and inelastic weft yarns onto a uniform warp. Depending on the direction of the lighting, the puckered areas will most often appear lighter than the smooth areas. Light strikes the raised texture of the puckered stripes, making them seem lighter; concurrently, the raised texture shades the smooth stripes, less light hits them, and they appear darker.

Basket Weave

Basket weave is a slight variation on plain weave. It is usually defined as two or more warp ends woven as a single unit with one or more weft threads. Basket weaves contribute two major properties to a fabric: texture, and drapes. If the fabric weave is sufficiently coarse to make the weave readily visible, basket weave can provide an interesting and pleasant change from regular tabby because of its more pronounced texture. It creates some shadow on the surface, which tends to appear slightly darker than when the same yarn is used in a smoother plain weave. With proper use of scale, or possibly with warp and weft done in contrasting colors so that the interplay of the two can be readily seen, an attractive and effective fabric design can be based solely on the contrast of tabby areas and basket weave areas (see Figure 4-37).

4-37. **Basket weave.**

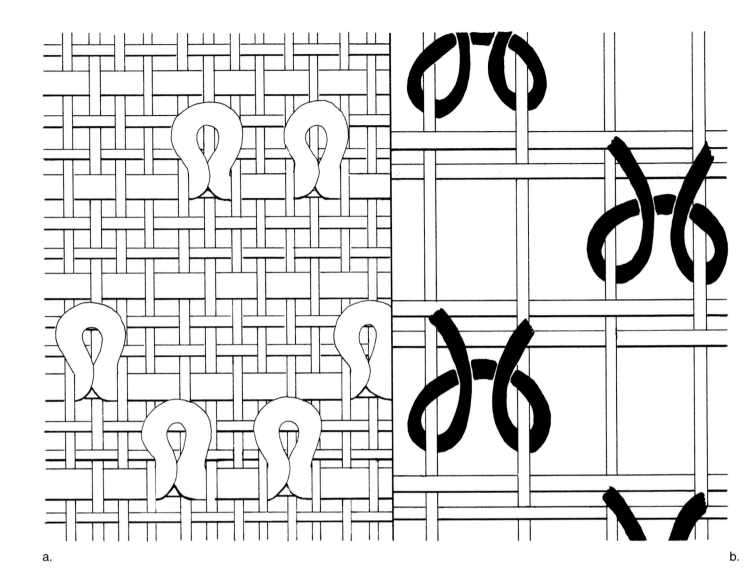

a.
b.

4-38. **Pile techniques: a. looping; b. rug knots.**

In addition to texture, basket weave produces a softer, more flowing drape in fabric than the same amount of yarn per inch would produce in a tabby weave. Because two or more warp or weft yarns are used as one, fewer interlacings occur in basket weave than in tabby weave of the same weight; this helps create a softer fabric with more give, more flexibility, and a softer, more form-fitting drape. Monk's cloth, flat duck, hopsacking, and some coat and suit fabrics are basket weaves. Oxford cloth is a fine basket weave in which the two warp yarns are used as a unit (equal in size to the one weft yarn). Although when the basket weave technique is done with fine fibers it is not obvious to the eye, it creates a softer fabric with an attractive drape and is commonly used for shirt material. A fabric with a soft, flowing drape will have softer and more graduated shadows than a stiff fabric with a more awkward or abrupt drape. A color shift between the two fabrics may be difficult to identify, but a difference in the quality of light and shadow on the two fabric surfaces will be visible.

Pile Techniques

Pile techniques create a deep texture on the fabric surface. As with yarn texture, the deeper and more pronounced the fabric texture is, the darker, richer, and more intense the color of the fabric will appear because of interreflection. In traditional hand-weaving, pile is created by a variety of knotting techniques, by woven float techniques, or by looping. *Looping* is simply pulling up loops of the desired height across the weft, every few rows (see Figure 4-38a). The loops are held in place by succeeding rows of plain weave. A limited color pattern can be developed across the fabric by inserting two (or possibly more) different-colored loop yarns into each shed and drawing up the color needed for each part of the pattern.

128

The various types of *rug knots* used by hand-weavers are also pile techniques (see Figure 4-38b). The knots can be made with a continuous weft that is wound on a small shuttle, made into a butterfly, or threaded through a large needle. Alternatively, the yarn can be precut and tied into the warp ends, either by hand or with the aid of a latch hook. Although knotting is a slow technique, the artist has complete freedom to introduce different colors and textures at any point in the rug or tapestry. Different textural effects can be obtained by varying the yarn weight, the length of the loops, or the spaces between the rows of knots. Short pile, when knotted close together, will stand up straight. The loops can be cut for a velvetlike texture and maximum interreflectance within the pile, making the colors appear dark, rich, and saturated.

Rows of long pile, when knotted farther apart, will allow the pile to flop down randomly on a rug surface or cascade down the surface of a wall hanging. This presents the side of the fiber and creates more reflectance, less interreflection, higher value, and lower intensity. The loops can be left uncut for one textural effect, or they can be cut evenly or unevenly for other effects.

Handwoven corduroy is not the same as the ribbed, cut pile, cotton fabric available commercially. Rather, it is a flat weave method that leaves long weft floats on the surface that can be cut to form a pile.

In the textile industry, pile fabrics are woven with an extra set of warp or weft yarns interlaced with the ground weave so that loops or cut ends are produced on the surface of the fabric. Weft pile fabrics are made with two sets of weft and one set of warp. The extra set of weft yarns floats over three or more (usually five or seven) warp ends. After the fabric is woven the floats are cut and brushed to a pile. Velveteen and corduroy are made in this way. In corduroy, the floats are arranged above each other to form rows when the floats are cut. In velveteen, the floats are staggered for an all-over effect. Pile yarns can interlace with one or three warp yarns; interlacing with three warp yarns forms a more durable cloth.

In *warp pile fabrics*—such as velvet, velour, and Wilton rugs—the pile is formed with an extra warp yarn. These fabrics are constructed by double cloth method, the wire-cut method, or the looped pile method. In the double cloth method (one of the most common techniques), five sets of yarn are used: two weft, two warp, and an extra warp used exclusively for the pile. Two separate fabrics are woven simultaneously, each with a set of one warp and one weft. The pile yarn is interlaced in one fabric and passed to the other fabric, where it is interlaced and passed back to the first fabric. When the fabric is finished, the two halves of the double cloth are cut apart, leaving a pile composed of cut ends that can be sheared so that they are evened up. Velvet is made in this way.

In the wire-cut method, two sets of warp and one set of weft are used. One warp is lifted up from the ground cloth, a wire is inserted across the fabric, and the warp is returned and woven into the fabric with the weft. At least three picks of weft should be woven before the pile warp is again lifted and the wire inserted for another row of loops. The loops can be left looped (in which case the wire is smooth) or they can be cut (in which case the wire has a knife on one end and cuts the loops as it is removed). Wilton rugs are commonly made using this technique.

In *terry pile fabric* (or looped toweling), the loops are woven on both sides of the fabric. This is accomplished by leaving slack on separate beams the set of pile warp, while the base fabric warp remains tight as usual. Several picks of warp are woven without beating. When the three or more acumulated picks are then beaten, the beating raises loops in the slack warp. Soft, fluffy, absorbent, low-twist yarns are used for the pile yarn. Although many of these warp or weft pile techniques have been used mainly in industry, some of the techniques (such as terry) could be taken by an inventive craftsperson and explored as a medium for artistic expression.

Cut pile fabrics demonstrate most dramatically the color changes due to interreflection, the absorption of light, and the filtering of color by the texture of the fabric. The fabric naps created by corduroy, velvet, cut rug piles, or any other fabric structures that orient fibers side-by-side with the cut ends pointing toward the viewer create the richest, most intense colors and the most dramatic color changes between dark areas (where the pile ends point directly at the viewer) and light areas (where they are crushed or positioned with their sides toward the viewer).

Looped (or uncut) piles show considerably less color shift due to interreflection than do cut piles because the uncut loop of yarn always presents a light-reflecting side of the yarn to the viewer. Consequently, more total light is reflected from the surface to the viewer's eye, making the looped fabric higher in value. At the same time, less total light is absorbed and filtered in the fabric texture, so a looped pile surface also appears less intense in color than a cut pile surface. This is a matter of degree, however: a looped pile surface is still darker and more intense in color than a flat tabby weave surface made from the same yarns would be. Interreflection is a specialized case of color control by fabric construction, in which the effects of surface texture and fiber orientation meet and reenforce one another to cause dramatic color change in the fabric (see Figure 4-39).

4-39. **Reflectance changes in different stitches of the same thread.**
Design: Mary Fry
Photo: Patricia Lambert

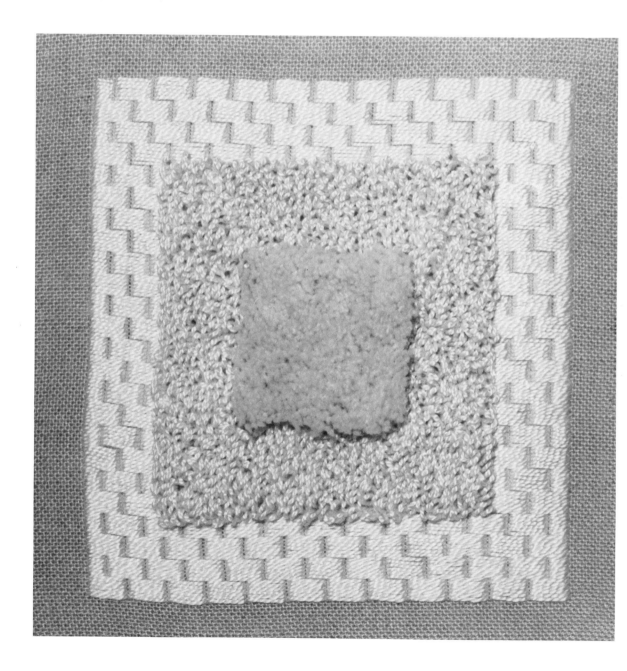

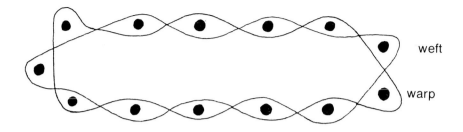

weft

warp

4-40. **Tubular weave, or cloth cylinder.**

Some fibers show a more obvious value difference than others when they are converted from a flat surface texture (such as the light-catching satin stitch or float weave) into a pile stitch. The greatest difference is seen in a smooth silk filament thread that has almost no twist. When sewn in a smooth, flat, satin stitch, the silk appears very lustrous and high in value. In addition to its highly oriented molecular structure and smooth surface, the silk fiber's triangular cross section and fineness create many good reflecting surfaces. The filament fiber—with little twist and no texture in the yarn to interrupt the flat, smooth reflecting surface of the long float—presents a virtually shadowless surface. When the same fiber is placed on end in a pile weave, however, the same characteristics of fiber structure that created high surface reflectance in the satin fabric also create a high degree of interreflection within the pile. The fineness and high luster of the fiber enable it to serve as a very efficient light filter, bouncing the light again and again off the many fiber surfaces in the pile before reflecting it to the viewer's eye as a much darker and more intense color.

Not surprisingly, a raw, short staple cotton shows the least difference in value and intensity between a flat stitch and a pile stitch, since it diffuses white light so effectively that the color created by selective reflection is difficult to see. The general light diffusion of the fiber also overcomes to a large extent the interreflective effect of the pile stitch. The random reflecting surfaces produced by the crumpled shape and rough surface texture of the fiber, its short staple length, and its less highly oriented arrangement in the uncombed yarn all contribute to the diffusion of light. The flat stitch is moderately high in value and not particularly lustrous because of its general diffusion of light; the pile stitch is equally unremarkable as a filter and is fairly high in value, as a result of diffusion. Although a noticeable difference in intensity and value between the flat stitch and the pile stitch is evident, the difference is much less remarkable here than in other fibers. Perle cotton (a mercerized, combed cotton) shows more difference than raw cotton does, but less than the various types of wool fibers do. The characteristics of man-made fibers vary depending on their structure and its influence on light reflectance and interreflection.

Other Double-element Techniques

Textural effects other than those classed as pile weaves can be created with the use of double elements. Welts and piques use two warps on two separate beams to produce a three-dimensional effect. The extra warp is not woven as a separate cloth, but instead produces detaining backing floats to force the woven face of the cloth into raised rounded ribs that run horizontally across the fabric. Welts are straight ribs and piques are curved ribs. As happens with other textured fabrics, the value of a yarn is lower on welts and piques than it is on a plain weave.

Double cloth is another essentially plain-weave fabric that can be made with three or more elements. In this case, two or more fabrics are woven simultaneously, one above the other on the same loom, and can be linked in various ways. If the double weave cloth is joined at both edges, the result is a tubular weave or cloth cylinder (see Figure 4-40). If the treadling sequence for tubular weave is reversed at planned intervals, the fabric comes together where the treadling is reversed and then reseparates, creating a series of little horizontal tubes within the fabric that can be stuffed during weaving to produce a bas relief—a sculptural three-dimensional effect.

The play of highlight and shadow on the surface curves of the fabric is important to the visual effect of all stuffed three-dimensional fiber pieces, whether they are double weaves, bas reliefs, fiber sculptures, or quilts. In such pieces, the drama of the highlights and shadows and the shifts in color can be played up or down according to the general reflectance of the fibers chosen and according to the reflectance or interreflection created by the surface textures of the pieces. Tremendous differences in the reflectance of light, the color quality, the value, the intensity, the emotional impact, and the general effect would exist among, for example, a stuffed bas relief done in satin, another done in a pile surface such as corduroy or velvet, and a third done with some areas of high-reflectance satin and other areas of high-interreflection velvet.

Quilting

Quilting is the sandwiching of two or three layers of fabric, or of a top and bottom layer of fabric with a nonwoven batting for the middle layer. Quilting stitches, which are small running stitches, or knots are used to hold the layers together in a variety of patterns or designs. Air trapped in unstitched areas prevents the surface from being uniformly flat. The most depressed areas are those where the layers are forced together by the stitching; these areas, which resemble valleys between hills, reflect the least amount of light. Conversely, the raised areas reflect the most light, creating a pattern in light and dark value contrast on the surface of the quilt.

The function of the quilting stitches is to hold the layers together, but in some cases they also act as the principal design element. Patterns of value formed by the quilting stitches show best on plain fabric that is high in value and has no other kind of design or texture.

Trapunto is a type of quilting that relies on value changes produced by changes in light reflectance on stitched and padded surface contours. A design is stitched through two or more layers of fabric; then some or all areas in the design are stuffed, creating a surface that resembles bas relief. High-luster fabrics yield the most dramatic trapunto effects. More subtle value changes result when less lustrous fabrics are used.

Italian quilting is similar to trapunto in that it is stitched and padded. A thick yarn padding is inserted between two parallel rows of stitching. The space between the two rows must be wide enough to allow insertion of a needle for carrying a heavy thread padding. Fabric with a high luster creates the most dramatic value changes in this technique, as in trapunto.

English quilting is characterized by a decorative top layer made of many small pieces of fabric that are sewn together. The process of sewing the pieces of fabric together is called piecing, pieced work, or patchwork. Instead of being pieced, the top layer can be appliquéd; appliqué is the technique of applying or adding additional pieces of fabric to the top layer. The top layer can also be embellished with free stitching or embroidery. In patchwork, when the top is made of many printed or colored fabrics, the design impact relies on contrasts in the shape, color, print, and structural texture of the fabric patches. Because the quilting stitches become lost in the surface in any case, they often follow the edges formed where the small pieces are joined in the top layer.

It is exciting in piecework quilting to use fabrics that have a decided nap or direction and to exploit the rich color variation that can result from consistent patterning of the nap direction. When the nap faces toward the viewer, the interreflection of light causes the color to appear rich, intense, and dark. When the nap faces away from the viewer, light is reflected uniformly by the parallel fibers of the nap (as it would be by any smooth-surfaced fabric), giving the dyed fabric color a higher value. If the viewer changes position in relation to the quilt, areas that were previously lighter will become dark, and visa versa, because the nap direction of the different patches has been reversed. Knowledgeable handling of nap direction can make or break the overall effect of a quilt that uses napped fabrics. Sloppy handling of nap can create chaos in an otherwise beautifully planned quilt by randomly causing napped patches to appear lighter or darker.

Some fabrics do not have a nap but nevertheless must be watched as the pieces are joined. A fabric such as a chambray is woven with a warp of one color and a weft of another. As a result, it reflects one color more than the other, depending on the direction from which the viewer looks at it. The dominant color is reversed when the fabric is turned 90 degrees. Fabrics with a distinctly corded look can also cause problems if the cording runs horizontally in all but one or two pieces, where it has been accidentally arranged vertically.

Quilters must develop an eye for how light reflects from the surface of fabrics as well as for how the print orientation of the colors and designs in the fabrics affect the overall pattern. Quilters must also be conscious of whether or not the threads of a piece of fabric are running parallel to the straight edges of the shape when it is cut and pieced. A piece of fabric cut slightly off the grain will not only reflect light slightly differently, it will not lie as smoothly as the others. When the artist must use pieces cut at an odd angle, extra care must be taken to ensure that they lie flat.

4-41. Patchwork quilt: *Triad* **(Detail).**

Artist: Nan Carter
Photo: Patricia Lambert
Collection: Barbara Thexton

4-42. Trapunto: *Poppies II* **(27" x 44").**

Artist: Analee Reutlinger
Photo: Analee Reutlinger
Courtesy of the artist

133

Embroidery

In both counted and free types of embroidery, texture is used to create a variety of light and color contrasts.

Texture can be achieved in many ways: by changing the length and slant of stitches; by superimposing stitches on top of each other; and by using knots and loops. Parallel stitches reflect light more uniformly creating lighter values than when the same thread is worked in stitches that are not parallel.

The value of the thread used helps determine how much influence textural changes have in the perceived value of an area. A light-colored thread shows greater value changes when worked in different textures than does a dark thread. Thread luster is another factor influencing the amount of value change that can be accomplished through textural changes. A lustrous white thread is most responsive to texture in creating value changes, while a black matte thread shows very little value change from one texture to another.

Stitches must have equal tension in order to create a surface of uniform texture. Stitches pulled too tightly sink below the others and loose stitches stand above the others; the resulting valleys and ridges catch light and reflect it, ruining the surface of the work.

When two or more threads are in the needle, care must be taken that one thread does not become tighter or looser than the other during stitching. In addition, the embroiderer must make sure that the two (or more) threads remain parallel to each other in the stitch; if they are allowed to twist in some stitches and not in others, light will reflect unevenly, and the surface will appear uneven.

Fabrics can be manipulated with stitches in a variety of ways, either by hand or on a machine. Smocking is one technique in which stitches are used to gather the fabric into decorative folds. Light reflection off the surface of the folds contrasts with the lack of reflection from the deep recesses. These contrasts are more noticeable in shiny, lustrous fabrics than in nonlustrous fabrics. Plaiting and pleating are other methods of manipulating fabric. Reversing the folds of pleats in some areas creates a change in texture and results in contrasts of light and dark. Soft sculpture is a three-dimensional fabric form that combines techniques of embroidery with light effects of contoured surfaces produced in ways similar to quilting techniques.

4-43. **Value changes in stitch technique are seen most clearly in light threads.**

Artist: Mary Fry
Photo: Patricia Lambert

Chapter 5.

Finishes and Color

Finishes include both commercial and hand processes that alter structure in some way and in turn alter the behavior of the fabric. Many finishes change and improve the behavior of different kinds of fabric. Among these are flame-proof, water-proof, moth-proof, stain-resistant, soil-release, water-repellent, wrinkle-resistant, shrink-resistant, antiseptic, antislip, antiabrasion, and absorbant finishes. This book deals only with finishes that affect the light reflectance and/or color of a fabric. Commercial finishes used in the textile industry and finishes traditionally used in home crafts are both considered. Commercial finishes are important here because quilters deal with commercially made and finished fabrics; therefore, the advent of wrinkle-free fabrics (for example) is important in the final appearance of their artwork.

Mercerization

Some finishes alter reflectance and color at the fiber level; others work at the fabric level. Mercerization of cotton is an important textile finishe that works at the fiber level. It changes the structure and properties—especially the color properties—of cotton. Cotton in its natural form has a matte look.

Although cotton fiber is very absorbent, it does not accept dye very well because cotton has a highly crystalline molecular arrangement that does not provide many spaces in the fiber structure for dye molecules to enter through. The fact that cotton does not dye easily, plus the fact that its surface diffuses light, makes it impossible to get a good rich color in dyed raw (or unfinished) cotton.

In 1844, John Mercer discovered that cotton fibers submerged in caustic soda (lye) plumped up, became more lustrous, and increased in strength by nearly one-third. Filling the fibers with caustic soda while stretching them causes each fiber to pump up into a cylindrical shape. The wrinkles disappear, giving the fiber a rounder, more uniform reflecting surface. Mercerization makes the fiber smoother and more transparent, allowing light to enter it and to make contact with the dye molecules—thereby creating color. It increases the fiber's reflectance and gives the treated fiber its characteristic soft shine.

Mercerization causes a physical change in the fiber at the molecular level, too. The arrangement of the molecules alters, becoming less crystalline and more balanced in sharing stresses (which makes the fiber stronger). Since crystalline areas are not susceptible to dyestuff, the decrease in crystallinity also creates more spaces between molecules, allowing more dye molecules to enter the fiber. Mercerized cotton can be dyed to the same intensity as unmercerized cotton with one-third less dye; if dyed in the same dyebath, mercerized cotton appears darker in value and more intense in color than raw cotton.

Scrooping

The luster of silk can similarly be increased by a process called scrooping. Mild acids are applied to the absorbent silk fiber; the fibers are then dried under tension and steamed. Scrooping not only adds luster to the fiber, it also contributes to the rustle typical of some silks.

Wool Finishes

Wool fibers can be given a finish that prevents them from felting or fulling during laundering. When wool is exposed either to boiling water or to water, temperature changes, agitation, pressure, and an alkaline solution (such as soapy water), the wool fibers migrate in among one another and interlock—a process known as felting (see Figure 5-1). When wool is exposed to water, the fiber's interior fills with water, its crimp straightens out, and the scales along it open out. Because the scales all open out in the same direction, the fiber is able to move ahead one way but cannot go back (see Figure 5-2). Agitation and the change of scale position caused by heat or by abrupt temperature changes encourage the fibers to move ahead and become further entangled. When the fibers dry, the crimp resets and the scales clamp firmly, interlocking the fibers permanently.

5-1. **Wool finishing: a. unfulled; b. fulled.**

a.
b.

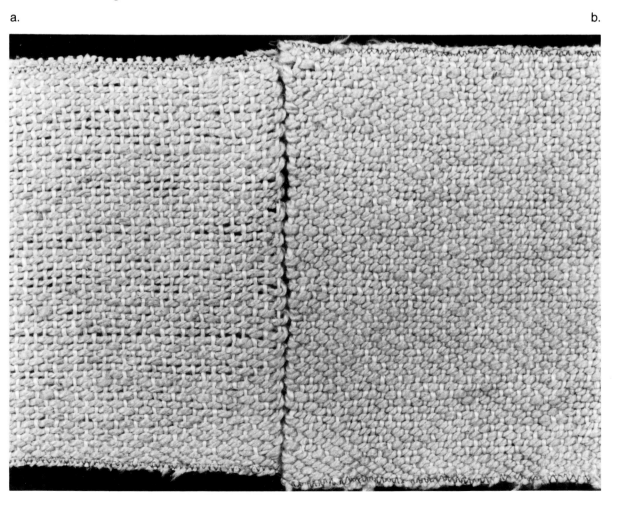

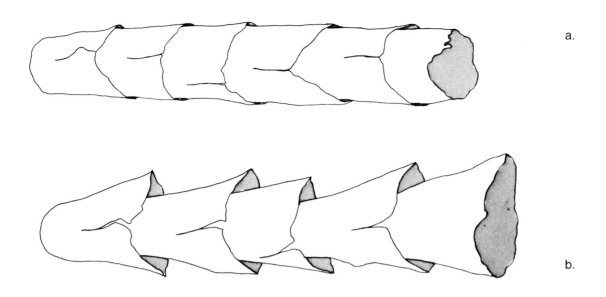

5-2. **Wool fiber: a. scales closed normally; b. scales open when exposed to hot water.**

The felting process results in shrinkage. It also changes the surface texture of the fabric and (to some degree) the fiber orientation. As the fibers entangle, the surface of the fabric becomes a denser, softer, and more uniform texture that translates into reduced luster, lower value, a fuzzier look, and more intense color. In comparison, the unfelted fabric has a more clearly defined yarn and fiber orientation, a more clearly defined yarn shape and weave texture, greater luster, higher value, and lower color intensity.

Sometimes felting is desirable, and sometimes it is not. For the latter situation, finishes have been developed that prevent wool fibers from felting and shrinking and make them more washable. One of these finishes coats the fiber with a thin layer of polymeric chemical that seals them so that they cannot become entangled. Another finish softens the cementing material between scales and seals the scales to the main body of the fiber. This, too, prevents the scales from opening and interlocking and thereby reduces felting. If not controlled properly, however, this finish can remove the scales entirely, resulting in a weakened fiber.

Optical Finishes

Some man-made fibers such as rayon, acetate, and nylon have a high degree of luster as a result of their highly oriented molecular structure, their smooth surface, their external shape. Fiber luster can be greatly diminished by taking advantage of yarn and fabric construction techniques that produce small and disorganized reflecting surfaces, by following fancy spinning and yarn-texturizing techniques, or by using textured weaves (such as crepe weaves). When these are not practicable or are inadequate to extinguish the brilliance of a fiber, however, substances can be added, either to the fiber solution or in finishing procedures, to reduce luster.

A common method is to add pigments such as titanium dioxide to the spinning solution before it is extruded through the spinnerette. A delustered fiber has microscopic pits on its surface that break up the uniformity of the fiber surface and reduce luster by scattering light reflection, thus creating an opaque fiber. External delustrants—such as barium salts, china clay, aluminun oxide, zinc oxide, and methylene urea—can be applied as a fabric finish to form an insoluble deposit on the outside of the fiber, disrupting the smooth surface of the fiber and again scattering light rays.

Optical brighteners are the other side of the coin. Many fabrics lose their whiteness or color purity during processing and maintenance; optical brighteners act to keep the whites white and the colors distinctly colored. They can be added as finishes or in the form of home laundering agents. The substances

138

attach themselves to the fabric and alter or increase the fabric's light reflectance. When exposed to sunlight, they absorb nonvisible ultraviolet light and convert it into visible blue light, thus increasing the total amount of light reflected by the fabric. White fabric looks whiter in consequence, and the value and intensity of colored fabric are raised.

Hand Finishes

Most fabrics require some degree of finishing, and the majority of finishes are applied after fabric construction. Hand finishes include simple washing, starching, ironing, bleaching, and dyeing. Blocking is a hand-finishing technique required of many knitted, crocheted, embroidered, or woven fabrics. Each type of hand finish alters in some way the light reflectance from the fabric and to some degree the color effect of the fabric.

Commercial Finishes

At the fabric level, two distinct kinds of commercial finishes are applied to cloth: smooth finishes, and raised finishes.

SMOOTH FINISHES

In smooth finishes, all loose fibers are removed or flattened into the surface of the cloth, leaving a smooth, lustrous surface that has more reflectance, higher value, and greater uniformity of color than the unfinished material had. The simple ironing or pressing of a fabric comes under this category. Removing wrinkles in a fabric changes the reflectance of the fabric's surface making it more organized, lightening its perceived color, and making its color more uniform.

The industrial equivalent of ironing is called *calendering,* a process in which the fabric passes through heavy, heated rollers and is pressed. Many variations on the calendering process are practiced. The permanence of this treatment depends on whether or not the fibers used are thermoplastic—or alternatively on whether or not the fabric is permeated with resin before calendering. Cotton and other cellulosic fibers (linen, rayon, cellulose acetate) tend to wrinkle easily, making them good candidates for the calendering process.

If one roller is sped up, the friction on the surface of the cloth *glazes* the surface, producing the type of effect found on chintz or polished cotton. The finish becomes permanent if the fabric has been impregnated with resins before calendering; Nonpermanent glazes use wax, glue, starch, or shellac in place of resin.

Cire is a high polish sometimes applied to silk and silk blends. The fabric is impregnated with wax or a thermoplastic material and then passed through the friction calender. The naturally high luster of silk and the added luster introduced by calendering create a fabric with a highly polished (or wet) look.

The calendering process can be used to create textured finishes as well as smooth ones. If one roller is engraved with a pattern, the result is an embossed relief pattern. This textured finish reflects light differently from the way a glazed surface does, creating definite areas of high reflectance and definite areas of low reflectance or shadow.

Schreinering involves use of a roller engraved with fine lines and set at an angle parallel to the twist of the yarns, to create a subtle, soft luster. This process is often used on cellulosic fibers such as cotton and linen. In addition to creating a soft luster, this finish flattens the yarns and produces smoother, more compact cloth. Schreinering is used on nylon and polyester tricot knit lingerie fabric to flatten the fabric and make it more opaque.

139

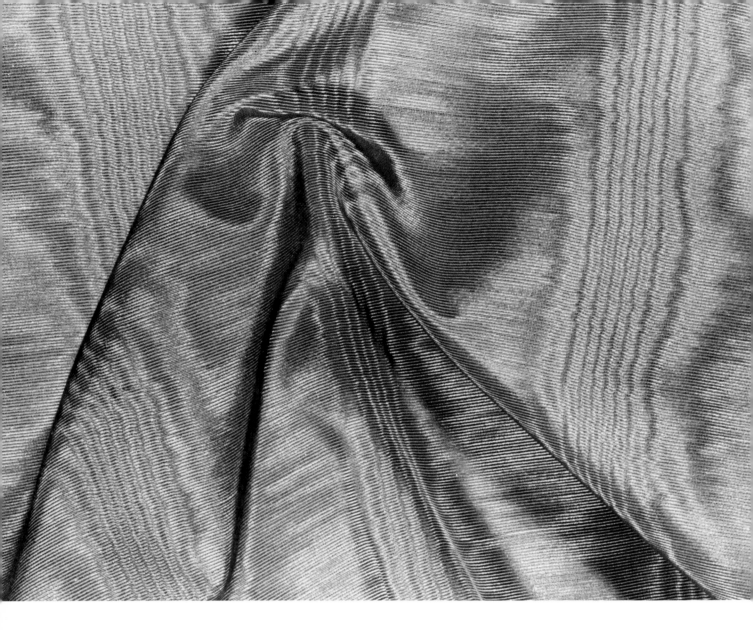

5-3. **Moiré Pattern.**
Photo: Patricia Lambert

Moiré is a lustrous patterned finish that depends for its effect on differences in light reflection. Before man-made fibers appeared, moiré was known as watered silk because the finish was primarily used on silks and because it resembled the patterns seen on the surface of water. Now, however, it is used on such man-made fibers as acetate and nylon, as well (see Figure 5-3).

Moiré can be produced by either of two methods; ribbed fabrics such as taffetas, failles, and bengalines work best. One method consists of doubling a ribbed fabric and feeding it between rollers (to introduce heat and pressure) so that the rib of one thickness is printed over the rib of the other, flattening some of the ribs. In the second method, a ribbed fabric passes slightly out of true under a roller engraved with a rib pattern resembling that of the fabric; a pattern of light reflectance is formed from the areas of flattened and nonflattened ribs. In certain areas, the ribs of the cloth fall exactly beneath the ribs etched on the roller and are flattened by them. Where the two patterns mesh, the fabric ribs remain rounded. The flattened ribs reflect more light and create lighter areas while the rounded ribs are relatively dark. The perceived areas of light and dark move as the viewer's eye moves with respect to the light source, or as the fabric moves, presenting different areas of reflectance to the eye.

Beetling is another mechanical finish often applied to cotton and linen fabrics. It is a smooth finish that increases the luster of these fabrics by flattening their yarns and providing more area for light to reflect from. The fabric is fed through a machine that pounds it with large hammers, simultaneously flattening the yarns and closing the weave. Tablecloths are often beetled so that they lie flat and look more lustrous.

Decating is a pressing process used on wool, silk, rayon, and blends. On wool, it is used to set luster and develop a permanent sheen. On synthetics and silks, it acts to reduce shine, to soften luster, and to help even the grain of the fabric. Decating makes use of heat, pressure, and moisture. In the dry method steam and then cold air are forced through the fabric, which is then pressed. In the wet method, hot water and then cold water are forced through the fabric before it is pressed.

Heat-setting is often used with man-made thermo-plastic fibers to increase the fabric's dimensional stability, but it can also be used to make the fabric wrinkle resistant (increasing light reflectance) or to introduce permanent pleats, creases, or surface embossing to the fabric (reducing light reflectance). Each type of thermoplastic fiber becomes soft, malleable, and receptive to heat-setting at a particular temperature. If it is then pressed into a new shape and cooled, it will retain the new shape. Any further heat-setting must occur at a temperature higher than that of the previous heat-set. To prevent heat-setting from occurring accidently, laundering and drying must be done at temperatures well below the initial heat-setting temperature of the fiber.

Singeing is another method used to produce a clear, smooth surface with more organized reflectance, higher value, and more uniform color. It consists of burning off the fuzz of fiber ends that stick out from a fabric made of staple fibers. The fabric is first brushed to remove loose fibers, and then passed (flat, without wrinkles or curled edges) over a red-hot plate or red-hot rollers, where the surface is singed. Another system, called gassing, passes the fabric quickly over open gas flames. The fabric moves fast enough to prevent damage to the fabric proper and is dipped in water afterward to extinguish any sparks.

RAISED FINISHES

Raised finishes draw fabric fibers to the surface, creating a nap that light penetrates to produce more saturated or intense color. If the surface fibers (or nap) are made to lie in one direction, the color will be of a higher value than if they are made to stand vertically.

When wool fabric is removed from the loom, it is often somewhat loosely woven and hard to the touch. Woolen fabrics are traditionally woven a little open and then washed and agitated to produce a *fulling* (or slight degree of felting), in which the scales on the fibers open out and entangle, the fabric shrinks a little and becomes loftier, warmer, and softer, and the fabric surface becomes more integrated. Worsteds are usually fulled less then woolens. A surface *nap* can then be raised by brushing. After brushing, the fabric becomes darker and more intense in color because of interreflection. Any optically mixed colors in the yarns or fabric structure become more intimately mixed in the nap, and the actual yarn and fabric structures are lost under the nap.

Napping can be done on other fibers than wool—including cotton and rayon. Fabrics used for napping should contain soft spun yarns with low twist and comparatively loose fibers. Fabrics with napped surfaces include flannels, blankets, and some coating and suiting materials. Suede cloth (a napped cotton) and duvetyn (a velvety, short-napped twill fabric) are made by napping the original fabric and then shearing the nap to produce a smooth, compact, and uniform surface. Napped fabrics are not the same as pile surfaces: piles are produced by means of a special process of fabric construction, whereas napped surfaces are produced on regular weaves by means of a finishing process.

Flocking is a finished process sometimes used in the textile industry that adds what appears to be a nap (but in fact is an aggregation of short fibers glued onto the fabric) to all or part of a fabric. If the flocking is to be done in a pattern, the glue is applied to the fabric in a pattern, the flock fibers are applied over the whole surface, and the adhesive is allowed to set; then the unglued fibers are removed, leaving a textured pattern that behaves with light much as napped and pile materials do—using interreflection to deepen colors, lower their value, and increase their intensity.

The application of corrosive chemicals (as in mercerization) can also be adapted to produce certain textured finishes. Plisse is a crinkled crepelike cotton that resembles seersucker to some degree. It is created not in the weave (as seersucker is) but as a finish in which caustic soda in paste form is painted on the fabric in a particular pattern. The treated areas shrink and the untreated areas pucker, resulting in a textured fabric after the paste is removed. Ironing tends to restretch the chemically shrunk fibers, canceling the textured effect.

Similar effects can be achieved with snythetics (treated with chemicals) or with the use of yarns having different shrinkage factors in a weave pattern (after which the shrinkage factor differential is developed in the finishing process under hot-weave processing).

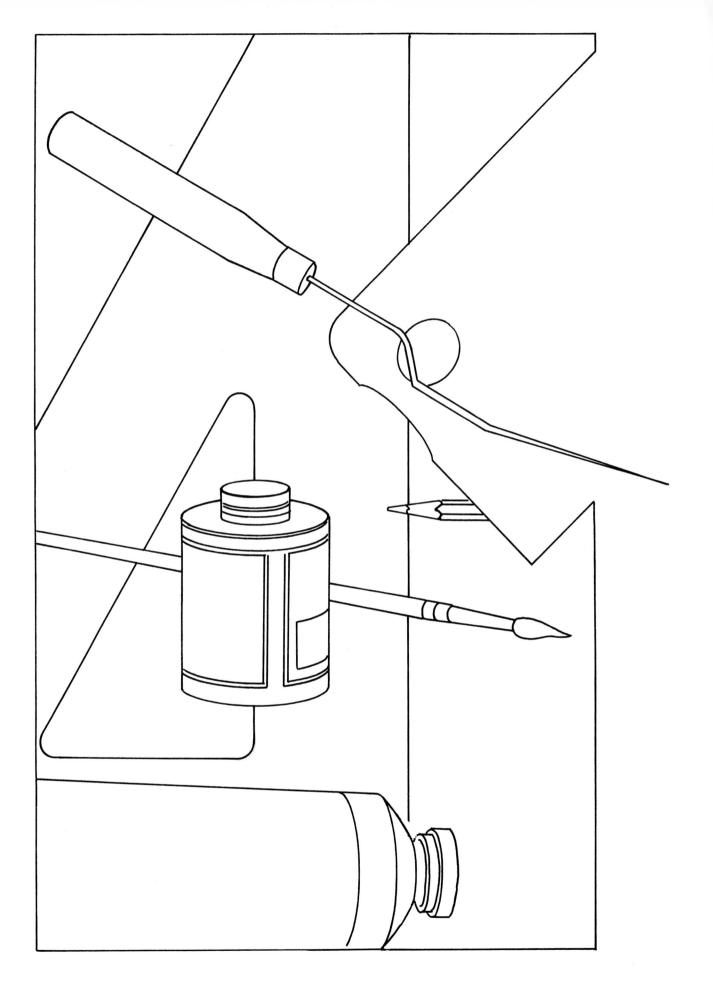

Part Three

Attaining Predictable Results

The primary purpose of studying color theory is to enable the artist to attain predictable results in the use of color—that is, to design with and control color. Color is an active sensation in its ability to provoke strong responses in a viewer. Either alone or in combination with other colors, it can be used to elicit a particular emotional response in a viewer: conflict or tranquility, excitement or languor, joy or sorrow, nausea or equanimity, anger or cool restraint. Color can create a sense of space whether a feeling of distance between two areas in a work or an illusion of transparency in a nontransparent medium. Color can make an area appear larger or smaller, and it can make the surface of a work seem to move, shift, undulate, or vibrate.

Part Three of this book presents practical applications of the study of color. Chapter 6 explores the relativity of color—how different colors interact with one another and how they change when combined in different ways. Chapter 7 discusses several color systems and comments on the emotional message and special effects that can be communicated with each. Chapter 8 suggests an approach fiber artists can use for translating newly learned color designed techniques into their fiber medium. Finally, chapter 9 contains projects, arranged by subject and order of difficulty, that are designed to help fiber artists bridge the gap between theory and practice so that they realize through experience the power and vitality their work can achieve as a result of color designing and color control.

Chapter 6

The Relativity of Color

Color is never static. Color is relative, and fluid, always changing its characteristics and its impact on the viewer; red is not simply red, and a particular red does not always have the same effect in every situation. Rarely in our surroundings or in art do we find color isolated from any contact with a neighboring color. Even a work done in a single color is usually viewed against a background or wall of some other color (or of black or white), and that context influences it in a unique way. Color may be found working in frank partnership (as with the pink petals and green sepals of a flower) or in a less obvious partnership (as with an object and its background or environment). Whenever colors are seen together, they influence and change one another.

Because color is relative and because it can be changed by other nearby colors, it can be deliberately manipulated to produce a particular planned effect. The other possibility is that color may change unexpectedly and by accident in the work of an inexperienced designer. Most of us have had the experience of choosing for a project a lovely selection of yarn colors that looked good in the yarn shop, only to find when they were worked up in the planned project, that they had changed in hue, in value, in intensity, or in a way harmful to the impact of the work.

These color shifts can occur as a result of either of two processes: optical mixing, and simultaneous contrast. Both optical mixing and simultaneous contrast are subjective visual phenomena that involve not only light waves and eye function, but the way the human brain is predisposed to interpret visual information. The size of the areas of color that are placed next to one another determines which process operates. Simultaneous contrast occurs most dramatically when large areas of intense color are placed next to one another in a design. When those same large areas of intense color are broken up into a small grid or into dots of color, however, and intermingled (as often happens in weaving and other fiber arts), optical mixing occurs, changing the colors in a different way.

Optical Mixing
When small dots or narrow lines of color are placed close to one another, our perception consists of an immediate impresssion of the total effect. The term *optical mixing* refers to the blending together of small dots to create the impression of a new color. The new color tends to be an average of the hue and value of the parent colors.

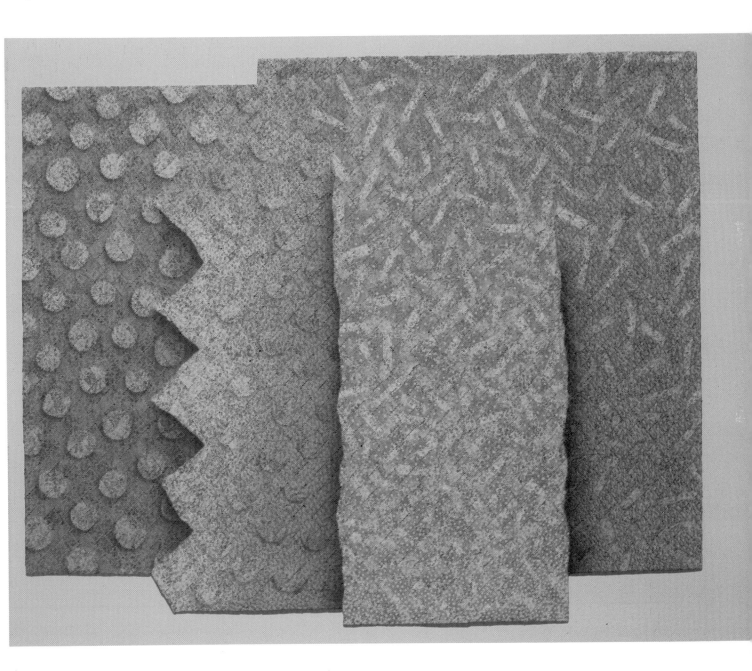

6-1. **Optical mixing:** *Cool Quarters* **(45'' x 57'', mixed media on woven paper, 1984).**

Artist: Glenn Brill
Photo: M.Lee Fatherree
Courtesy of Allrich Gallery; San Francisco, California

As discussed in Part One additive mixing involves color mixing with different wavelengths of projected light. As two or more wavelengths are added to the light mixture, the color of the mixture becomes lighter; and the sum of the wavelengths of all three light primaries (red, blue, and green) yield white light. In practical terms, full-spectrum white light is available to the fiber artist either in the form of daylight or (to a less perfect degree) in the form of some type of light bulb—incandescent, fluorescent, or special full-spectrum lights.

The artist most often creates visible color in a fiber work through subtractive mixing of dye colors or through optical mixing of different-colored fibers. Subtractive mixing starts with full-spectrum white light from which the colorants contained in dyes and pigments subtract (through absorption) certain wavelengths of light, leaving the remaining wavelengths to be reflected and become visible to the eye. When pigments or dyes are mixed, more colorants are added to the mixture, more wavelengths are absorbed (subtracted), and the combined colors become darker. The sum of all three subtractive primaries (yellow, cyan, and magenta) is a dark color that approaches black. It is not pure black only because the pigments are imperfect in their selective reflectance and allow a small amount of light to continue being reflected.

Instead of the colorants' being physically mixed (as occurs in subtractive mixing), optical mixtures are achieved when the wavelengths of light selectively reflected by small areas of different colors are additively mixed in our perception. Optical mixing combines elements of selective reflection from the colored dots with elements of additive mixing by our perception to create a kind of visual average of the hue and value of all the colors presented (see Figure 6-2). Because optical mixing creates a new color that is a visual average in both hue and value of the parent colors, the sum of an optical mix of all three primaries (yellow, cyan, and magenta) is a medium value.

6-2. Optical mixing
a. *Yellow ?* **(Detail) (noil silk, double Idat, 42½'' x 49'').**

Artist: Sarah Vincent
Photo: Sarah Vincent
Collection: Phillip Morris Company
Detail courtesy of the artist

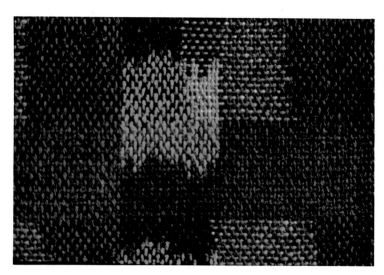

a.

violet is perceived

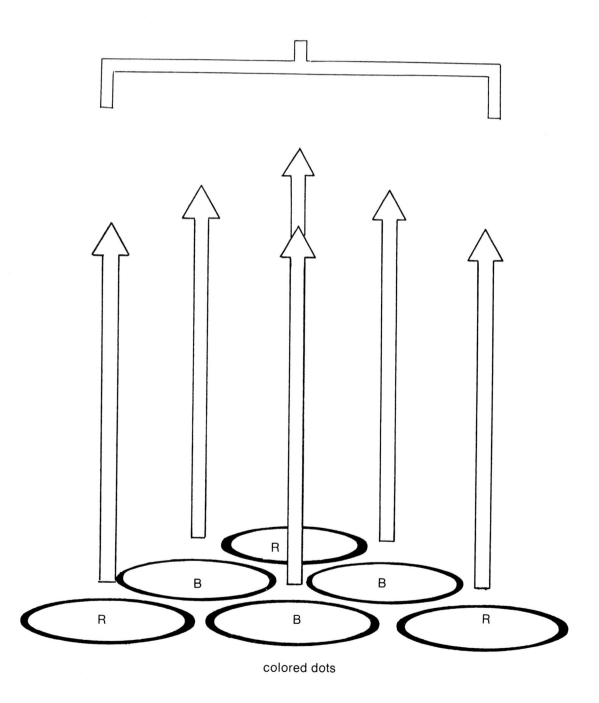

colored dots

b.

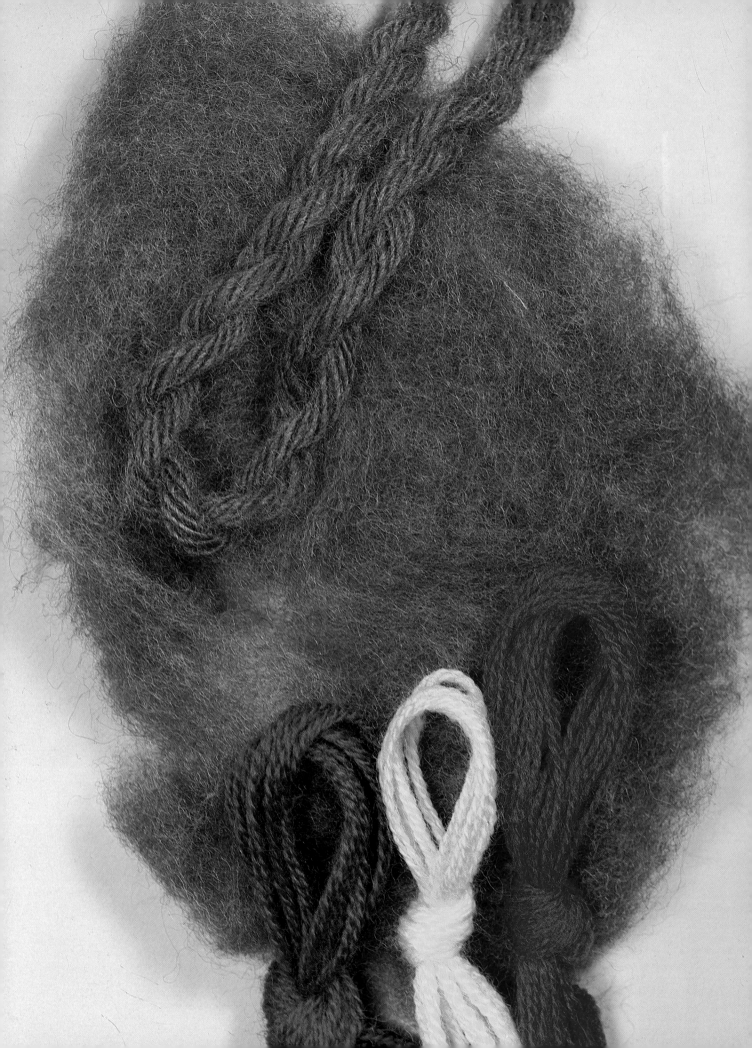

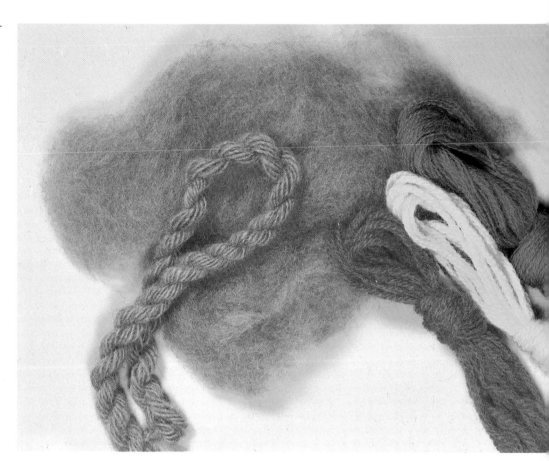

c.2.

c.1. Red, yellow, and blue, carded and spun.
c.2. Magenta, yellow, and cyan, carded and spun (equal amounts produce yellow dominance).
c.3. Magenta, yellow, and cyan, carded and spun. Magenta and Cyan dominant.

Carding/spinning: Carol Russell
Photo: Patricia Lambert

c.3

c.1.

PRACTICAL ADVANTAGES OF OPTICAL MIXING FOR THE FIBER ARTS

Use of optical mixing broadens the range of colors available to the fiber artist. It can be an exciting and practical alternative to yarn company color cards or the dyepot. If, for example, a fiber artist who does not dye would like to design a work using ten colors (or their tints) modulated in regular intervals from orange to violet, but finds that commercial sources of dyed fleece or yarns are limited to the primary and secondary hues, plus gary, white, and black, the artist can use optical mixing to blend as many steps in the modulation as are needed for the work—without the time, mess, and effort (or the technical skill and experience) needed to produce the same colors by hand-dyeing them (see Figure 6-3).

6-3. **Optically mixed color modulation: color blanket.**
Artist: Carol Russell
Photo: Patricia Lambert
Collection: Barbara Staepelaere

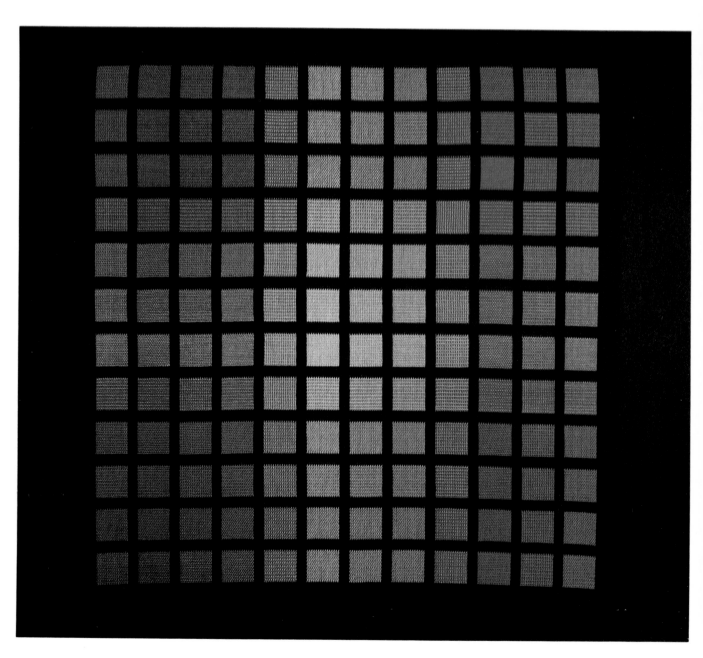

150

Optically mixed colors have a beautiful visual quality unlike that of yarns uniformly dyed with physically mixed colorants. This visual quality of optically mixed colors adds another expressive tool to an artist's color palette. Under certain specific conditions, optically mixed colors can be more vibrant and intense than any of the uniformly dyed parent colors in the mixture; this happens only when the parent colors being combined are very close in hue and value. For example, two slightly different reds—so close in color that they might represent different dyelots of the same hue—will make an optically blended red that is more vibrant and intense than either of the original reds (see Figure 6-4).

Most often optically mixed colors tend to be more grayed less intense, and softer than any of the component colors in the mixture and also to be more grayed than the product of a physical, subtractive mixture of the two dyes would be. Thus, an orange yarn blended optically from yellow fleece and red fleece will be less intense in hue than would a yarn uniformly dyed with an orange dye composed of the identical yellow and red parent dyes.

The clarity and intensity of the colors achieved by an optical blend depend on several factors. If an intense mixture color is to be achieved, the parent colors must be fully intense and analogous hues. If the parent colores are dull or broken, the mixture cannot be otherwise. If the parent hues are not strictly analogous—that is, if when combined they represent in some amount all three primaries—the mixture will be a dull, broken color, whether mixed subtractively or optically. A brilliant red warp and an intense green weft will create an optically mixed gray fabric similar in value to the red and green.

Other factors specific to optical mixing influence the ability of optically mixed colors to impart hue to their blend.

6-4. **The optical mixture (c) is a result of weaving one thread (a) with another (b).**
Weaver: Mary Fry
Photo: Patricia Lambert

a.

b.

c.

FACTORS THAT INFLUENCE
HUE IN AN OPTICAL BLEND

The first factor involved is the size or scale of the dots of the parent colors being blended. This factor is sometimes referred to as the intimacy of the blend. In pointillism, an optimum size exists (at any given distance) at which small areas of painted color will blend and impart hue to the mixed color. Dots or areas of color smaller than the optimum size tend to produce a grayer blended color, while larger dots refuse to blend at all and so remain areas having individual colors.

In work with fiber, however, it appears that the smaller the scale and the more intimately the different colors are blended, the easier it is for the viewer to perceive the optically mixed hue and the closer the mixture comes to a pigment mixture of the same colors. For example, a yarn made from cyan fleece and yellow fleece more readily appears green if the cyan and yellow fleece are thoroughly carded and blended together than if the fleeces are combined into a two-ply yarn made from one strand of the cyan and one strand of the yellow (see Figure 6-5). Similarly, a piece of fabric made from an even, alternating combination of cyan and yellow yarns in warp and weft appears greener (and less gray) if the fabric is brushed in finishing, to blend the surface fibers in a nap, than if it is left unbrushed.

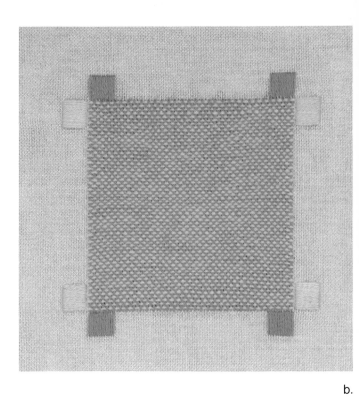

b.

6-5. **Optical mixing with yellow and cyan: a. fleece and ply; b. yellow and cyan weave; c. combinations of yellow with tints of different blues (including cyan).**

Carding/spinning: Carol Russell, Mary Fry
Photo: Patricia Lambert

a.

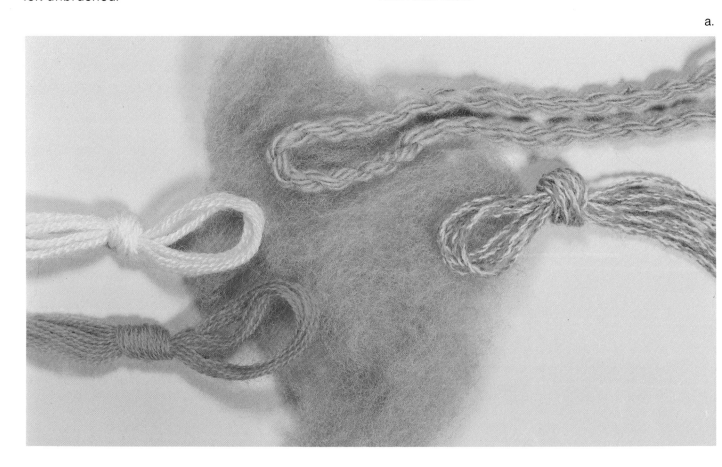

152

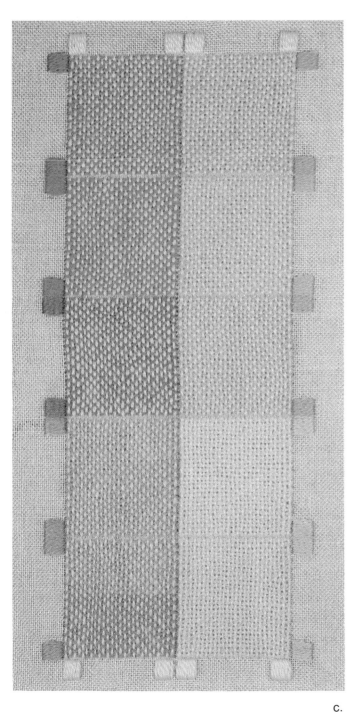

c.

Two things happen when a fabric is brushed: first, the blend becomes more intimate because individual hairs from the cyan and yellow yarns lie next to one another, rather than just the cyan and yellow yarns themselves lying contiguously; second, a nap is created. Although it is unclear what accounts for the difference in optimum scale between paint and fiber, the interreflection of light in the fibers and (particularly) in the brushed nap of a fabric would seem to play a significant role in intensifying the visual hue of an optical blend in a fiber medium. A comparison of three forms of a fabric made of yellow and cyan warp and weft—unbrushed, brushed, and brushed and then pressed (to flatten the nap and largely negate inter-reflecton)—showed that both the brushed sample and the brushed and pressed sample were more intense in hue than the unbrushed sample, and that the unpressed nap was more intense than the pressed one. This suggests that the hue intensity of an optical blend in fiber is due in part to the intimacy of the blend and in part to the interreflection of light in the nap of the fabric.

153

Since size, scale, and intimacy of blend all affect the intensity of an optical color, distance and angle of viewing are obviously additional factors in the apparent intensity of an optically mixed color. Viewing a fabric from a greater distance or at a sharper angle to its surface diminishes the scale. Thus, if the scale of an optical mix is too large to blend well in the eye of the viewer, viewing it an an angle or from a greater distance tends to create a smaller scale and make the colors blend better (see Fjgure 6-6a). Angle of viewing is an important factor in the color effect of optically mixed clothing fabrics, as well as in other fabrics that hang with a drape. The portions of the fabric plane that directly face the viewer's eye tend to show the individual colors making up the fabric, while the parts of the drape that angle away from the viewer appear more blended (see Figure 6-6b).

Distance works in a similar way, up to a point. At an optimum distance from the fabric (given a particular scale), the viewer see the optimum optical mixture. Beyond that distance, however, the optically mixed colors tend to lose their characteristic hue and move from a color to the relative value of that color. When the optimum distance is passed, high-value colors such as yellow typically become light gray or white and finally disappear. Middle-value colors such as orange and certain greens become a middle gray, and low-value colors such as blue and purple become dark gray or black and finally (at even greater distance) a less dark gray.

Optically blended colors are not the only kind that turn gray with distance. Subtractively mixed colors also lose their characteristic hue with distance but not as quickly as optical mixtures. The amount of distance needed for colors to gray also depends on the size of the area: a solid green area 1" square grays much faster than does a 12" square area of the same color.

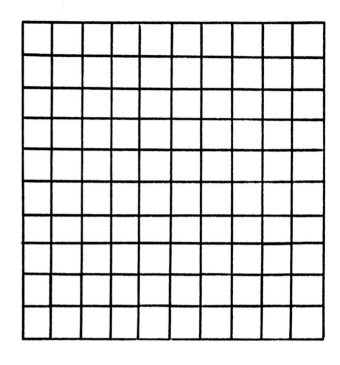

a. areas too large to blend

6-6. **Fabric optical mixing**

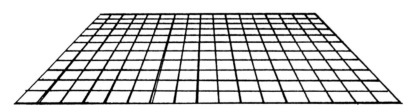

viewed at angle may blend in part

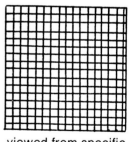

viewed from specific
distance will blend

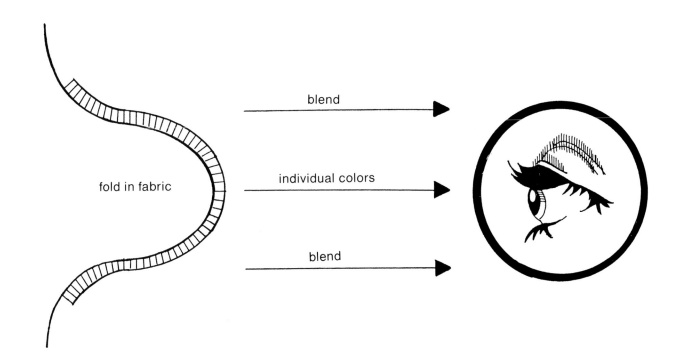

fold in fabric

blend

individual colors

blend

b.

The general graying of all colors with distance has several causes. At a greater distance, the amount of selectively reflected colored light reaching the viewer's eye from the colored object decreases because small particles of moisture, dust, and pollutants in the atmosphere between the eye and the colored object serve to scatter some of the light reflected from the object so that it does not reach the eye. In addition, as distance increases, the relative size of the colored area being viewed decreases in relation to the rest of the visual field; this decreases the proportion of light coming from the colored object relative to the total amount of light entering the eye, making the object's hue harder to perceive.

A fourth factor in the ability of two colors to impart hue to an optical blend is the relative values of the two colors used. The closer the values of the original colors are, the more easily the original colors blend in the eye/brain process and the more hue is visible in the blend. For example, for blending green from yellow and blue, cyan works better than an ultramarine blue. Yellows are high in value and blues are low, so if the value difference between blue and yellow is minimized by using cyan, the result is a greener color than would result if a low-value ultramarine blue were used. Cyan not only is closer in value to yellow, it is closer in hue as well; it also eliminates any possibility of a red undertone in the blue, which would negate any hue effect of the blue/yellow optical mixture by introducing the third primary.

155

b.

6-7. A tint of cyan and yellow hue produces a better green than does a mix of cyan and yellow (b).

Weaver: Mary Fry
Photo: Patricia Lambert

The relative value of the two parent colors is such an important factor in the ability of optical mixtures to produce hue that—in mixing pure hues of such widely divergent values as yellow and cyan—a person can get a greener green by sacrificing the intensity of the blue somewhat (by tinting it a bit with white) to bring the values closer together (see Figure 6-7). The proper adjustment of values to make in an optical mixture must be based on experimentation to find the point of balance between value and intensity that produces the most intensely hued mixture. The value factor helps explain why a color resulting from the optical mix of two analogous colors can appear livelier and more intense than either of the two component colors, whereas a color resulting from the optical mix of two colors of significant hue and value difference has a softer, less intense, and more grayed quality than either of the component colors.

Although fairly hard-and-fast rules can be formulated about optical mixing in paint, the corresponding rules for fibers are not quite so clearly definable because of the myriad factors influencing light and color behavior in fiber. The chemical makeup of both the fiber and the dye, as well as the physical structure of the fiber, yarn, and fabric, influences the refraction, transmission, and interreflection of light. In addition, finishes such as optical brighteners—which absorb nonvisible (ultraviolet) energy and translate it into visible light—alter the visible results. The fiber artist must therefore experiment with the color effect of a planned project, using the exact materials intended for the actual work.

The result of an optical blend is always rich and visually satisfying. This can be seen by comparing a uniformly dyed gray fabric to a gray fabric created by weaving, knitting, crocheting, embroidering, or working fine threads of any combination of colors in uniform arrangement that results in a balanced complement— for example, a mixture of all three primary and/or all three secondary colors. Equal portions of each color seem to create a gray with a dominance of yellow (see Figure 6-8). Experimentation with samples, in which the relative amount of each color is adjusted, will be necessary to find the exact ratio needed to create a neutral gray. An optically mixed neutral gray fabric presents rich, subtle, and beautiful changes; soft hue and temperature variations appear in the folds and ridges of the overall gray effect of the draped fabric. In comparison, the uniformly dyed gray fabric shows only value changes in the folds and ridges of the draped fabric. This demonstrates the special beauty of an optical mix.

a.

b.

c.

6-8. **Optical mixing (equal parts of each primary produces a neutral with a yellow dominance): a. loops and pile in both RYB and MYC systems; b. woven with equal amounts; c. woven with decreased yellow.**

Designs: Mary Fry
Photo: Patricia Lambert

AREAS WHERE OPTICAL MIXING
IS APPLICABLE IN FIBER

By using a little imagination, most fiber artists can enrich their work by adding optically mixed colors to their color choices. The optical mixing of colored fleece can easily be applied to felting, since colored fibers blended as loose fibers create the most homogeneous and (therefore) the most colorful blend (see Figure 6-9).

6-9. **Optically blended color in felt:** *Tetons* **(felt inlay, 3' x 5', 1982).**
Artist: Barbara Staepelaere
Photo: Patricia Lambert
Courtesy: Boeringer Ingleheim Company; Danbury, Connecticut

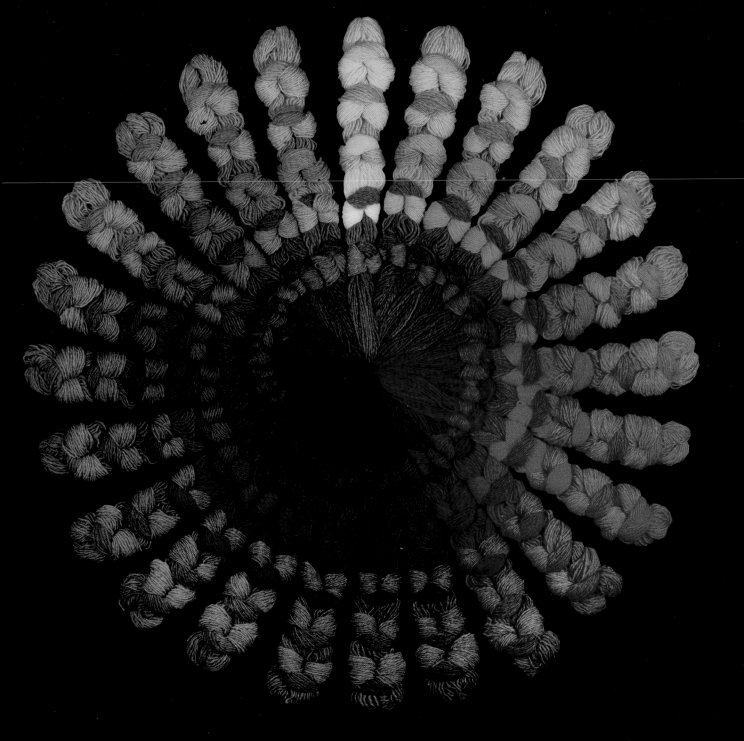

Another area where optical mixing has traditionally been used to advantage is in the spinning of yarns (see Figure 6-10). We are all familiar with the rich, soft hues of heather yarns created from two or more colors; with the soft tints created by blending white fibers and a hue; with the subtle shades that result from an optical blend of black and a hue; and with the beautiful ranges of grays in natural colored yarns (such as the Icelandic yarns) that extend from almost white to dark charcoal. Close inspection of these undyed natural grays reveals that in these yarns, as in natural gray fleeces, the different values of gray are the product of an optical blend of different proportions of individual black and white wool fibers.

6-10. **Optically mixed hue circle, showing tints and shades.**
Artist/Dyer: Antonia Kormos
Photo: Patricia Lambert
Courtesy of the artist

When an optically mixed yarn is created from two different-colored fleeces, the scale of the optical mix and the resulting intimacy of the color blend in the yarn can be varied at different stages of the spinning. In carding, the hand-spinner simply cards until the colored fleece on the cards reaches the uniformity of blend desired in the yarn. In commercial spinning, the colors can be blended at various stages of production to produce different degrees of color blending.

Spinners are in an excellent position to create and enjoy the subtle changes in optical color effects that result from changes in scale, intimacy of blend, and value relationships. Fiber artists in all of the fiber art disciplines have the opportunity to use these optically mixed yarns in the structure of their fabrics and thus to incorporate the qualities of optically mixed colors in their work. Moreover, each discipline offers opportunities for combining threads or yarns of different colors in its method of construction.

Weavers have traditionally used optical mixing to advantage in their blend of colors in warp and weft, creating color effects through manipulation of the weave pattern and of different warp and weft colors. One of the most exciting aspects of weaving and braiding involves planning the final color effects of different color possibilities in warp and weft and planning the method by which these colors will interact in the weave pattern.

Plaids provide a virtual roadmap of optical mixing by the clear, systematic way in which they introduce color A and color B, and then produce optically mixed color C where the two intersect. Chambray combines a colored warp and a white weft to create a slightly mottled tint. Shot fabrics are lustrous fabrics that combine a warp of one definite color and a weft of a contrasting color to make a fabric that is generally an optical blend of the two but that—because of the fiber luster and orientation—shimmers back and forth between a dominance of one hue or the other, depending on its folds and on changes in the direction from which it is viewed.

In weaving and braiding, as in most other fiber arts such as knitting, crochet, macramé, embroidery, and some kinds of basket-making, optical mixes can be created simply by using two or more threads or yarns as one in the needle, the heddles, or the shuttle. The scale and resulting color effects of this kind of blend depend on the fineness of the yarn and the fabric gauge. An embroiderer who was previously limited to the selection of colors on the color chart but who looks with a new eye at the possibilities of blending several different-colored threads in one needle can find a new range of color expression suddenly possible (see Figure 6-11a). A smooth modulation of optically mixed color can be created by slowly rotating the selection of several colored threads in the needle. Besides using multiple threads in the same needle, the embroiderer

a.

6-11. **a. Optical mixing in a blend of four threads.**
Design: Mary Fry
Photo: Patricia Lambert

161

can work stitches of one color over a ground of another color so that small areas of ground color and stitch color are presented commingled in an optical mix. A second possibility is to work over layers of stitches in one color with another color, again presenting two or more colors in small commingled areas.

This layering effect of positive and negative spaces in a pattern can also be exploited with lace, tatting, sprang, macramé, netting, knit, crochet, and some of the more open weaves (see Figure 6-11b).

Patchwork quilters can make use of all of the woven techniques of optical blends in their choice of fabrics for piecing. In addition, many small prints on cotton fabrics that are typically used for patchwork create an optical blend when viewed from a distance, giving the quilt a different color effect at a distance of 10 feet than it has at a distance of 2 feet. Quilters using patchwork techniques can also take advantage of the fact that in some weaves the face and back sides of the fabric may be noticeably different in intensity or hue. Depending on the structure of the weave, more or fewer warp and weft threads of certain colors may appear on the face or back of the fabric, creating color blends of different proportions and thus creating different optical mixes.

Quiltmakers also have the option of embroidering over their work, using all the stitch and ground techniques and blended yarns available to the embroiderer. Another exciting possibility in quiltmaking is to create optical blends through the layering of a fine sheer fabric or net fabric of one color over an opaque fabric of another color, or through using several layers of the transparent fabric. The color possibilities of optical blending in the fiber arts are almost endless.

b. Optical mixing of red/green, orange/blue modulations with net.

Design: Ann Harris/Mary Fry
Photo: Patricia Lambert

Simultaneous Contrast

Colors need not be broken into small dots and blended together in order to be changed in a design; larger areas of color can elicit color shifts of hue, value, intensity, or temperature in one another as a result of simultaneous contrast (see Figure 6-12). Optical mixing and simultaneous contrast are opposite manifestations of the relativity of human color perception. Optical mixing creates a unity or commonality of color in which differences in small specks of color are negated so that we perceive a larger whole consisting of a single color. Simultaneous contrast, on the other hand, enhances the perceived differences between two colors in a design. Both processes contribute to the human brain's ability to process and make order out of the chaos of visual stimuli, grouping some stimuli together and separating others.

Simultaneous contrast is a shift in a color created by that color's proximity to another color. The phenomenon occurs because any given color produces an afterimage (an illusory color generated by human perception) that is the color's opposite in both hue and value. Afterimages have a transparent, diaphanous quality. They seem to float over the colors in our field of vision, lending their qualities of hue and value to these actual colors as if a transparent wash had been added to them.

162

6-12. **a. Small areas of color produce optical mixtures; larger areas of color create color shifts by simultaneous contrast.**

Artist: Benita Wolffe
Photo: Patricia Lambert
Courtesy of the artist

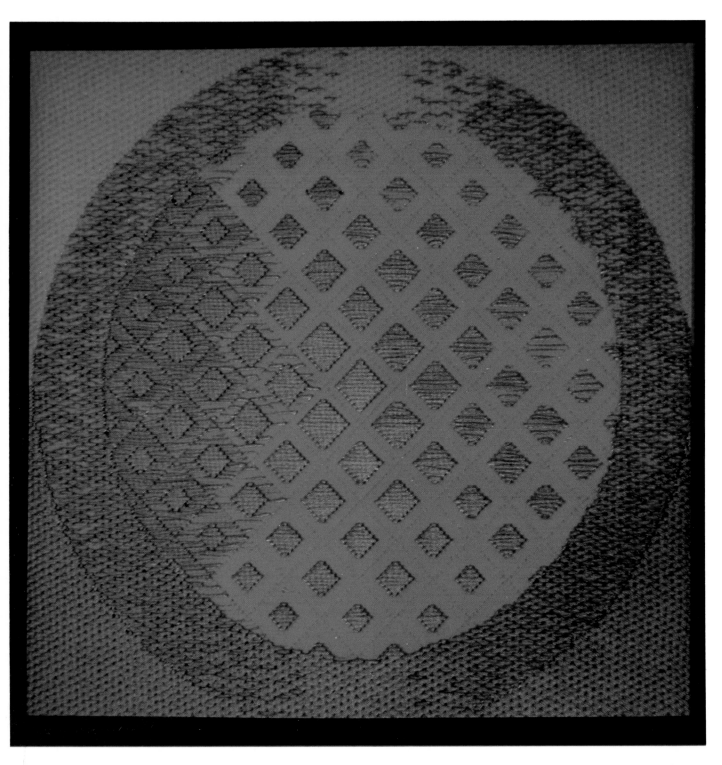

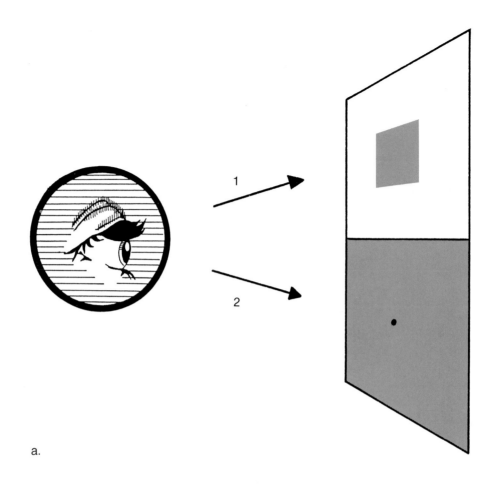

a.

6-13. **Relativity of middle gray: a. placed on a light background, it produces a light afterimage on a dark background; b. placed on a dark background, it produces a dark afterimage on a light background.**

The afterimage generated by the hue characteristic of a color is called its *complementary afterimage.* Complementary afterimages are much less intense than the stimulus color. The afterimage generated by the value characteristic of a color is called its *negative afterimage.* Any dark stimulus color (or black) produces a light negative afterimage; any light stimulus color (or white) produces a dark negative afterimage; middle gray (or a middle-value color) produces a light afterimage if viewed on a white background (because, by contrast to the white ground, its value is low) and produces a dark afterimage if viewed on a black background (because by contrast to the black, its value is high) (see Figure 6-13). Contrast between the stimulus value and its ground is thus as important as

the actual value of the stimulus in producing negative afterimages.

The production of afterimages and the color shifts of simultaneous contrast raise some questions. How can these phenomenon be controlled? Can they be reinforced, reduced, or negated altogether? How can they be used to enhance color effect in a design? A first step in answering these questions is to focus on the types of afterimages separately—first on negative afterimage and its effect on the other colors in a design, and then on complementary afterimage and its effects. After this, the effects of negative and complementary afterimages can be considered from the standpoint of changing other colors in a planned direction in a design.

164

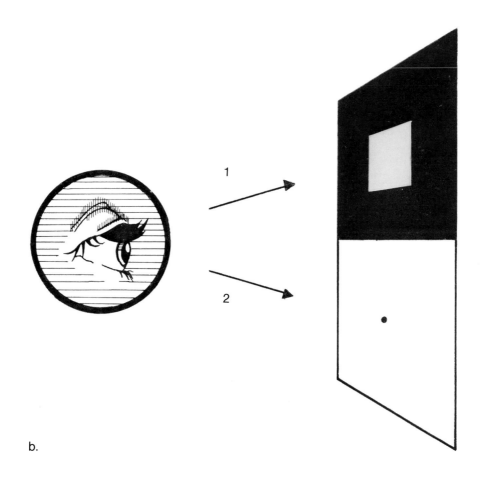

b.

CHANGING VALUE WITH NEGATIVE AFTERIMAGE

By stimulating negative afterimages, colors in a design can influence the relative values of their neighboring colors. Although negative afterimage is created by the value of any stimulus color, grays are best used to demonstrate negative afterimage because in them only the value change is seen—without interference from complementary afterimages that a color would create. The value of any color can be changed by simultaneous contrast exactly as the values of grays are changed. The effects of simultaneous contrast can best be seen when a large area of stimulus color surrounds a relatively small area whose color the artist wishes to change, when no interfering colors are present to confuse the perception of the afterimages, when the colors are viewed in full spectrum daylight but not in direct sunlight, and when the viewer's eyes are kept on the stimulus color steadily for 30 seconds.

Practice improves a person's ability to perceive afterimages. Such practice should not be attempted over extended periods because the eyes fatigue fairly quickly and lose their ability to perceive afterimages. A large dark background generates a light negative afterimage, which washes over a figure on that ground and makes it appear lighter. Correspondingly, a large light ground generates a dark negative afterimage, which washes over a figure on that ground and makes it appear darker.

6-14. **Values change hue: a. colors appear darker when surrounded with white; b. they appear unchanged; c. they appear lighter.**

Design: Mary Fry
Photos: Patricia Lambert

a.

Making One Value Look Like Two

Start with a 6" x 12" white board. On the left half of the board glue a 6" square of black paper. Leave the right side white. Choose a middle value gray and cut two identical 1" squares. Glue one of the gray squares in the center of the black side. Glue the second gray square in the center of the white side. Stare steadily at a point between the two sides for 20 seconds. The two gray squares will appear to be different in value, even though they are both cut from the sheet of gray paper. The black ground has made the square on it seem lighter by simultaneous contrast i.e. negative after-image; the white ground has made the square on it appear darker.

An observable difference in figures of the same value is produced when they are placed on grounds of dissimilar value—black and white grounds creating the greatest difference. This effect can be incorporated in a work either for the fun of manipulating color behavior or for practical reasons. If, for example, the values available for a particular fiber piece are limited

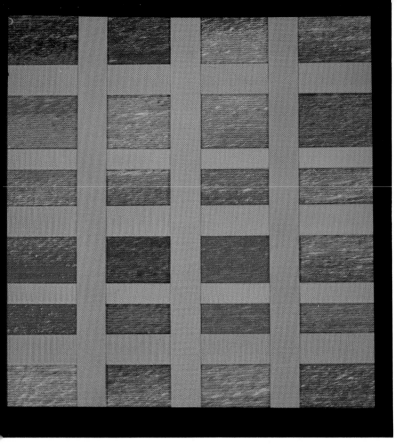

b.

c.

to four values, juxtaposing the darkest and lightest values as alternate figure and ground areas can give the piece the effect of having six values rather than four—one darker than the darkest of the original four, and one lighter than the lightest of those.

This phenomenon can also be applied in mounting or displaying art work. Any color or hue looks noticeably lighter and more intense when displayed against a black ground; the same color or hue maintains its original intensity and value when displayed against a gray ground, and it appears noticeably darker and less intense when displayed against a white ground (see Figure 6-14). An artist who has created a work of low-intensity, minor relationships and wishes to maintain exactly that mood in the work should therefore mount or display the work against a gray background. Conversely, an artist who has created a vibrant, intense design and wishes to keep that feeling might do well to mount or display it against a black background. Displaying a dramatic, intense color study against a white wall subdues the color intensity and lowers the study's value.

b.   (read horizontally)

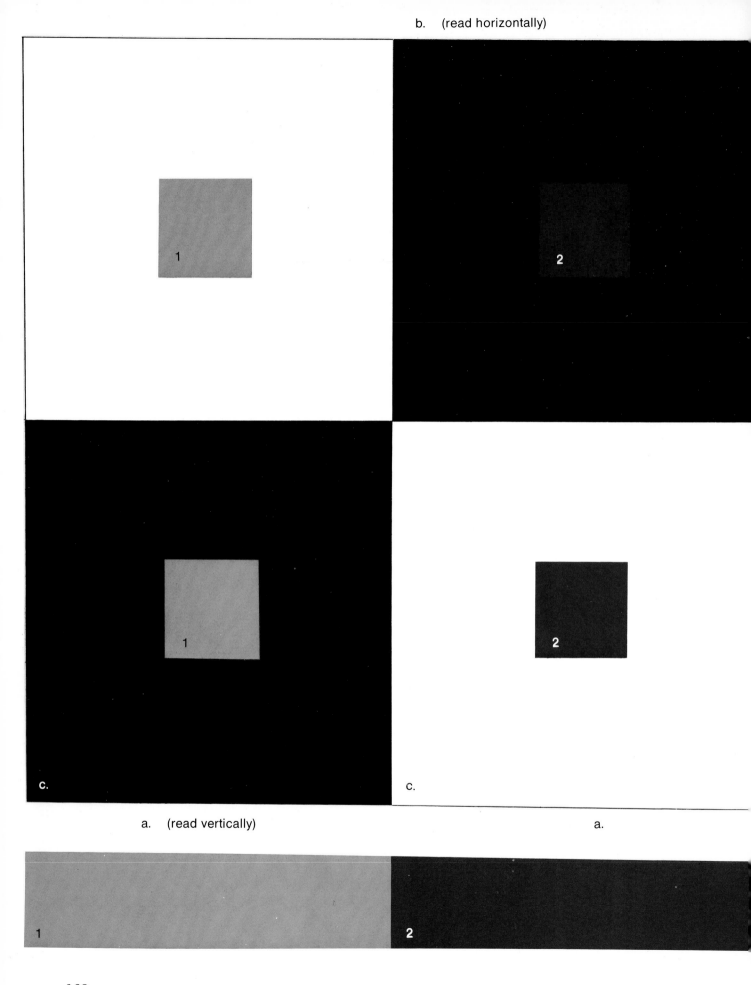

c.

c.

a.   (read vertically)

a.

168

Making Two Values Look Like One

Two figures of the same value can appear different when placed on different grounds; by means of the same effect, two values can be manipulated to look identical. The background area in such a case must be sufficiently large to stimulate a strong afterimage. Figure 6-15a illustrates very different values that have been placed on black and white grounds; the darker figure has been placed on the black ground, and the lighter figure has been placed on the white ground. The lighter figure is darkened by the white ground and the darker figure is lightened by the black ground to a point where the two figures appear to have the same value. In figure 6-15b, the difference between the figure values is reinforced when they are reversed on the grounds. A value limit exists in the capacity to create the illusion that two values are the same. The black and white grounds used in figure 6-15 establish the outside limits of what is possible. The grounds do not have to be black and white, but the actual difference in values that can be chosen for the matching figures becomes proportionately smaller as the background values approach one another.

6-15. **Value manipulation: a. one value looks like two; b. two values look like one; c. figure 6-15b reversed.**

a.

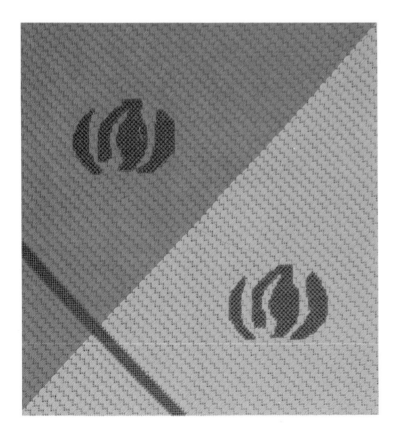

b.

6-16. **Intensity is changed with complementary afterimages: a. background values are similar; b. background values are changed to make a value shift in the figure.**

Artist: Liz Gordon
Photo: Patricia Lambert

CHANGING HUE, INTENSITY, AND TEMPERATURE WITH COMPLEMENTARY AFTERIMAGES

In order to manipulate color by means of complementary afterimage, an artist must plan to combine the characteristics of hue, temperature, and intensity already present in the colors used in the design with the characteristics of their complementary afterimages. As with other kinds of color mixing, the hue of the afterimage has the potential to change not only the hue of its neighboring colors, but also their intensity and temperature at the same time. For example, if a bright green ground surrounds a low-intensity green figure, the green stimulus of the background will generate a magenta afterimage that will wash over the low-intensity green of the figure, changing its hue, making it less intense (magenta + green = gray), and increasing its color temperature.

In figure 6-16a, the background values are kept similar so that the relative values of the two figures remain the same. The green figures in both grounds are the same color, as is shown by the green stripe. After a viewer looks at the dividing line for 30 seconds, the green figure on the green ground will seem to grow duller as a result of the magenta afterimage. The red ground, on the other hand, stimulates a greenish afterimage that enhances the green already present in its figure, increasing the intensity of that figure's green.

The easiest way to anticipate the approximate hue of a complementary afterimage is to refer to the light primaries and secondaries or to their mirror image, the magenta-yellow-cyan (MYC) pigment system. Afterimages are related to light complements rather than to the traditional red-yellow-blue (RYB) pigment complements—an important factor in obtaining predictable results in work with simultaneous contrast. The afterimage of magenta is green and the afterimage of middle green is somewhere in the magenta range. The complement of cyan is red-orange and the complement of yellow is blue; the colors of these afterimages are somewhat subjective, and it is very difficult to anticipate exactly the color afterimage that will be produced or to keep afterimage colors memorized.

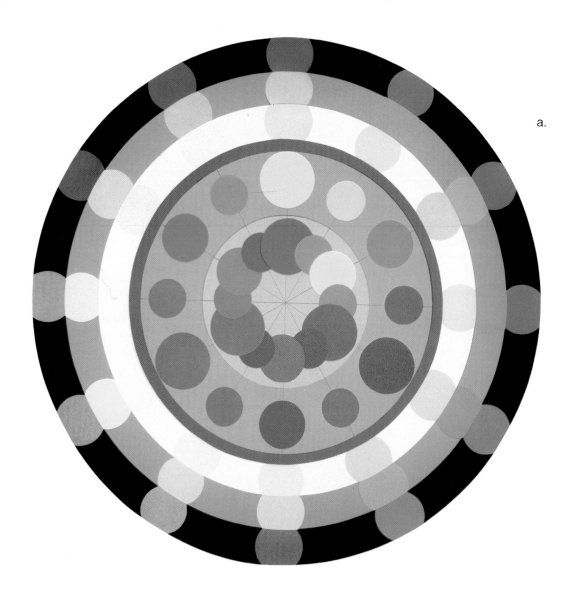

a.

The afterimage circle in figure 6-17 is designed to help artists visualize afterimages and anticipate the effects of simultaneous contrast in a design. The innermost ring in figure 6-17 graphically shows the light primaries and secondaries, which can be used to predict afterimage. For those who prefer to work with the RYB color wheel as a design reference, the RYB primaries, secondaries, and intermediaries are shown in the second ring from the center, lined up in relation to the light primaries and secondaries. The green on the light circle lines up with the yellow on the pigment circle, for example. In light, green is a primary and yellow is a secondary.

In this illustration, the hues of the red-yellow-blue hue circle are used as the stimulus colors in the visualization of the afterimages. Each individual disk of color has three colors extending from it (shown on the white, gray, and black rings respectively). Each color on the white, gray, and black rings approximates the afterimage stimulated by the pigment color as it would be seen on a white, gray, or black surface. When the afterimage is seen on white, it looks tinted; when seen on gray, it seems to have a more intense color; and when seen on black, it looks shaded. Making allowance for individual sight variations, these approximations are accurate. They can be made by successively looking at each hue for 30 seconds under a strong light and then looking at a white surface and recording the afterimages, looking back at each hue for 30 seconds and then looking at a gray surface and recording the afterimages, and so on. Since the eye tires very quickly from this kind of stimulation, the approximations must be done in stages.

6-17. **Afterimage hue circle: a. RYB hue circle, showing inner circle of light hues (in pigment), pigment hues, and afterimage hues of pigment hues on white, gray, and black (done in paper); b. MYC hue circle showing MYC as primaries (center) progressing to eighteen-hue circle and showing each related afterimage color. (the outer circle is an optical mix of each hue and its complement).**

Designs/Execution: Mary Fry
Photos: Patricia Lambert

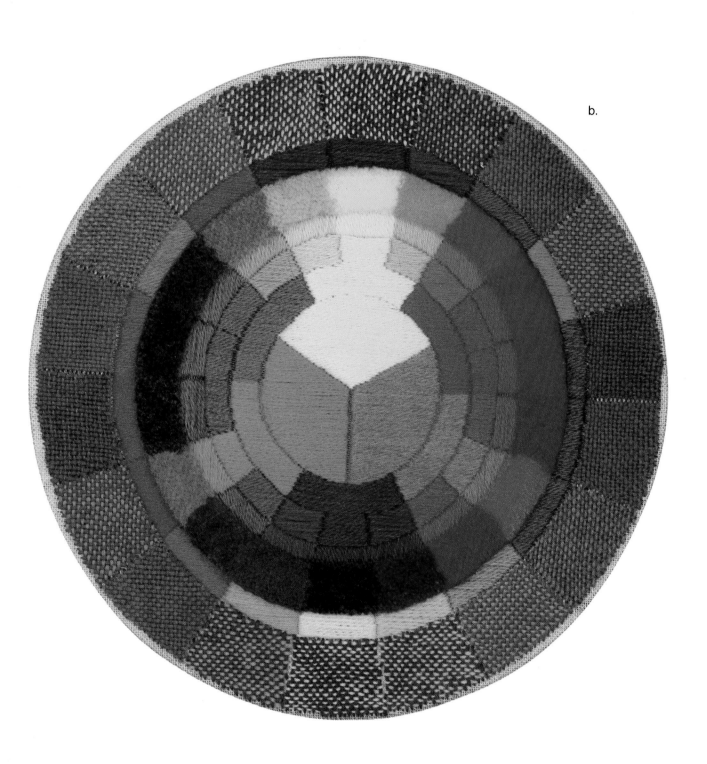

b.

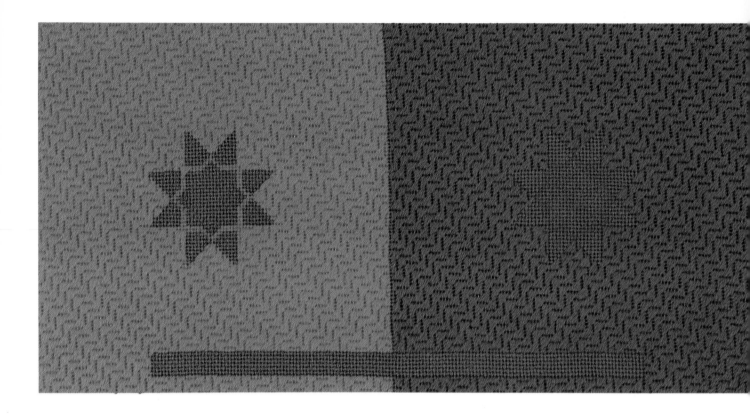

CHANGING HUE INTENSITY, TEMPERATURE, AND VALUE WITH AFTERIMAGE

Since afterimage is both complementary and negative, simultaneous contrast can be used to change all color characteristics—hue, intensity, temperature, and value. The first step in doing this is to decide the direction in which a particular color is to shift. Then the artist should determine what hue and value qualities in an afterimage would mix with the color to produce the desired shift. The next step is to choose a stimulus color of opposite value and complementary hue to that required in the afterimage. Once the colors are chosen, the design should be planned; the artist must keep in mind that the afterimage is produced most effectively if the design makes use of a large area of intense stimulus color in proportion to a smaller area of color to be shifted. The color shift is most obvious if the afterimage washes over a low-intensity color or a gray. It remains visible on a more intense color but is more readily identifiable on a color of low intensity.

In figure 6-16b, as in figure 6-16a, complementary afterimage has been used to change the intensity of the green figure. The value of the green background has also been raised, so the figure on it appears darker and less intense because of negative afterimage. The combined effect of negative and complementary afterimages creates an especially noticeable change of intensity between these two figures. Experiments with colored papers can be undertaken to produce similar effects.

6-18. As a result of changing backgrounds, one color looks like two.

Design: Liz Gordon
Photo: Patricia Lambert

Making One Color Look Like Two

One color can be made to look like two in much the same way as the intensity of the color was changed in figure 6-16b. Figure 6-18 demonstrates how negative and complementary afterimages can be used to achieve maximum color change. The blue-green stripe running through the grounds of dark blue and of red is the same color; however, the blue-green in the star patterns changes dramatically when viewed on grounds that differ widely in value, hue, and temperature. When the stripe is masked out and the dividing line between the two background squares is stared at, negative afterimages will make the star in the red ground appear darker and the star in the blue ground appear lighter (because the red ground is lighter in value than the blue ground). In addition to the value difference in the grounds, which creates a change in value in the figures, a strong difference of hue exists, producing different complementary afterimages. The red ground produces a blue-green afterimage, strengthening the blue color and cool temperature of the star in that ground. The blue ground produces a yellow-orange afterimage that combines with the blue-green of the star, pushing it toward yellow-green and warming the temperature of the figure considerably.

174

Making Two Colors Look Like One

The blue-green color of the two stars in the above illustration was shifted in two different directions—one toward blue, and the other toward yellow-green. The process can also be used to shift analogous colors toward each other and make them appear the same. This can be accomplished only with analogous or closely related colors; although a planned use of simultaneous contrast can be used to change color to a noticeable degree, the transparent nature of after-image limits how much change can be created. In figure 6-18, for example, the blue-green of the stars appeared to change quite significantly, but it still remained within the range of analogous colors.

The two star colors in figure 6-19 are analogous, as is shown by the color stripe below the yellow-green and red-violet squares. If the stripe is masked out and the dividing line between the two squares is stared at, the stars soon look remarkably similar in color. In order for the two colors to look like one through simultaneous contrast, the compound yellow-orange color must first be distinguished from the simpler primary yellow color in terms of hue and value. Since the yellow-orange has a small amount of red in it, washing the primary yellow with a reddish afterimage (by putting the yellow figure on a green ground) would seem to be an appropriate way to solve the problem. This procedure does help bring the figures closer together, but not close enough. The figure colors must both be shifted with negative and complementary afterimages.

When a red-violet hue of a slightly darker value than the green is placed behind the yellow-orange star, a lighter yellow-green afterimage is formed. The red quality in the yellow-orange is neutralized by the greenish quality of the yellow-green afterimage, while the yellow already present in the figure's color is reinforced by the yellow of the yellow-green afterimage. The slightly darker value of the red-violet background also lightens the yellow-orange figure, bringing its value closer to that of the primary yellow figure. When a green hue of slightly lighter value is placed behind the primary yellow star, the green stimulates a red afterimage; simultaneously, the slightly lighter value of the green darkens the red afterimage to a small degree, making the yellow appear more yellow-orange. In response to these arrangements, the figures' colors move closer to one another in appearance. The longer a viewer looks at the figures, the harder it becomes to discern that they are two different colors.

6-19. **As a result of changing backgrounds, two colors look like one.**
Design: Liz Gordon
Photo: Patricia Lambert

a.

Simultaneous contrast has definite possibilities as a color-designing tool. With careful planning, it can be used to enhance the expressiveness of color arrangement. Several specific methods can be used to reinforce the effects of simultaneous contrast in color designing.

(1) One of the simplest methods of creating strong simultaneous contrast is to use large areas of intense complementary colors together (see Figure 6-20a). Since the afterimage created by each color is already present in its complement, the colors in the design all look more intense because they are reinforced totally, both by body color and by afterimage. It is reasonable to ask why there should be an afterimage at all if all the wavelengths of light are present to make white light. If two equal-sized areas of complements are scanned by the eye very quickly, the theory holds up. No afterimage is formed because the cones are totally stimulated as if by white light. However when looking at an art work our eye often browses leisurely about the design rather than rapidly scanning it. We look at one color for a few seconds, create an afterimage from it and then look to another color. Afterimages are formed and complementary colors enhance one another. This strong contrast often makes colors appear to vibrate, or glow along the border between two complementary colors. This is an exciting color effect and creates a tremendous impact, but it can bother the eyes and make the work difficult to look at for long periods of time. Just how much visual stimulation is desirable depends on the situation, the purpose of the work, and personal taste.

(2) Another method of creating visible simultaneous contrast is to use large, intense ground areas with small neutral or low-intensity figures (see Figure 6-20b). In some ways, the color effect produced by this means is less intense than that of the first method, but it does allow the artist to play with the subtle but visible afterimages that develop on neutral figures in combination with saturated hue areas.

6-20. **Methods of reinforcing simultaneous contrast: (a) use large areas of intense complementary colors; (b) use large intense ground areas with smaller low intensity figure areas; (c) use a figure color that includes the afterimage color of the background (here, a blue-gray is used in the figure color); (d) use low-intensity areas of the afterimage color of the figures. Compare the contrast with and without these areas; (e) use light areas to surround dark, and dark areas to surround white.**

Designs: Mary Fry and Lois Dougherty (6-20d)
Photos: Patricia Lambert

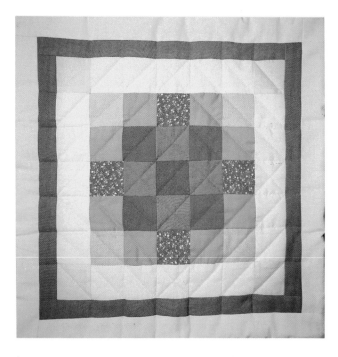

b.

c.

d.

e.

(3) To heighten the feeling of contrast produced by the method just decribed, a neutral that leans slightly toward the complement of the background hue can be chosen (see Figure 6-20c). This will compound and intensify the effect of the afterimage on the neutral figure area.

(4) A color in one area of a design can be intensified through simultaneous contrast by using low-intensity auras of complementary colors around that area of color (see Figure 6-20d). The stars with auras in figure 6-20d) take on greater brilliance and depth than the stars without auras, which appear flatter and less dramatic.

(5) Surrounding light areas of color with dark colors and surrounding dark areas of color with light colors can create a feeling of greater value contrast in a work (see Figure 6-20e).

(6) Using a black ground heightens the drama and intensity of figure colors (see Figure 6-14c).

In general, the greatest contrasts—whether in hue, value, temperature, or intensity—tend to heighten and dramatize afterimages and to reinforce simultaneous contrast.

6-21. **Black stripes show yellow-green afterimage (stare at center of design for 15 seconds.**

Design: Mary Fry
Photo: Patricia Lambert

CONTROLLING SIMULTANEOUS
CONTRAST IN DESIGNING

A fiber artist or commercial manufacturer often does not want colors to change quality when they are combined in a work. In these situations, the issue is how to reduce or cancel simultaneous contrast when the strong visual impact, color changes, and surprising intensities (or sudden losses of intensity) that may ensue from simultaneous contrast are not desired. When a black stripe is placed on a violet ground, for example, it acquires a yellow-green quality. Because the violet's value is quite low, its yellow-green afterimage shows up remarkably well on a black or dark gray (see Figure 6-21). The way to eliminate this

phenomenon is to neutralize the afterimage by mixing complements. If some of the violet background color is added to the black stripe, making it a dark shade of violet, the violet in the stripe will neutralize the yellow-green afterimage and cancel it out—just as one complementary color neutralizes another. Although a dyer could physically add violet to the black, many fiber artists do not have this option; for them, a better course would be to choose a very dark violet thread that appears to be a combination of black and violet. The illusory yellow of the afterimage and the actual violet of the pigment present in the dark stripe would thereupon seem to disappear, leaving black, the color desired in the first place. Thus, the final result is a rich, dense, black figure on a violet ground (see Figure 6-22).

6-22. **Controlling simultaneous contrast: a. black stripes in violet ground; b. black stripe and dark violet on white; c. dark violet stripes on violet ground.**
Design: Mary Fry
Photo: Patricia Lambert

If an artist wanted to create a woven rug that contained a violet, low intensity blue, and yellow hue pattern on an intense orange ground, simultaneous contrast would influence the pattern colors selected. The strong blue afterimage of the orange ground would create a violet that looked distinctly blue-violet, a yellow that had a greenish quality, and a blue of electric intensity. An artist wanting to avoid these color shifts in the finished work would have to change the original colors to compensate for the blue afterimage. To warm the violet and the yellow, respectively, the violet must be changed to a red-violet and the yellow to an orange-yellow. The low-intensity blue pattern color must be switched to a gray of the same value as the desired blue, allowing the afterimage to render it a low-intensity blue. Figure 6-23a and b shows the colors originally chosen and the colors as modified to get the desired effect. The colors are shown on a white ground so that they can be seen clearly, without the effect of the complementary afterimage. Figure 6-23c and d shows these same colors on the orange ground.

6-23. **Controlling simultaneous contrast of colored stripes in an orange rug: a. desired colors; b. shifted colors required to produce desired colors on orange ground; c. desired color effect; d. shifted colors (b) on orange ground; e. original colors (a) on orange ground.**

a.

b.

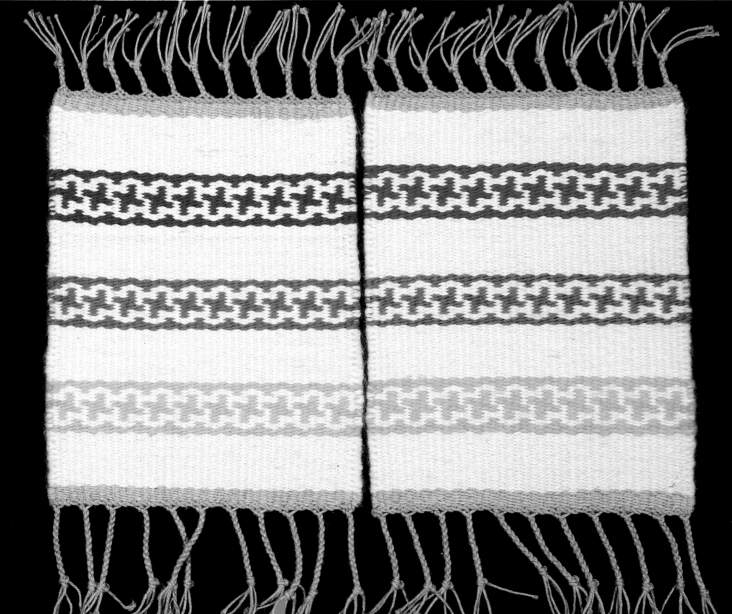

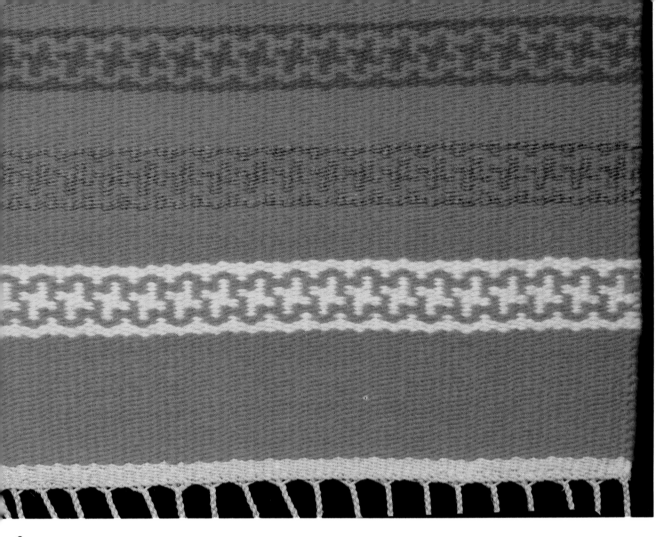

c.

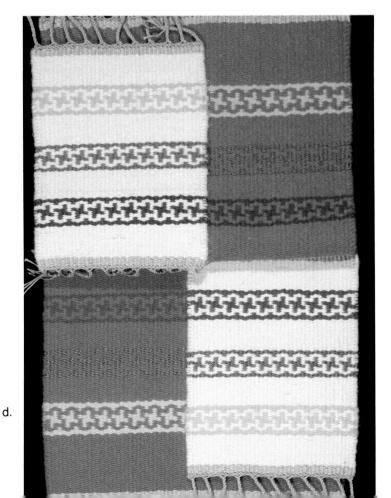

d.

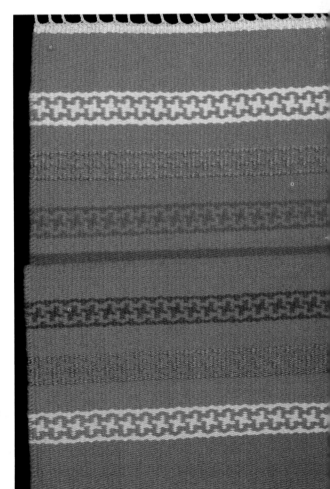

e.

METHODS OF REDUCING
SIMULTANEOUS CONTRAST

The color shifts of simultaneous contrast can be completely avoided in only a few ways. One way is to place colors sufficiently far away from each other, separated by a neutral area, that their afterimages do not affect one another. Another way is for the viewer to stand so far back from the work that the colors lose their intensity, and other elements in the field of vision intrude or become dominant. Short of these fairly drastic (and potentially counterproductive) steps, some methods of reducing the effects of simultaneous contrast in a work can be used.

(1) One approach is to keep values closely related and intensities low (see Figure 6-24a) since intense hues and strong value contrasts produce the strongest afterimages. Afterimages will still be produced, but they will be so weak that the viewer will not be aware of them.

6-24. **a. Reducing simultaneous contrast by keeping values closely related and intensities low:** *Sky Scrape* **(felt inlay, 24" x 30", 1982).**

Artist: Barbara Staepelaere
Photo: Patricia Lambert
Collection of the artist

a.

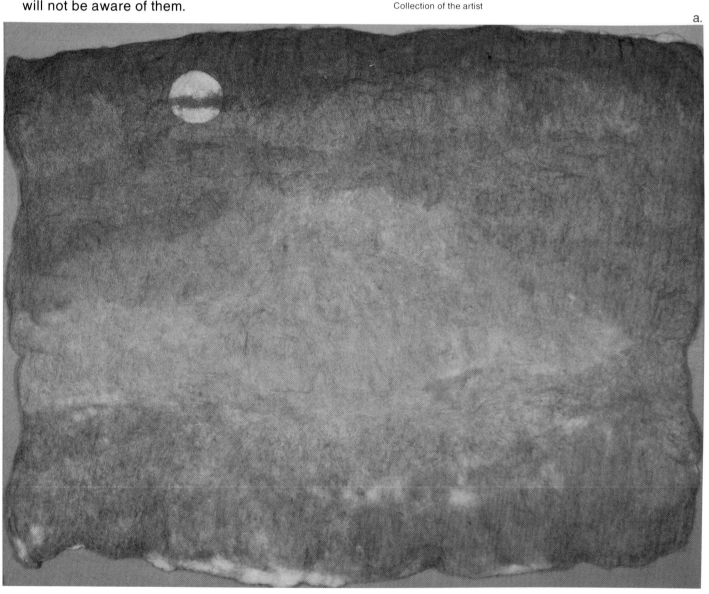

(2) Another method is to outline the figure in black, white, or gray (see Figure 6-24b). When two intense hues are placed next to one another, the complementary contrast along the borders where they meet may be uncomfortably high; in some cases (especially with red and green complements), the colors may even seem to vibrate or glow along the border. Outlining the figure in black, white, or gray or separating the two colors with a black line will greatly reduce this complementary contrast.

(3) Similarly, including small areas of black and white in the design reduces the overall vibrancy and color distortion created by the simultaneous contrast of complementary afterimages (see Figure 6-24c). The black areas should be kept small; if they are made too large, they will create a negative afterimage themselves, reintensifying the colors next to them. Small areas of black and white, however, seem to create rests for the eye from the contrasts of the hues. In this way, they relieve the effect of simultaneous contrast in the design.

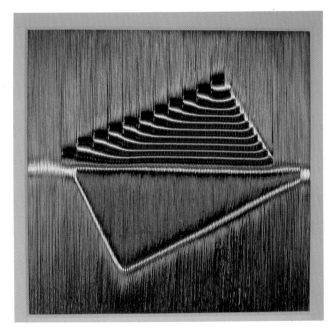

c.

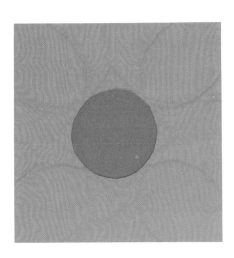

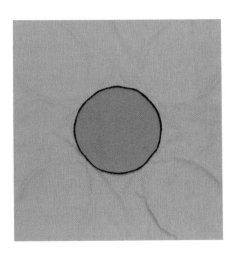

b.

b. Reducing simultaneous contrast by outlining color areas with black, white, or gray: (1) strong simultaneous contrast; (2) reduced simultaneous contrast.

Designs: Mary Fry/Nan Carter
Patricia Lambert

c. Reducing simultaneous contrast by including small areas of black and white as rest areas: *Series I #7* **(6'' x 6'', 1984).**

Artist: Ruth Gowell
Photo: Ruth Gowell
Courtesy of the artist

183

d.

d. Reducing simultaneous contrast by surrounding colors with large areas of white: *Robin's Rainbow* (detail) (quilt).

Artist: Nan Carter
Photo: Patricia Lambert
Courtesy of Robin Louis Sayre

e-1

e-1. Untitled

Artist: Mary Fry
Photo: Patricia Lambert

(4) Surrounding colors in the design with large areas of white create dark negative afterimages that tend to subdue the other colors in the design (see Figure 6-24d). Technically, simultaneous contrast is at work here, creating a negative afterimage, but its ultimate effect is to promote a feeling of reduced color contrast.

(5) A small-scale pattern can be used in designs to break up large areas of strong color (see Figure 6-24e). The concept of scale is important in the manipulation of simultaneous contrast. Afterimage can only be created through the mediation of large areas of unbroken color. Small areas—even of bright colors—if broken up and mixed with others in a pattern, reduce the ability of the eye/brain to respond to the separate hues by creating afterimages.

184

e-2

f.

f. Reducing simultaneous contrast by adding a small amount of the complement to a design (quilt).

Artist: Mary Fry
Photo: Patricia Lambert

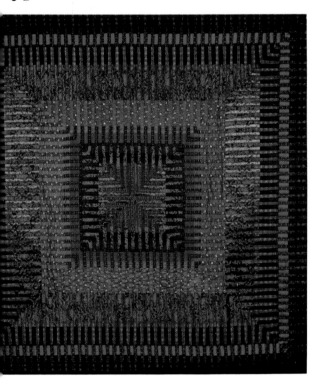

e-2. *Moroccan Measures* **(quilt).**

Artist: Nancy Herman
Photo: Kenneth Kauffman
Courtesy of the artist

e. Reducing simultaneous contrast by using small-scale pattern to break up large areas of intense color: *Moroccan Measures* **(quilt).**

Artist: Nancy Herman
Photo: Kenneth Kauffman
Courtesy of the artist

(6) A final method is to add a small area of the complement to the design (see Figure 6-24f). This may at first seem contradictory, since using large areas of complementary colors does enhance simultaneous contrast. The key word here however, is *small.* In a design that has a large amount of green in it, for example, as well as smaller areas of some other colors, the other colors are affected by a red afterimage from the green. If a small area of red is introduced into the design, the complement to the green is provided in the design and the eye/brain tends not to manufacture as strong an afterimage of that color. If the red area is small, it will not manufacture noticeable afterimages of its own, and so the startling contrasts of large complementary areas will be avoided.

Artists and designers have worked with simultaneous contrast intuitively ever since people first realized that color becomes more dynamic and interesting when contrasts are used. Not everyone reacts to color in the same way or even sees afterimages in entirely the same way. For some artists the idea of reinforcing simultaneous contrast to the point of producing visual vibrations is not desirable; for others, low-intensity colors executed in minor keys may be boring. Given that tastes differ, the artist must deal with simultaneous contrast from the standpoint of control—whether the goal of that control is to reinforce or reduce its effect.

185

Chapter 7

A Systematic Approach to Color Design

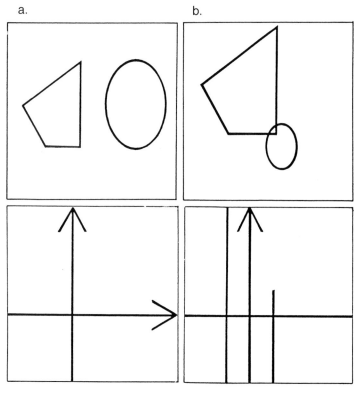

7-1. **Simple shapes, lines, size and direction demonstrate contrast and dominance: a. contrast alone produces unresolved tension; b. dominance produces unity.**

Color can serve as an emotional prod; conversely, our emotions can stimulate a feeling of color. Phrases describing emotion and linked to color are used in everyday language—feeling blue, red with anger, green with envy. Other descriptions allude to color—cool as a cucumber, a sunny disposition. The connection is made on such a regular basis that we pay little conscious attention to it, and yet it is a powerful tool for the fiber artist to use in directing emotional impact in a design. By learning to control the proportion and organization of color in a work, an artist can consciously produce an emotional response in a viewer.

Having a systematic way of choosing color and color relationships is helpful in developing an emotional message. Another valuable aid is an understanding of the concept of unity—the feeling of visual and psychological wholeness or completeness inherent in a work of art. Unity is established by first creating a tension within the design—by the use of contrasting visual elements such as color, value, line, shape, size, direction, and texture (see Figure 7-1a)—and then resolving that tension through use of a greater proportion or dominance of one of the elements (see Figure 7-1b). When a work lacks unity, either because an insufficient contrast is set up or because little or no dominance is apparent, the design lacks strength, clarity, and purpose. At times however, a nonunified design may be the only way of visually describing a particular feeling.

The primary interest of this text lies in producing unity with color. Color unity is achieved through a dominance over contrast of any color characteristics—hue, value, intensity, or temperature. For example, in a design where all the values are similar and all the intensities are low, presenting neither contrast nor dominance, color unity may be established by a greater proportion of cool colors than of warm ones (that is, by a temperature dominance). Color unity may also be established by repeating intervals between colors or by using a strong color pattern to create dominance (see Figure 7-2).

7-2. **Color unity produced by a strong color pattern making a dominance:** *Color Study in Greens.*

Artist: Jane Warnick
Photo: Patricia Lambert
Courtesy of the artist

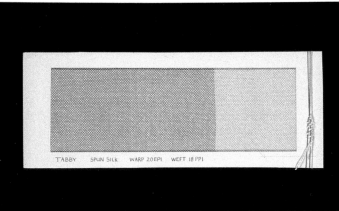

a.

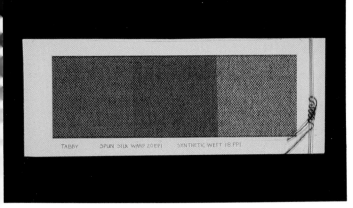

b.

7-3. **Value dominance studies: a. (tints) high value; b. (shades) low value.**

Artist: Sarah Vincent
Photos: Sarah Vincent
Courtesy of the artist

A hand-spinner can produce optically blended color dominance in a pattern of yarns by adding a small amount of a chosen predyed fleece to each of the yarns spun for a work. This holds the color design together with an overall feeling of the common color much as a wash or glaze does in a painting. Similarly, black, white, or gray can be added to each color in a design to give the feeling of a singular tonality or value dominance (see Figure 7-3). Weavers have used this technique for establishing color dominance with great success—for example, by weaving a multicolored warp with a single-colored weft. The weft color unifies any combination of colors in the warp by adding its color dominance to all of the warp colors (again, through optical mixing).

187

Any assortment of yarn colors can be put in a single dyebath (reject colors can be recycled this way), yielding an instantly unified palette through the dominance of the dyebath color over the widely contrasting assortment of yarn colors.

In addition to the emotional responses stimulated by color organization, many hues and colors have a history of symbolic meaning that can evoke strong and sometimes subliminal emotional reactions. The use of color as symbol finds its origins in prehistoric times. How color has evolved in the world's cultures, changing with time, place, and purpose, is a revelation in nonverbal communication. Although the subject cannot be addressed sufficiently in so short a space, figure 7-4 charts some of the elemental meanings of the various hues. (This is in no way meant to be a thorough treatment of the subject; see the bibliography for suggested additional reading.)

Meanings

Red. excitement, love, agitation, aggression, violence, anger, bravery, passion, fire, blood

Orange. warmth, security, fulfillment, happiness, earthiness, autumn

Yellow. happiness, cheerfulness, joy, fear, intellect, treachery, deceit, contagion, early spring

Green. stability, emotional balance, calm, cool, jealousy, anger, disease, poison, nature, trees, grasses, summer

Blue. serenity, spirituality, peace, detachment, depression, cold, coolness, winter

Violet. internalization, depth of feeling, passion, death, nature, opulence, spring

---

7-4. **Some elemental meanings of hues.**

Some hues have a rather confusing duality. For example, yellow gives a feeling of bright cheerfulness, and of being a sunny, happy color; but in a different context, it can denote disease or contagion, and in still another context, cowardice or fear.

Color systems can help the fiber artist maximize the viewer's emotional response to a work. They provide an organizational foundation on which to buiid the color contrast and dominance necessary for color unity and impact. Any organization of color must be thought of initially as belonging to a chromatic (color) system, an achromatic (value) system, or a composite (color and value) system. Each of these systems can in turn be subdivided into simple, straightforward color combinations.

188

The chromatic system can be divided into two large categories: hue and its combinations; and mixed or modulated colors and their combinations.

HUE AND ITS COMBINATIONS

Hue systems are built either on complementary contrasts or on analogous relationships. Since all three primaries are present to some degree in complementary systems, such systems impart a greater sense of contrast than analogous systems do, as well as a feeling of completeness and balance that comes from having the entire color range represented in the color mixtures and combinations.

Analogous color systems are created from closely related hue steps around the hue circle. Colors are analogous if they are contained on the hue circle within a range that includes only two of the primaries. For example, any two hues in the range from yellow (through green) to blue on the hue circle are analogous. Past blue toward violet on the hue circle, the third primary (red) is included in the violet combination, and so a complementary contrast to the yellows in the system is created. In the other direction past yellow toward orange, red is again introduced, and a complement to the blues in the system is set up.

Analogous systems, with their closely related hues, provide much less hue contrast than complementary systems do. Their strength is in offering a system in which the artist can effectively mute contrast and provide a peaceful, quiet, harmonious, and less stimulating work. The least contrast seems to come from the most closely related analogs, and the greatest contrast from the dyad (or single direct complement).

Complementary Hue Relationships

A dyad is any pair of complementary hues. The twenty-four-hue circle contains twelve sets of complementary pairs or dyads, each of which presents different value (key) and hue relationships as different proportions of the two hues are used. Since the dyad is a system using only two hues, color dominance in each dyad is created by increasing the amount of either one hue or the other.

Complementary pairs of pigment hues are found lying directly opposite one another on the hue circle. In combination, they contain all three primaries freeing the eye from making afterimages and creating a feeling of wholeness and color harmony in the work. Their emotional impact on the viewer depends on how and in what proportion the individual hues are used in the work. When used in large areas, they provide maximum contrast and evoke maximum excitement in the viewer. When used in small areas or points of color, however, they mix optically, neutralize one another into soft, peaceful, chromatic grays.

In addition to the direct, two-color (or dyadic) complementary systems, hue systems exist that are based on combinations of three, four, and more hues. Hue systems made up of three hues are called triads; visualizing triads on the hue circle may be easier with the help of a triangle superimposed over the circle. Different types of triadic relationships can be represented by different-shaped triangles.

An equilateral triangle, for example, when rotated in the hue circle, points out systems of equally separated hues (see Figure 7-5a). If it is placed so that each point of the triangle touches each primary, a primary system of yellow, red, and blue is immediately apparent. Depending on the color dominance, three primary systems are possible, each with a different primary dominating, and a different weighting of the emotional impact of the simple triadic design. The expressive quality and the value (or key) of each hue is different (see Figure 7-6). Because each hue is fully saturated the relationship of intensity to the other characteristics can be ignored here; thus, in these systems, temperature, value, and of course hue are the characteristics we can manipulate.

7-5. **Triadic hue systems: equilateral (a) and isosceles (b) triangles in hue circle.**

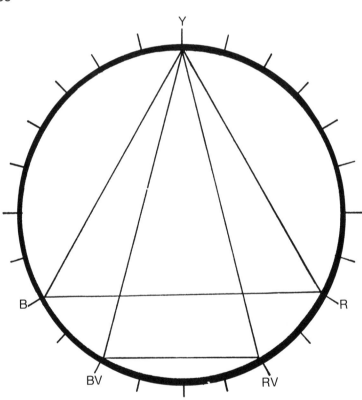

Figure 7-6		
Dominant Hue	**Key**	**Feeling**
Yellow	high major	happy, bright, uplifting
Red	middle major	strong, positive, direct
Blue	low major	dramatic, quiet, heavy

7-6. **Keys and feelings established by different dominant hues.**

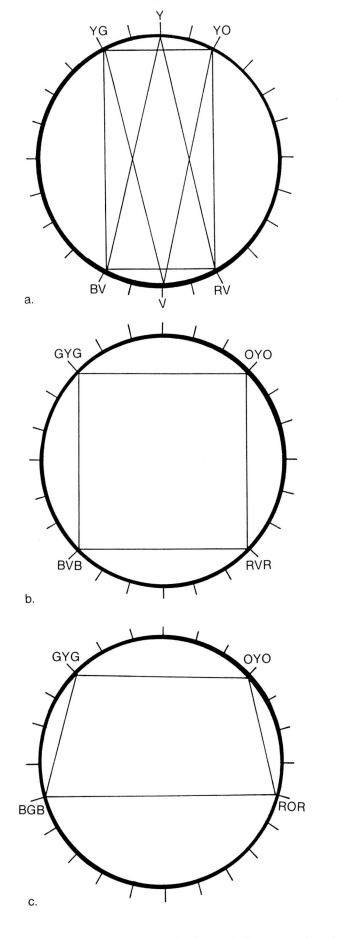

a.

b.

c.

7-7. **Tetradic hue systems in hue circle: a. rectangle (double split complement); b. square; c. trapazoid.**

If the equilateral triangle is rotated within the twenty-four-hue circle, any combination of three hues will consist of equally separated components and will produce a system incorporating each of the three primaries—but on a subtle basis, with varying changes in key that again depend on the values of the hues used and on the hue dominance. When the triangle is set on the secondaries (orange, green, and violet), for example, a relatively minor-keyed relationship is established. (Although the key of a primary—red, yellow, and blue—triad is not strictly major either, the feeling is far closer to major than to minor because of the great value interval between yellow and blue.) In all color systems—hue and modulated—the key formed by the color choice and color dominance in the design greatly influence the emotional impact of the work.

In the twenty-four-hue circle, the equilateral triangle can assume any of eight possible positions, with three different possible color dominances for each position, giving a total of twenty-four possible systems for this kind of equilateral triad.

Other hue systems based on triads can be derived by placing an elongated isosceles triangle on the hue circle so that the apex points to a hue and each of the two base corners points to a hue analogous to the hue that is complementary to the apex (see Figure 7-5b). This is called a split complementary system. An example of a split complementary system in a twenty-four-hue circle is yellow at the apex of the triangle and violet-red-violet and violet-blue-violet at the base corners—each of which falls on a different side of the complement of yellow (violet). This split complementary system constitutes a slightly subtler version of the direct complementary theme examined under dyads.

If two elongated isosceles triangles are placed over each other in reverse position on the hue circle and the apex of each is removed (leaving a narrow rectangle), the resulting four-color system is known as a double split complement or simply as a tetrad (see Figure 7-7a). The term *double split complement* is not quite fitting, since the direct complements (the apexes of the two triangles) are not present, but including them ruins the subtle nature of the tetrad, and produces a rather blatant pair of complementary analogs. The complementary tetrad, like other complementary systems, yields a feeling of completeness and color balance. The elongated rectangle of the complementary tetrad can be rotated in the hue circle to point out six color selections, each of which has four different possible color dominances.

Another basic tetrad system can be established by placing a square over the hue circle; the diagonal corners of the square point to two direct complementary pairs (see Figure 7-7b). This tetrad consists of a combination of two pairs of direct complements and can be called a double complement. As with the rectangular tetrad explained above, six possible com-

191

binations can be built on a square in a twenty-four-hue circle, each having four possible color dominances.

A trapezoid can be used to create yet another usable tretrad system in the hue circle (see Figure 7-7c). If a line is drawn between two analogous hues—not necessarily directly analogous, but in the same arc—and then lines are drawn to the immediate right and left of their complements, a tetrad is produced that is not exactly the same as the double split complement but yields the same sense of color balance. Once the trapezoidal shape is constructed, it too can be rotated to locate more color combinations.

A hexad is made by connecting three complementary pairs such that three equidistant groupings of complementary pairs are produced (see Figure 7-8). Four possible hexads exist in a twenty-four-hue circle, and each is completely balanced. Because hexads thoroughly represent the colors of the hue circle, a design done in this system has a rich, fully orchestrated color feeling. Each of the four possible hexads has six possible color dominances.

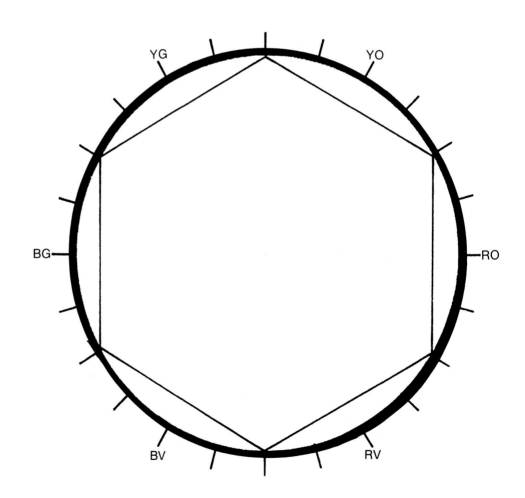

7-8. **Hexadic hue systems.**

7-9. **Hexadic relationship:** *New Wave Hits Echo Beach*
(wool and rayon-Lurex weaving 4' x 8').

Artist: Sheila O'Hara
Photo: Gary Sinick
Courtesy of the artist

7-10. **Tints, shades, and tints of shades of red/green modulation:** *A Peony for Irving Penn* **(tapestry weaving, 52" x 60").**

Artist: Mary Lynn O'Shea
Photo: Eric Borg
Courtesy of the artist

Analogous Hue Relationships

Analogous hues are hues that lie next to one another on the hue circle. Any combination of colors that fall within a single primary arc—that is, between two primaries on the hue circle—are analogs. As soon as one of the colors crosses into a second arc (thus introducing a third primary) the color combination is no longer strictly analogous, but contains some degree of a complement; if mixed, the colors in the combination would produce not a hue, but a lower-intensity (or grayed) color.

In practice, however, the word *analog* refers to any colors strongly related by a common hue. In accordance with this looser definition, the combination of hues can contain elements from more than one primary arc—for example, elements from red-orange through red to red-violet—and still be counted as an analogous selection. The impact of a design created from analogs in the strict definition (hues all contained in a single primary arc) differs subtly from that of a design created from analogs in the looser definition.

All analogous systems are harmonious. Strict analogs are especially closely related—almost to the point of being monochromatic, if only a few hues are used. The differences between yellow, yellow-orange yellow, and yellow-orange are slight; the colors are so strongly related by hue, similarity of temperature, and nearness of value that little contrast exists. Consequently, the key is always minor.

A system of more loosely defined analogs (such as one ranging from red-orange through red and red-violet to violet) is strongly unified by the red hue common to the entire range; however, a wider variety of hues and relatively more color contrast is present than in a strict analogous system. Because the color selection crosses from one primary arc to another, some complementary hue contrast is present; and although a strong dominance is created by the red hue and a sense of gradual harmonious change is sustained throughout, some contrast is also present to provide a stronger feeling of color unity, completeness, and balance in the color selection.

Other characteristics being equal the more analogous the color system, the quieter its impact. As the analogous system broadens to include all three primaries, it becomes more dramatic and more balanced. When analogous colors are used in a combined system of hues, tints, and shades, they behave more dramatically because of value contrasts that are introduced by the tints and shades. This fact connects analogous and complementary systems composed of pure hue to chromatic systems composed of mixed, broken, or modulated colors.

7-11. Split complementary modulation of yellow / red violet and blue / violet, with tins and shades: *Iris II* **(tapestry weaving, 46" x 44").**

Artist: Mary Lynn O'Shea
Photo: Eric Borg
Courtesy of the artist

MIXED OR MODULATED COLOR AND ITS COMBINATIONS

Modulated systems consist of colors produced by combinations of complements, secondary hues, or tints, tones, and shades. The system chosen can include the hues used to create the modulation, or it can omit the hues and include only the colors in the midrange of the modulation itself (see Figure 7-11).

Complementary Modulations

Whenever two complementary hues are mixed, the resulting color is a functon and product of the tinctorial strength and proportions of the two hues used. A considerable range of color can be obtained by varying the proportions of the two complements. Each variation in hue of either of the two original complements being mixed yields a different result. For example, a complementary modulation between a red-violet red and a green-blue green yields a different range of colors than does a modulation between red-orange and blue-green.

195

In a twenty-four-hue circle, twelve different pairs of complementary hues can be modulated to produce a range of colors which include sensitive and delicate chromatic neutrals when tinted. Chromatic neutrals are grays that show decided temperature shifts to warm or cool, depending on the colors next to them. The general emotional impact is a quiet, contained feeling of serenity; the characteristics of the midscale colors are closely related.

The colors found in complementary modulations are often colors found in nature. The colors of stems, grasses, and leaves—particularly in the fall and winter seasons—are marvelous examples of these closely related broken colors. In working out designs, the artist should not as a rule choose more than four or five colors per modulation. Of course, it is possible to do so with successful results, but in most cases the best tenet is "less is more"; Limits (paradoxically) broaden creative possibilities.

Secondary Modulations

The secondary hues—orange, green, and violet—also produce a modulated range of subtle beautiful broken colors like those found in nature. Modulations between any two secondary colors can be done in exactly the same way as complementary modulations, either with dye, paint or already dyed fiber mixed optically, with slightly different results. Figure 7-12 shows the relationship of primary, secondary, and tertiary colors. Although this illustration does not show the complete modulation of the tertiaries, it does show the kinds of soft, low-intensity color that result when two secondaries are mixed and tinted.

The emotional impact of the tertiaries is a calming, soothing one because of the low intensity of the palette. The keys resulting from these modulations are minor unless the colors are tinted or shaded for greater variation of value. Each system produces a strongly unified palette among the colors used, even if fully intense secondary hues themselves are included in the palette. The eye/brain responds subliminally in understanding the underlying unity of a system in which only two hues have been used to produce a whole series of offspring.

7-12. **Goethe's triangle, showing sample tertiaries mixed from secondaries.**

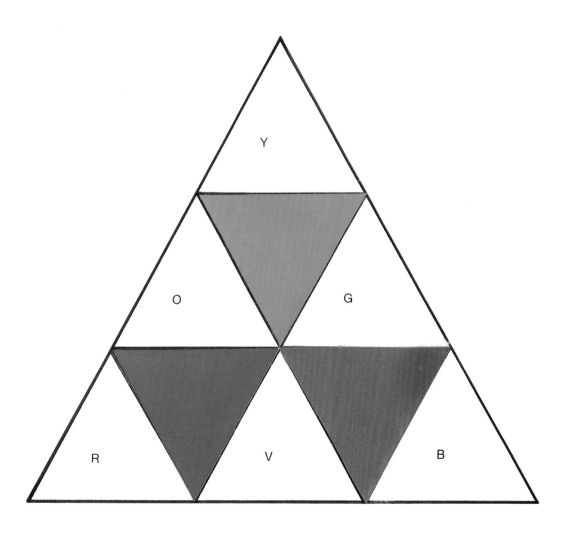

Tints, Tones, and Shades

Many more color modulations can be created by tinting, toning, or shading any hue in graduated steps.

A tint involves a scale of decreasing hue intensity and increasing value; a tone creates a modulation of decreasing hue intensity but with no accompanying change in value; and a shade creates a modulation of decreasing hue intensity and decreasing value. Keys again play an important part in the impact of these three kinds of modulations. In toning, when the relative value of the hue (and not just any gray) is used, the result is always minor. These beautiful systems depend on the subtle, low-intensity colors that appear in the midrange of the modulated steps and the strong feeling of space created by the advancing and receding properties of the different intensities (see Figure 7-10). In addition to the feeling of space created by the presence of areas of different intensities, modulated tones of a hue can produce interesting effects by using the more intense colors to set up a simultaneous contrast (and its accompanying hue influence) on the more neutral colors.

Some color shifts may occur in tinted and shaded modulations, too, but their bigger and more dramatic value changes tend to neutralize the hue effect of the simultaneous contrast. Key plays an important part in tinted and shaded modulations, and—since black and white are being used—the keys can be easily manipulated to produce a specific result. A monochromatic system for each of the primaries presents a straightforward example. Yellow is a high value. If yellow is tinted and four graduated tints plus the hue are used, the result will be a high minor key. If, on the other hand, the yellow is shaded as well as tinted, and if two shades are used in a design along with two tints and the hue, the key will be much more major. Only one hue is used, but the design's emotional impact is changed by the tinting and shading—that is, by the key change.

The same experiment can be done with blue, with slightly different results. Blue has a low value, so blue and its tints graduated to white create a major key. If the blue is shaded, the result is an extremely low minor, composed entirely of colors so dark that their gradation of intensity cannot be seen. It may be necessary to tint the shades to some degree in order to see these differences. Even though major or minor keys can be developed, the emotional impact of monochromatic and low-intensity systems seems centered on feelings of temperature shift. Even small changes in temperature affect the viewer: warm colors stimulate; cool colors quiet.

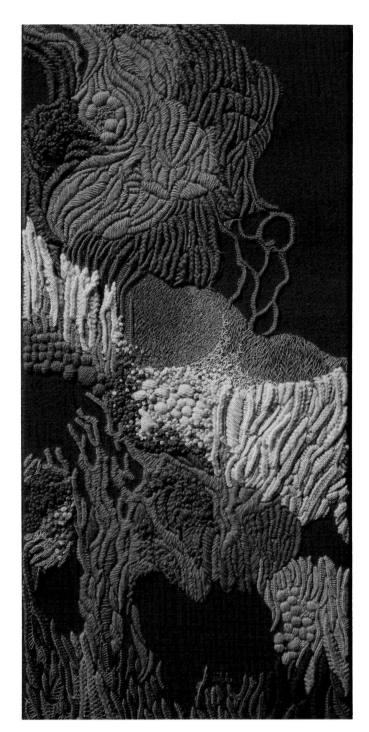

7-13. **Shades and tints of shades of yellow and tertiary colors** *Tierra Amarilla* **(wool and cotton on wool, 14" x 29". (detail)**

Artist: Wilcke H. Smith
Photo: Wilcke H. Smith
Collection: Elinor Grant; San Luis Obispo, California

7-14. **Chromatic system with tints:** *For Nellie* **(detail)**
(machine embroidery on predyed silk fabric).

Artist: Barbara Smith
Photo: Mark A. Smith
Courtesy of Irving Kupferberg

Any color can be tinted, shaded, or toned. Tints can be shaded and shades can be tinted, giving the artist considerable control in modifying color by small degrees. Another benefit of these kinds of modulations is that tinting, toning, and shading produce unexpected hue changes in the modulations as well. Tinting brings out the undertones in a color. Shading often changes hues by mixing them with the blue undertone in black.

For example, yellow mixed with black does not produce a grayed yellow, but a surprisingly beautiful range of soft greens that emerge as a result of the blue contained in black. Tinting out shades of colors often produces beautiful surprises from the mixtures of undertones that are made visible through the process. Tinting and shading give soft, low-intensity colors and close color relationships that cannot easily be obtained in other ways. It is neither necessary nor desirable always to limit tinting, toning, and shading to monochromatic color systems—that is, to a single hue plus its tints, tones, and shades.

All of the chromatic systems discussed above can be altered by tinting, toning, and shading to create color systems with very different feelings. For example, a hexadic system containing a full range of brilliant hues can be modified and quieted through slight shading or tinting of all of the hues; alternatively it can be manipulated for different effects by selective tinting and shading of some of the hues. As another example, a design formed around fairly large areas of a complementary dyad of orange and blue might produce an undesirably high level of contrast. If the orange, the blue, or both are modulated to lower intensities and different values through tinting or shading, the drama of the excessively high contrast is tamed, controlled, and manipulated to conform to a particular palette with a particular emotional impact decided upon by the artist. A lifetime could be spent exploring the endlessly satisfying possibilities of these color systems.

7-15. **Chromatic system of analogs:** *Winter Sky in Vermont* **(detail, Ikat weaving).**
Artist: Candiss Ann Cole
Photo: Patricia Lambert
Collection of the artist

Achromatic Systems

The second basic category of color systems, the achromatic systems, are concerned with values and value relationships (or keys). Not only are keys a tool for designing in colors, they can be used to create truly exquisite and satisfying designs (see chapter 2 for a complete description). Each key itself produces feelings of light and a unique emotional impact.

7-16. **High minor key (value changes are the result of directional lighting):** *White Peony* **(white on white embroidery).**
Artist: Betty Chen Louis
Photo: Patricia Lambert

The eye/brain system's ability to understand spatial relationships in our three-dimensional world is something we take for granted. It is only when this faculty is upset that we are made aware of just how instinctive depth perception and spatial orientation actually are. Unfortunately, our ability to produce and control the illusion of three-dimensionality (or space) on a two-dimensional surface is far less intuitive; some intellectual decision-making is required in order to produce the illusion that areas or objects in a work are advancing toward or receding away from the viewer.

7-17. Composite color relationships *Doric II: Blue Mode* **(quilt, 30" x 40").**

Artist: Jan Myers
Photo: Mark Karell
Courtesy: Kan Am Realty Company; Atlanta, Georgia

A third category of color combinations covers chromatic-achromatic systems: those that involve the use of a hue or other color in an otherwise achromatic system; and those that involve the addition of black, white, or gray to an otherwise chromatic system.

The use of grays and hues in simple combinations is an effective method of augmenting a hue's expressive quality by minimizing the influence of other colors and thereby allowing the viewer to focus on one color. The hue makes a clearer, bolder statement (certainly a different statement) then could be achieved with values alone (see Figure 7-17).

The eye/brain perception system is continually trying to simplify, interrelate, and order the chaos of the visual world. Careful planning of color designs and thoughtful use of color systems can heighten an artist's expressive effectiveness by reinforcing our natural way of seeing and our natural inclination to achieve visual order. Strangely, the more carefully a color system is thought through in terms of goal, the more effective and spontaneous the finished design appears. Although some will argue that the spontaneity of creation—the "happy accident"—has been lost, in its place grows the true and free creativity of an artist who understands color and can use it expressively.

A work can be realistic, representational, abstract, or pure design. The control of space is personal. A plaid weave can achieve as much or as little spatial sense as a bowl of flowers sitting on a table in front of a window. It depends on the artist's taste and ability.

The term *picture plane* is often used to describe the immediate surface on which space illusion appears. It refers to the actual two-dimensional surface of a work. The kinds of pictorial space possible range from deep space—where parts of a work seem to float well in front of or far behind the picture plane—to flat space that exhibits little or no depth distance between areas in the work (see Figure 7-18).

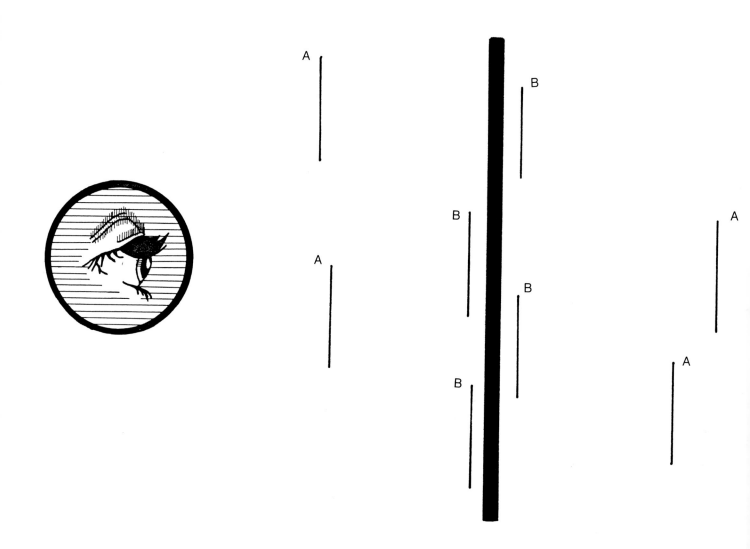

7-18. **The picture plane and illusions of space (a = Deep space; b = Flat space).**

SPATIAL TECHNIQUES

Two categories of techniques can be used to produce the visual illusion of flat or deep space through careful use of color and/or value relationships: chiaroscuro, and perspective.

Chiaroscuro

Chiaroscuro is an Italian word meaning "light/dark." It refers to a technique of arranging values in a logical progression from light to dark to describe a curved surface or form, implying a light source with its visually understandable high, middle, and low light. Chiaroscuro produces a limited kind of space by describing a flat shape as a three-dimensional form through the careful placement of value (see Figure 7-19).

7-19. **Chiaroscuro, changing values to show form:** *Egg and Fish* **(detail) (tapestry weaving, 7.54 square meters, 1970).**
Artist: Helena Hernmarck
Photo: Henena Hernmarck
Courtesy of the artist

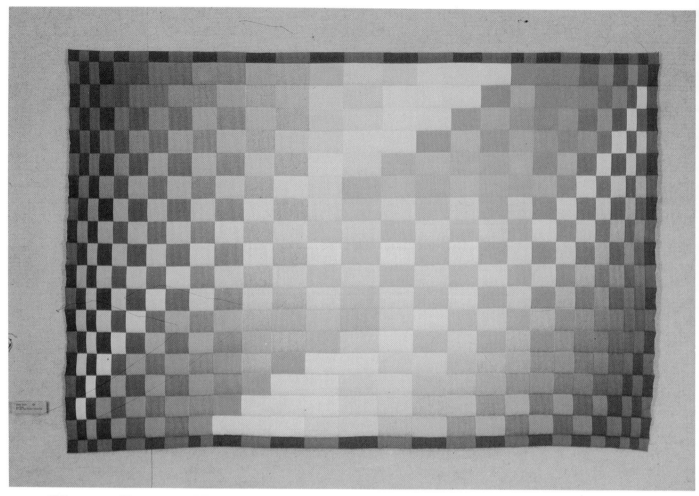

7-20. **Chiaroscuro, the illusion of curved surfaces:** *Orange Galaxy* **(quilt), 1980).**

Artist: Jan Myers
Photo: Jan Myers
Courtesy of Gretchen and David Porter; Minneapolis, Minnesota

7-21. **Notan, positive and negative shapes:** *Winds of Fire* **(Detail) (Banner).**

Artist: Ann Harris
Courtesy of the artist

Perspective

The two basic kinds of perspective, *linear* and *aerial* can be used separately or in combination.

Aerial perspective creates a feeling of space through the use of advancing and receding colors; contrasts in value, intensity, and temperature; and texture and detail. Aerial perspective relies on varying degrees of contrast to produce a sense of deep or flat space.

Deep Space

The first principle involved in creating a feeling of deep space is to work with high contrast in the color characteristics of value, intensity, and temperature: The second principle is to make a logical and consistent arrangement of these characteristics in a design, from the most advancing to the most receding (see Figure 7-22).

7-22. Contrasts of hue, value, and intensity (detail and nondetail), all producing the illusion of space: *Bluebonnets* **(tapestry weaving, 11' x 20').**

Artist: Helena Hernmarck
Photo: James F. Wilson
Collection: Carrozza Investments Ltd., Dallas Centre, Dallas, Texas

Linear perspective refers to the principal geometric system in which a feeling of realism and space is created through the scaled use of line, making objects become progressively smaller and closer together as they (seemingly) recede into the distance. The result is often virtually photographic—as though an actual scene were being viewed from a single vantage point. Railroad tracks converging in the distance to a single vanishing point on the horizon of the picture plane is a simple, classic example (see Figure 7-23). The technique can of course be applied to abstract work as well.

7-23. **Linear perspective, the illusion of space with line:** *Steel I* **(woven tapestry, 89" x 117", 1973).**

Artist: Helena Hernmarck
Photo courtesy of the artist
Collection: Bethlehem Steel Corporate Offices

An excellent way of understanding deep space is by reference to actual distances in nature (see Figure 7-24). A mountain range gives us an example of value, intensity, and temperature of color at one viewing. Mountains or hills that are closer appear darker or lower in value, while those in the distance appear lighter. Similarly, trees or other objects closer to the viewer are darker; as they recede into the distance, they become lighter in value. Light and dark values worked in abstract patterns or designs very often advance or recede unpredictably (notan). At one moment a dark shape advances, but at the next it seems to drop out and become a hole in the design. This spatial flexibility is tricky and has its origins in the way we perceive positive and negative shapes. Areas that describe solid shapes or objects are called positive space; areas around those shapes are called negative space. Areas of high contrast can be perceived as moving either in or out, or at times they may appear quite stable (see Figure 7-21).

Intensity and temperature tend to diminish with distance. The intensity of color seen in the New England hills in autumn is brilliant at close or middle distances, but becomes bluer and less intense as the distance from the viewer increases. This phenomenon of heightened value, cooler temperature, and lowered intensity at greater distances is caused by the atmospheric scattering of light by particles of dust, pollen, moisture, and other pollutants in the air. These small, airborne particles also tend to absorb longer wavelengths of light, shifting color toward blue.

7-24. Aerial Perspective, the illusion of space with values: *Canyon (tapestry weaving, 3' x 5').*

Artist: Barbara Staepelaere
Photo: Patricia Lambert

7-25. Consistent arrangement of shapes to reinforce a sense of space: *Intarivasion* **(wool weaving, 105" x 144", 1982).**

Artist: Sheila O'Hara
Photo: Charles Frizzell
Courtesy of the artist

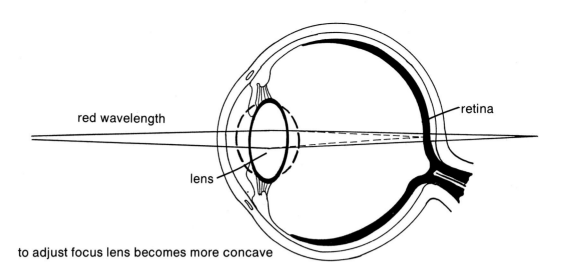

red wavelength

retina

lens

to adjust focus lens becomes more concave

Warm colors tend to produce a sensation of coming forward or advancing in space, while cooler colors seem to recede. The reasons for this are founded in physical and physiological fact. When white light is refracted by a prism, red wavelengths are bent the least, and blue and blue-violet wavelengths are bent the most. When light is refracted by the lens of the eye, the same thing occurs: red wavelengths are refracted only slightly by the eye lens, so in order for the lens to bring the red wavelengths into sharp focus on the retina, it must become rounder or more convex (just as it would on a close object of any color); blue wavelengths, on the other hand, are refracted at a sharper angle by the eye lens and, therefore, in order for the lens to make the blue wavelengths come into sharp focus on the retina, it must become more elongated or concave (just as it would for a more distant object). Because the eye must react to red as it would to a closer object, we perceive it as closer than it really is—thus the term *advancing color*. Conversely, the lens's response to blue is as if it were viewing a more distant object, which makes the blue seem to *recede* (see Figure 7-26).

7-26. **a. cross section of eye. Dotted lines indicates correction of (1) red wavelengths of light focused on retina, and (2) blue wavelengths of light focused on retina.**

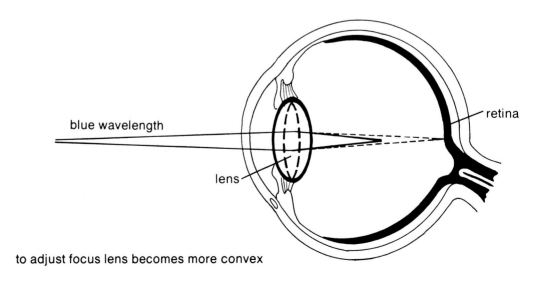

blue wavelength

retina

lens

to adjust focus lens becomes more convex

b. Temperature contrast, showing advancing and receding space (the red-violet advances in the cool circle and recedes in the warm one).

Design: Mary Fry
Photo: Patricia Lambert

Although yellow is grouped with the warm colors and violet is grouped with the cool colors, both of these colors can be focused on the retina with the lens at or near its normal shape; thus yellow and violet neither advance nor recede.

Intensity and temperature, unlike value, advance and recede in abstraction much as they do in realistic work.

The spatial code based on use of high-contrast color characteristics in a consistent arrangement of gradation can be augmented by other visual clues, including the amount of detail and/or texture used and the degree of gradual color contrast present in an area of a work. The presence of detail, of textural contrasts, or of generally large, bold textures and small color contrasts creates a feeling of nearness. Uniformity, or a lack of these contrasts, adds to a feeling of distance. We perceive detail, textures, and subtle contrasts of color at close range, and we cannot see these things clearly at a distance.

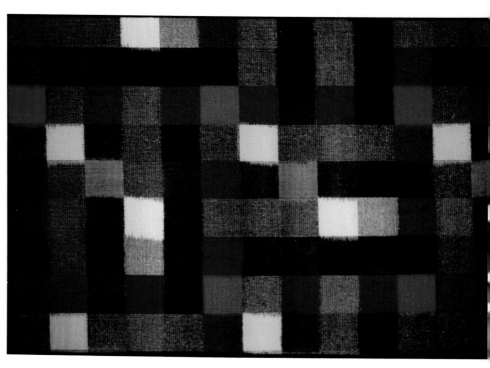

Another spatial clue is the physical arrangement of the colored shapes in the design. Shapes in a design can be arranged to reinforce its linear perspective—creating an illusion of deep space (see Figure 7-25)—or to overlap one another in a design (see Figure 7-28). The planes indicated by overlapping shapes can be strengthened by color contrasts or negated by a lack of contrast between shapes. If a shape with warmer, more intense, advancing colors is placed in the design so that it appears to be lying on top of an area of cooler, grayer, receding colors, the sense of space in the design will be enhanced by the placement.

7-27. **Colored shapes and deep space (afterimages):** *Pot Holder III* **(detail).**
Artist: Sarah G. Vincent
Photo: Sarah G. Vincent
Courtesy of the artist

7-28. **Colored shapes and deep space (mixed media embroidery, 11'' x 14'').**
Artist: Joan Schulze
Photo: Joan Schulze
Courtesy of the artist

7-29. **a. Temperature/intensity shifts to flatten space:** *Shift in Thirds* **(detail) (cotton and rayon weaving, 1983).**
b. Temperature shifts with tints to increase space *Night Vision* **(worsted wool, 45" x 79", 1984).**

Artist: Lois Bryant
Photo: Lois Bryant
Courtesy of the artist

Flat Space

Major keys, contrast between hues and broken color, and differences in temperature are the ingredients for producing deep space. A sense of flat space can be produced by minimizing these features to a point at which no visual space exists and the work becomes totally two-dimensional. Closely related values or minor relationships reduce the sense of space and reinforce the sense of the picture plane.

Reducing contrasts in color intensity in the work also reduces the spatial impact. The degree to which space can be developed by means of low intensities is quite interesting. A work done in a high-intensity palette of both warms and cools has a greater spatial quality than one done in low-intensity equivalents of the same hues (see Figure 7-29). Both the high- and the low-intensity palettes, however, will tend to appear much flatter than a palette that includes both high- and low-intensity colors.

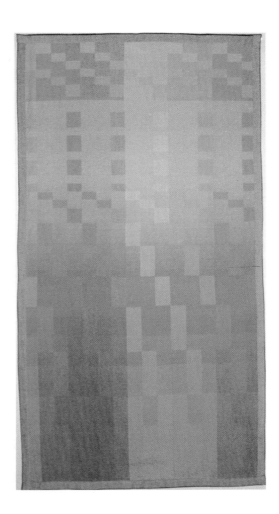

b.

211

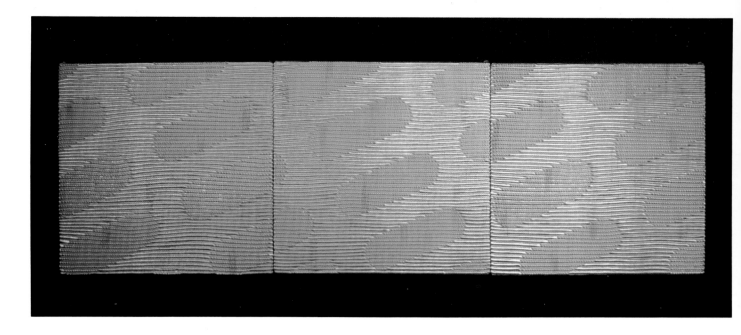

7-30. **Flat space (low-intensity, high-value) tints with temperature change:** *Spring Clouds* **(warp-faced weave, 24" x 72" x 1", 1982).**

Artist: Ruth Gowell
Photo: Ruth Gowell
Courtesy of the artist

In much the same way, a feeling of flat space can be achieved by limiting contrasts of temperature. A work done in all-warm or all-cool colors will tend to be flatter than one done in warm and cool colors (see Figure 7-30). If the fiber artist wants to achieve a feeling of flatness with a palette containing both warm and cool colors, contrasts must be minimized and the colors should be arranged so that even small contrasts in value, intensity, and temperature do not group in a way that emphasizes the advancing and receding qualities of each. The darkness of a darker-value, low-intensity, cool color, for example blue-gray, juxtaposed with a higher value of a higher-intensity, warm color, such as a tint of orange, will restrain the natural tendency of the cooler color or lower intensity to recede thus reducing the space; conversely, the tendency of the higher value to recede can be offset by the tendency of the warmer color or higher intensity to advance.

For spatial effects to be truly flat, all contrasts must be kept to a minimum. Controlling the degree of contrast in a work allows the fiber artist to control spatial illusion. Sometimes, however, unexpected results occur. Because, value and space are tricky, results should be checked on a small scale first to ensure that the effect obtained is the effect desired.

Transparency

Overlapping shapes and color contrasts can be manipulated in designs to produce beautiful illusions of transparency and space. These illusions are the result of carefully chosen color relationships created by using any two colors in company of a third color that appears to be a mixture of the first two.

212

When two actual colorants are combined, the color they produce subtractively depends on the proportions of each of the colors used. For example, if red and yellow are mixed to create orange (depending on the proportions of the two parent colors) the resulting orange may be a red-orange, a yellow-orange, or a middle mixture of orange approaching neither parent color. Visually, the color mixtures and their parent colors inhabit different spatial planes: the red-orange appears closer in space to the red, and the yellow-orange appears closer to the yellow (see Figure 7-31).

This spatial effect can be used dramatically in a design of overlapping colors to make one color seem opaque and the other transparent—or to make both colors seem transparent. If parent colors of red and blue are used as two shapes and a violet mixture color is placed in the area where the two parent color shapes overlap, an illusion of transparency results, with one shape appearing to be transparent and floating in space over the other. Which shape reads as transparent depends on the hue, value, and intensity of the mixture color especially on whether it is a middle mixture equidistant from each parent color or is closer to one parent or the other.

7-31. Illusion of transparency and opacity.

Artist: Mary Fry
Photo: Patricia Lambert

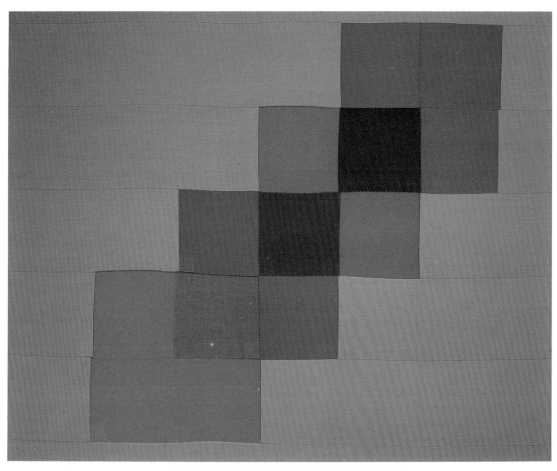

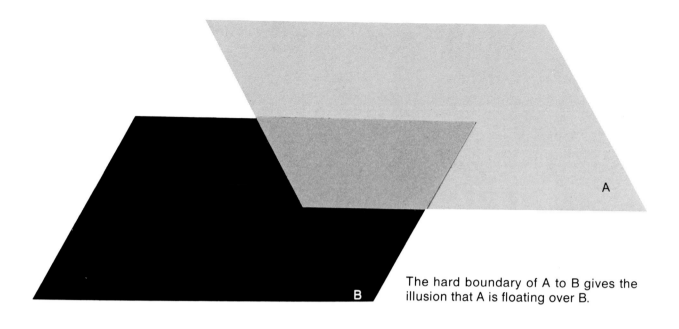

The hard boundary of A to B gives the illusion that A is floating over B.

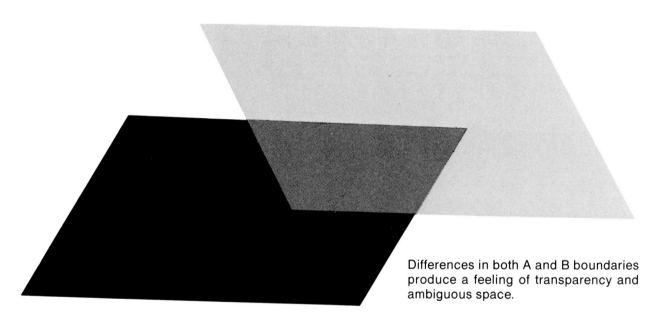

Differences in both A and B boundaries produce a feeling of transparency and ambiguous space.

The spatial behavior of colors that create an illusion of transparency can be expressed in terms of their common boundaries. The softer boundaries—those nearer one another in value—imply physical nearness and connection. The harder boundaries—those with greater value contrast—imply distance and indicate separation from one another. Certain color areas in the design unite as a result and seem to be transparent, floating over seemingly. more distant opaque areas. When the mixture is a middle (or *medial*) mixture, the boundaries are equally soft or hard and exhibit an equal value difference. The medial mixture appears to be the sum of two overlapping transparent colors with light behind them (see Figure 7-32).

7-32. **Changes in boundary contrast produce illusions of transparency and space.**

214

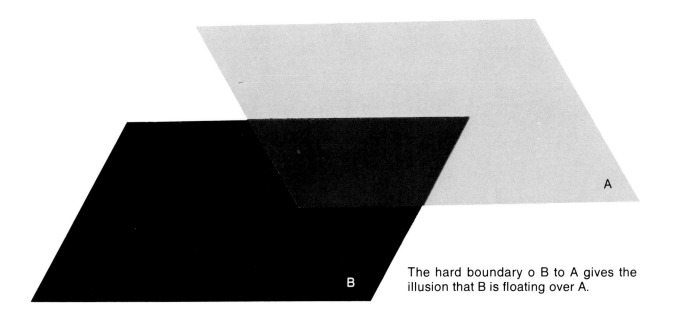

The hard boundary o B to A gives the
illusion that B is floating over A.

7-33. **Color boundaries.**

Whether the transparent shape appears to lie directly over the other shape or appears to be floating above it, with space between the two, depends on the advancing or receding behavior of the contrasts in value, intensity, and temperature between the two parent colors chosen. If one of the parent shapes is a high-value, low-intensity, pale gray-blue, and the other is red, and if the violet (mixture) color where they overlap is closer to red than to gray-blue, two things will happen to reinforce the sense of space in the design: the boundaries of the middle mixture of red-violet will unite with those of the red (because the red-violet is closer in color and value to the red than to the gray-blue) to form a single red transparency overlapping a gray-blue opaque area; and the red will advance and the gray-blue will recede, creating a strong sense of space between the red transparency and the gray-blue opaque shape beneath it. If two parent colors that have a balance of advancing and receding characteristics are chosen instead, and the boundaries have nearly the same qualities, the shapes will appear to be two backlit transparencies on closer planes in the design (see Figure 7-33).

7-34. Illusions of transparency and opacity produced by optical mixing (canvas work).

Artist: Benita Wolffe
Photo: Patricia Lambert
Courtesy of the artist

216

It is important to remember that these third colors produced as transparency illusions do not necessarily mimic how real transparent materials of the same colors behave when overlapped or held over opaque surfaces. The eye/brain system accepts a number of third-color possibilities as plausible mixtures, and this allows the fiber artist broader color expression. In practice, the use of actual transparent and opaque materials (when possible) provides a good jumping-off point. Such use acts as a guide in establishing possible combinations of colors, and it helps in controlling the spatial plasticity of the final mixtures.

7-35. **Ambiguous space:** *Triple Grid Overlap* **(knotting, linen, 10" x 16", 1982).**
Artist: Diane H. Itter
Photo: David Keister
Courtesy of Mr. and Mrs. Emanuel Gerard; New York, New York

7-36. **Well-defined space:** *Quilt Quartet* **(knotting, linen, 9" x 17", 1983).**
Artist: Diane H. Itter
Photo: David Keister
Courtesy of Mr. and Mrs. Richard Bloch; Santa Fe, New Mexico

Structural Color Effects

Iridescense, opalescence, and luminescence are all results of interactions of light with structure. As a medium, fiber seems particularly suited for imitating these natural color effects because its own structure gives it numerous possibilities for a dialogue with light. Pushed a little farther, the fiber medium can be made to produce modulations of light and color that can dazzle the eye with the illusion of structural color.

Developing skills of accurate observation is an important prerequisite of learning how to imitate the particular contrasts of hue, value, intensity, and temperature—as well as the patterns of color and light reflectance—that are typical of iridescence, opalescence, and luminescence. After carefully observing an example of structural color such as an abalone shell, an artist may begin the sensitive task of reproducing (in simplified form) the patterns, hues, values, and intensities of color seen in the natural object (see Figure 7-37). It takes practice to see and simplify the characteristics that identify a color effect as structural.

b.

7-37. **Opalescence: a. abalone shell (realistic interpretation—counted technique); b. abalone shell (work in progress); c. abalone shell on gray background, negating afterimages of black and producing heightened effect of opalescence; d. abstract color interpretation of abalone shell (weaving).**

Artist: Mary Fry
Photo: Patricia Lambert

a.

c.

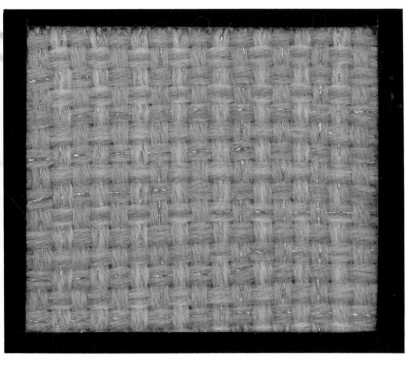

d.

HUE

Hues often shift back and forth in complementary patterns, as they do in an opal (see Figure 7-38). Other forms of iridescence, such as in bird feathers, may show a slow gradation along a surface curve through certain sets of analogous hues—blue-green to blue-violet, for example, or yellow-green to a blue-green. As a feather changes angle around a curve, it may go from black (where the angle is steep to the viewer's eye) through deep blue to blue-green and thence to yellow-green (where the curve faces the viewer's eye), and then change abruptly back to black as the angle of the curve again turns away from the viewer. These kinds of analogous or complementary hue changes and the exact character of the colors present must be observed closely; careful attention to exact color detail heightens the sense of structural color.

7-38. a. Dark opalescence: opal (3x)

Loaned by D. Goldfarb, Goldsmith
Design Studio; Stamford, Connecticut
Photo: Patricia Lambert

b. Abstract interpretation of dark opal (canvas work).

Artist: Benita Wolffe
Photo: Patricia Lambert

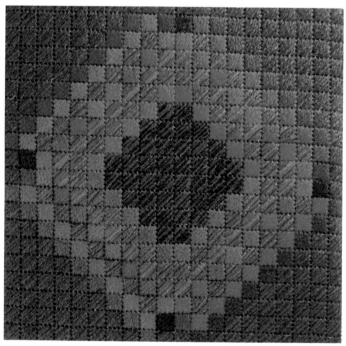

220

VALUE

In order for the artist to design realistic structural color patterns, the exact values (keys of the color patterns) must be matched. In opalescent colors the complementary hues are likely to have a high-value, low-intensity magenta next to an equally high-value, low-intensity green. The similarity of values and intensities creates a high minor key (see Figure 7-39). The more dramatically iridescent bird feathers range from a deep velvety black to a lustrous high value yellow-green, giving the feather overall a middle major key.

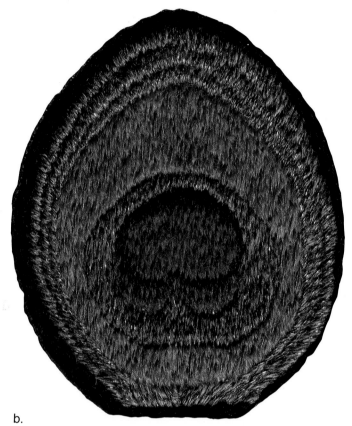

a.

7-39. **Iridescence: a. peacock feather; b. realistic interpretation of peacock feather (free stitchery); c. abstract interpretation (canvas work).**
Artist: Mary Fry
Photo: Patricia Lambert

b.

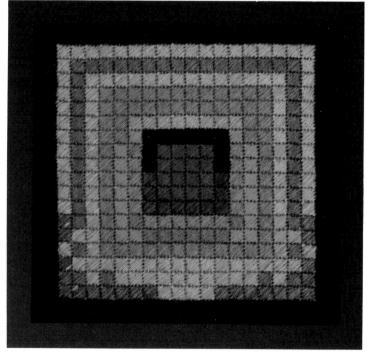

c.

THE USE OF BLACK

A dark outline or areas of dark velvety black, like those seen in the iridescent "eyes" of a peacock's tail, enhance the richly intense colors nearby by simple contrast. The fiber artist can use black in this way to separate and dramatize the intensity of the colors and to give them a more iridescent or luminescent quality.

7-40. **Luminescence and space: Tie dye and counted technique.**
Artist: Mary Fry
Photo: Patricia Lambert

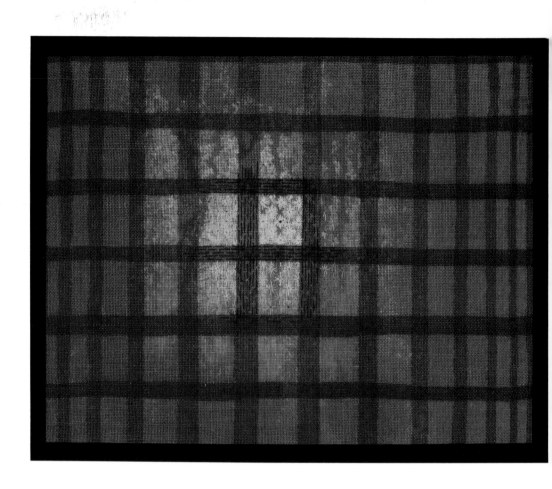

INTENSITY

Many iridescent animal species exhibit iridescence only on part of their body. A fish may have a row of light blue-green iridescent spots on an otherwise light gray body; a damselfly may show areas of intense blue iridescence surrounded by black; a hummingbird may have an iridescent flash of maroon or red on a body that is otherwise a soft, dull gray-green.

Even within the iridescent area itself (depending on the viewer's angle of vision), areas of no color may lie next to areas of intense iridescent color. The structural nature of the color makes the spectral hues visible only when viewed from a certain angle, and areas that are not at the moment showing their structural color often appear gray, black, or a chromatic gray. The dull, low-intensity areas only serve to augment the intensity of areas seen as iridescent. If the areas of intense color in a design are surrounded by low-intensity low-middle- to low-value colors such as chromatic grays, the more intense color (of as high a value as possible) will become brighter by contrast and will seem to glow. The more saturated the color, the more dramatic the contrast. Close attention to this particular detail of iridescence—contrast of color intensity, the exact imitation of the low-intensity color as well as of the patterns of high- and low-intensity colors—helps to create a realistic structural color effect.

The same technique can be used to evoke a stronger sense of luminescence. If the background is kept dull and low (even black) in value, the area of high value and high intensity placed on that dark ground will appear to shine with an inner light—particularly if the areas of intense color are composed of high-luster materials such as rayon or a high-gloss synthetic, possibly even combined with metallic threads (see Figure 7-40).

7-41. **Luminescence:** *Harbor Lights*
(detail) (Ikat, dyed mercerized woven
cotton, 1983).
Artist: Jayn Thomas
Photo: Don De Feo
Courtesy of the artist

GRADATION OF INTENSITY

Gradation of intensity can be used along with the contrast of intensity to give a three-dimensional quality to luminescent shapes. Values and intensities can both be graded to give a feeling of form, as with a light tube or a firefly's abdomen. If the lightest value is progressively graded down—or if the color of greatest intensity is graded to a less intense version of the original color—while the background is kept very dark or black, the feeling created is one of a three-dimensional luminescent shape. This kind of gradation can be done by tinting, toning, shading, or complementary modulation.

LUSTER

One advantage of using fiber to imitate structural color is that great variation in luster is available in different fibers—from extremely high-gloss synthetics of metallic and plastic-coated fiber to rich, matte, woolen yarn. The variety of ways that different yarns reflect, transmit, and absorb light allows the fiber artist to come very close to matching the particular types of reflectance that are such an important part of the appearance of structural colors.

The textures of materials exhibiting iridescence, opalescence, or luminescence show a considerable range in their luster or lack of luster. In a single iridescent peacock feather, areas of matte black appear next to highly lustrous, metallic-looking bronze areas. Some iridescent surfaces, such as a beetle's back, appear to be shiny or satiny like hard porcelain, others, such as opalescent abalone or mother-of-pearl, appear nacreous or pearly. In addition, an iridescent area, such as a butterfly wing, may appear to have an extremely high gloss or a totally matte surface, depending on its angle to the viewer. Not only do hue, value, and intensity change with the angle of the iridescent object to the viewer's eye, so does the degree of total reflectance or luster. The iridescent object may contain gradations from shiny to matte, as well as areas of extreme gloss and areas of no luster at all.

After observing all of these subtleties of surface luster in an object, the artist chooses threads or yarns that come as close to these effects as possible. Sometimes, in imitating a lustrous area of intense hue, a color effect can be made to appear even more scintillating and shimmering if a touch of fine metal thread is added among the lustrous silk or synthetic threads. The metal thread heightens the feeling of glittering or glowing light, even though the metal thread does not itself possess a spectral hue.

7-42. Iridescent movement and color play (magenta/green weave, high-luster rayon fabric).

Photo: Patricia Lambert

SPECIAL MATERIALS

Many different types of liquid pigment available today may be of interest to fiber artists working with a particular technique, such as with painted fabric or fibers. These pigments can be used to produce glittering, shimmering, or metallic effects.

Luminous pigment colors—including fluorescent paints, dyes, and inks—are interesting because they constitute the most vivid and brilliant pigments available. Their principle drawback is that they fade. Permanence may not be a consideration in certain types of fiber projects, however, and where it is not, all kinds of novel effects can be obtained at no disadvantage through the use of these fluorescent materials.

Metallic substances are another possibility. Paint sold as iridescent or luminous often contains finely divided metallic powders in suspension; a typical example is Grumbacher's Thalo Bronze. In addition to being able to purchase metallic powders in suspension in a paint or paste, the artist can buy a can of the powder itself. When sprinkled over a transparent glue solution (called a *size* or *sizing*), the powders give a metallic luster to a surface. A fiber or fabric piece can be painted in the appropriate places with a thin layer of size, and then dusted with a thin layer of copper, bronze, gold, or silver (actually, aluminum) powder. After the size is dry, the excess powder is removed by shaking or vacuuming; the powder sticks only to areas that were sized. One word of caution: some sort of mask should be worn when dealing with these finely divided particles, and as few air currents as possible should be allowed in the work area.

Gilding a fiber surface with gold, aluminum, or copper leaf is also a possibility, but effective gilding takes a little practice. The metallic surfaces can then be glazed with a color or applied over another color, or surface appliqué can be worked over them.

MOVEMENT

The most illusive quality to capture in working with actual structural colors is that of constant change. Natural colors are made dynamic by movement of the structures that produce them or by changes in the viewer's angle of vision. Although imitating this dynamic characteristic of structural color effectively is difficult in a static design, several approaches are possible.

A weaver can use a shot fabric to create this sense of iridescent movement and color play. Shot fabric is woven in a plain or tabby weave, with a warp of one color and a weft of another. It is often made of silk or some other highly lustrous fiber, spun so that the fibers lie in a highly organized, parallel way in the yarn and reflect light in an organized way (see Figure 7-42).

Partly because of the highly lustrous, highly organized quality of the yarn, and partly because the colors are separated and organized in two different perpendicular directions in the warp and weft, the resulting fabric color appears not as an optical blend of warp and weft colors, as would normally happen, but as either the color of the warp or the color of the weft (depending on the angle of light reflectance and the viewer's angle of vision). As the fabric surface ripples or bends around a fold—or as the fine, lightweight fabric moves with air currents—it presents a moving, alternating pattern of the two colors to the viewer. This is very similar to the way natural structural colors behave.

The quality of iridescence in the fabric can be increased by choosing colors in warp and weft to match the colors present in the iridescent model. The use of black or matte areas further heightens the similarity of the work to the iridescent model. For example, in an iridescent blue-green butterfly wing, the dominant hues in the iridescent area are a low-value, intense blue (almost blue-violet) and a relatively high-value blue-green. When the wing structure is turned so that the color is not visible, the wing appears to approach black. The iridescent area of the wing is also surrounded by a very light brown (commonly called beige, but technically referred to as a tint of a shade of red-orange). If the weaver designs a cloth with a black warp and a weft that includes areas or stripes of blue-violet and blue-green (both of fine, lustrous yarn), bordered by or alternating with a fine, lightweight, matte-finish fiber of beige, the color of the fabric and its ability to change with movement will closely resemble the iridescence of the butterfly wing.

raised wings

extended wings

7-43. **Iridescence: color changes produced by movement.**

Fiber artists in the other disciplines can adapt their techniques comparably to replicate structural colors—making use of light reflectance and fiber luster, organization, and direction to approach the exact hues, values, and intensities found in the model. An embroiderer can use satin stitch arranged at differing angles, in conjunction with the kinds of fibers and colors appropriate to the model. Analogous color gradations typical of the iridescent model can be created by carrying several different-colored threads in the needle and slowly rotating the colors.

A quilter can use highly lustrous patches of satin material in appropriate colors, sewn so that the floats in the fabric are oriented to catch light in an appropriate positive-negative pattern, simulating the play of light and color in an iridescent model. The light-and-color pattern created by the direction of the floats in the satin fabric can be combined with a pattern of low-intensity color and matte-finish patches of material to heighten the iridescent feeling of the lustrous areas further.

For a tapestry weaver, an embroiderer, or any fiber artist working with heavier techniques, another possible method of achieving dynamic feeling is visual sequencing (see Figure 7-43). Designing with a sense of sequence allows the artist to show progressive changes in hue, value, intensity, and surface luster that result from changes in the viewer's angle of vision when looking at structural colors. Thus, the series of sequential patterns produces a sense of movement, light, and color.

Chapter 8

Transition to Fiber

Materials

Designing directly and spontaneously with color is challenging and often plays an important role in teaching and self-discovery; however, planning a work on a smaller scale, with paint, paper, or other materials, has several significant advantages. Through a series of renderings, a fiber artist can develop and complete a design before committing it in its final form to fiber. Making several smaller versions of a fiber work not only presents an opportunity for previsualizing color relationships, it allows changes in approach to correct flaws in a design and to try new ideas without sacrificing materials.

Because the system of production with most fiber techniques is time-consuming, the use of renderings as a tool to establish the direction or goal of a piece and work out the design problems involved before production actually begins can save considerable time and money. This process can also help in determining the scale of a finished work—especially in case of doubt about the finished size.

Sometimes a design will read well as a small piece but change character when enlarged. If a large-scale piece is to be planned, a small-scale rendering can be put into an opaque projector or photographed as a transparency and projected. The fiber artist then gains an excellent sense of what the actual finished work will look like in scale. This technique saves hours. If something is not quite right in the small-scale version, the artist can make corrections, adjustments, and comparisons of different renderings and then choose the most successful one.

Colored papers are an excellent material for making preliminary designs. Various companies maintain good quality control and make a vast number of hues, tints, shades, and values that can be bought at relatively little cost from a good artists' supply store catering to the commercial art trade. Art stores also have swatch books of the color systems on hand or available on order. Such systems often include not only papers but transparent overlay colors and matching dye markers.

As well as being inexpensive and coming in a wide variety of colors and values, colored papers have a uniformity of surface that allows their color effects to be seen with a minimum of effort. Professional colored paper systems are easily obtainable and can be matched and replaced repeatedly. They do have a tendency to fade, however, so they should be used for working models or for teaching purposes only; as a rule, swatch and sample books should be replaced with new editions every year or so. Ultraviolet light causes fading of nonpermanent pigments, but if the papers are kept away from light when not in use, they will fade very slowly. The same goes for small paper renderings kept in notebooks or in drawers.

Still another advantage of using papers is the small amount of equipment needed for working with them. A good brand of heavy rubber cement is the adhesive of choice because—although it is impermanent and eventually loses its adhesive qualities—it neither shrinks nor curls the paper. Papers laid down with good rubber cement can also be peeled up and replaced, as desired. The solvent (or thinner) in rubber cement is volatile and should be used with good ventilation. Because it can stain certain colored papers, rubber cement should be used sparingly and cleanly; a novice ought not be surprised if gaining proficiency takes a little practice. Scissors, a mat knife, a single-edged razor blade, and a rubber cement pick-up for removing extra cement round out the list of basic equipment. Working with paper and rubber cement may seem tedious at first, but with a little practice it becomes easier, and the results in color control are well worth the effort.

Other artists' materials in addition to colored papers can be useful to the fiber artist in planning and previsualizing a design. Most fiber artists use one or another graphics arts medium (pencil, pastel, or crayon, for example) at some stage in preparing their work. Many large art supply houses publish yearly catalogs that are either free for the asking or are available at nominal cost. These catalogs can be an important source of new ideas, new materials, and new techniques for preplanning works.

Physically mixing paint or other media to obtain new colors gives the fiber artist yet another dimension in exploring color and in experimenting with new dye combinations. Through paint mixing, an artist can develop a glossary of mixed colors that can later be translated into terms of dye and kept for future use and referral. Even without being a dyer, a fiber artist can find that a color catalog makes a helpful reference tool in designing.

Paint mixtures produced with pigments of known quality—such as those compounded by Grumbacher, Winsor-Newton, and other well-known manufacturers—are permanent and nonfading. Any fugitive color (a color that is not fast) is marked as such. Some of the opaque watercolor paints known as gouache may fade to a small degree, but the permanence of these is identified on the package, and if a doubt as to a color's permanence exists, the company will always be glad to furnish the information. Most oil and acrylic colors are completely permanent. One noteworthy property of acrylics and other water-soluble paints, however, is that they usually dry down; that is, they dry to a somewhat darker color than they appear to have when wet. With experience an artist can anticipate the amount of value shift that will occur in water-soluble paints with drying. Transparent watercolors are not recommended for mixing and developing a color glossary because of their transparent nature and because of the variation in the way they dry; they are recommended for previsualizing designs, though, if the paint quality provides the density and weight of color and the general feeling that the artist wants.

The yarn samples in this text were all dyed to match color swatches originally mixed with acrylic paints. Acrylic paints are extremely satisfactory for making swatches, for several reasons. First, they dry quickly; but if the drying time is too fast, a few drops of glycerine (which can be purchased at a pharmacy) will slow down the drying time without changing the color effect of the paint in any way. Second, they are water-soluble, which makes cleanup and dilution simple and inexpensive. The paint is made by dispersing pigment, a dry colorant powder, in an acrylic emulsion that is soluble in water. When the paint dries, the resin particles in the emulsion bind together to form a strong, water-insoluble film. This last characteristic makes cleaning dried acrylic paint off a brush (without a solvent) virtually impossible; for this reason, brushes should be kept suspended or sitting in water while in use. They should not be stored in water between uses, however, because prolonged exposure to water loosens the brush hairs or bristles. Brushes should be shaken out after cleaning, to remove as much excess water as possible from under the metal ferrule crimped around the hairs.

Some artists may find it simplest to use a painting knife instead of a brush in making color samples. If so, the following equipment is appropriate for paint mixing: a trowel-shaped painting knife, at least 2 inches long; tube colors of the artist's choice (a color chart may be obtained from the paint company or from an art supply dealer); one large tube each of black and white; a disposable palette (or equivalent) a pad of two-ply bristol board or canvas paper; the appropriate solvent for the paint; rags; containers; paper towels.

Water is the appropriate solvent for acrylic and gouache paints—with perhaps a few drops of glycerine to retard drying, if needed. An excellent solvent for oils is mineral spirits, probably better than turpentine, because it evaporates completely, is essentially odorless, is relatively inexpensive, and causes fewer allergies. Mineral spirits can be purchased under many different names, including Varnolene, Ortho paint thinner, and Nankee pollution-free paint thinner. Thinning oil paints with a little linseed oil is also recommended.

8-1. **Mixing and applying paint: preparing to make value swatches, painting knife with black and white paint on disposable paper palette; a., b., c. mixing a value; d. thorough mixing is essential; e., f. scraping the palette surface while mixing, to ensure an even blend; g. loading the knife as if spreading butter; h. knifing out an even film of paint (when dry, a value or color swatch may be cut out and used in a scale for reference).**

Mixing Technique

The mixing technique is the same no matter what paint medium is used. Oil, acrylic, and gouache are all opaque media, although they can be thinned to a dilute wash or glaze and their opacity makes it easier to see their color quality. The consistency of the mix should resemble soft butter and colors should be completely and uniformly blended. This is done with the painting knife, in the manner as is used in mixed icing for a cake. It takes time and patience to get a thorough mix.

When the mix is complete, a portion of it should be taken on the (clean) painting knife and troweled as evenly as possible onto the bristol board. The surface of the paint should be flat and textureless. The paint film should be as thin as possible but thick enough to remain opaque throughout. Achieving this takes a little practice, but it soon becomes simple. After the sample has been made, a 1" x 2" (or larger) piece should be cut from it and arranged in a scale or modulation of other colors. The color sample can be treated in a group or alone; but it makes a more understandable reference tool if it appears in some sort of scale, such as one of tints, shades, hues, or other modulations.

It is generally a good idea when mixing paint to experiment with small amounts of color at first. The tinctorial power of a color (its ability to change the character of another color) may be surprising. In some instances, a large amount of a color will be needed to change an existing one; in other cases, very little will be necessary. A good rule of thumb is always to add dark color to a light color in small amounts if the end result is to be a lighter color, and to add light color to a dark color in small amounts if the end result is to be a dark color.

a.

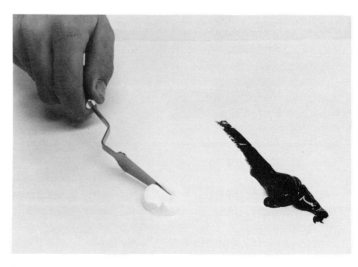

b.

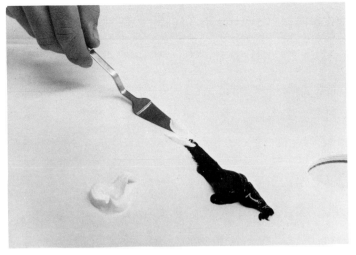

c.

f.

d.

g.

e.

h.

Every artist prefers certain materials and techniques. The principal reason for using familiar materials and techniques is that, over a period of time, there is no need to prethink a technical situation. Making renderings is only the first stage of fiber work; it is important to experiment freely, and knowing materials and methods permits that freedom. An artist should begin early on to search for methods, to try different materials, to experiment with ideas, and to find materials and methods that fit different situations: anything that might produce a desired effect is worth a try.

Chapter 9

Projects

The following exercises and projects are meant to supplement information in the text for purposes of expanding color awareness and expression. The accompanying table of abbreviations (Figure 9-1) is included as a quick reference tool to color abbreviations.

Simple Hues

R = red
B = blue
Y = yellow
G = green
M = magenta
C = cyan

Paired Hues

Combination hues referring to a balanced appearance

YO = yellow/orange
RO = red/orange
RV = red/violet
BG = blue/green

Compound Hues that show a dominance in the RYB system:

YOY = yellow/orange/yellow—a yellow-orange that has a quality closer to yellow than to yellow-orange on the hue circle.

RVR = red/violet/red—a red-violet that has a quality closer to red than to red-violet on the hue circle.

MYC System:
Hue circle based on subtractive primaries or light secondaries—magenta, yellow, cyan

An 18-hue Circle of the MYC system, showing primaries, secondaries and intermediaries (capital letters show dominance of color quality):

Y, Yro, ROy
RO, ROm, Mro
M, Mbv, BVm
BV, BVc, Cbv
C, Cg, Gc
G, Gy, Yg

M, Y, C = primaries
RO, BV, G = secondaries

RYB System:
Hue circle based on traditional red, yellow, blue

Abbreviations for the 24-hue circle of the RYB system:

R, RVR, RV, VRV
V, VBV, BV, BVB
B, BGB, BG, GBG
G, GYG, YG, YGY
Y, YOY, YO, OYO
O, ORO, RO, ROR

R, Y, B = primaries
V, G, O = secondaries
RV, BV, BG, YG, YO, RO = balanced intermediaries. The remaining hues show a dominance of either a primary or a secondary.

Figure 9-1

It is advisable, in the beginning, to limit the extent of any design. Stripes and grid patterns are simple to execute and show color relationships clearly; they are also useful in preparing reference exercises as visual aids in teaching or for the studio.

Wherever possible, use your own technique— whether you weave, embroider, knot, hook, knit, crochet, mix media, piece fabric, or whatever. Some projects are suggested for only one technique, but even these may be adapted to others. Experiment! These projects are to be used as study guides and reference tools for design and inspiration.

Additive and Subtractive Color Mixing

1. Bring together three spotlights, flashlights, cannister lights, or projectors that can be fitted with colored gels. Tape a gel to the outside of each of the lights or lenses. Red, green, and blue-violet gels or colored acetate can be obtained from any art store. Using a white surface, project the red and green lights at the same area. What is the resultant color? Is it lighter than either the red or the green? Repeat the process with red and blue-violet gels. Is the resultant color lighter-than either the red or the blue-violet? Try the same thing with blue-violet and green gels. Is the resultant color lighter than either the blue-violet or the green? Overlap all three lights on one spot. The resultant white area is a product of additive mixing.

Using colored papers, make a reference poster for your studio that illustrates the results of this project, showing the primaries and secondaries of additive mixing.

2. Repeat project 1, using magenta, yellow, and cyan gels. Put all three gels on one light. What happens? When light secondaries are placed over the same light source all light waves are absorbed and no light is transmitted. This phenomenon demonstrates complete subtractive mixing.

Using colored papers, make a reference poster for your studio that illustrates the results of this project, showing the subtractive primaries and secondaries based on the additive system.

3. Mix the following pigments or dyes together: (a) magenta, yellow, and cyan; (b) yellow, red, and blue. Use the hue circles in the text as a reference for the hues. Observe the neutral that is produced in each case.

4. Make a reference chart of the traditional primaries and secondaries (red, yellow, blue, green, orange, and violet). Make a second reference chart of the subtractive primaries and secondaries based on the additive system.

Lighting and Perception

5. Mount a variety of samples of threads or fabrics on notebook paper. Note and record the apparent changes of the colors in terms of hue, value, intensity, and temperature when they are viewed under the following light conditions: daylight, tungsten, fluorescent, a combination of tungsten and fluorescent, full spectrum fluorescent, and low light (such as dusk).

6. Design pieces for different rooms in your home or office. Choose the colors under the same type of lighting in which each is to be viewed.

7. Carefully study the colors in a favorite plaid, quilt, dress, painting, or piece of fabric. Put it away and from memory choose the colors from color sample cards of yarn or paint. Compare your choices with the original. Record the results of your color memory.

8. Observe the difference in colors of things that are seen (a) in sunlight, and (b) in shade. Compare the differences in value, hue, intensity, and temperature.

Hue

9. Make a twelve-hue circle or a twenty-four-hue circle in paint, paper, or fibers in the RYB system. Label the primaries, secondaries, intermediaries, analogous groups (within each primary arc of the hue circle), complements, and warm and cool colors. Repeat, making a six-hue or eighteen-hue circle in the MYC system.

10. Mix secondaries in paint from the RYB primaries. Mix secondaries in paint from the MYC primaries. Compare the mixtures.

11. Mix tertiaries in paint (using both definitions of tertiary colors) in both systems. (Dyers should do projects 9, 10, and 11 with dye.)

12. Arrange the fibers in your studio according to hue families.

13. Choose five hues. Make a grid or striped pattern based on them. Use the same proportions of hues in a design, and translate it into fiber.

Value

14. Make a value scale with papers or paint consisting of fifteen or more steps in paint or commercial gray papers (see page 31 for instructions. Label white 0%, black 100%, and middle gray 50%. Indicate the high values as from 25% up to 0%; the high middle as from 50% to 25%; the low middle as from 50% to 75%; and the low as from 75% to 100%. Match samples of the primaries and secondaries of both the RYB and MYC systems to their relative values on the scale. (Dyers should make the scale in dyed fabrics or yarns, keeping careful notes as to techniques and quantities of dyes used.)

15. Make a second value scale, and punch a hole in the center of each step in the scale, (refer to figures 2-24 and 2-25). Determine the values of the fibers in your studio. Mount small samples of the fibers on the first value scale, at their relative value. Place the hues on one side of the scale and the less intense colors on the other.

16. Choose any five values from the value scale and

make a grid or striped pattern based on them. Translate this pattern into a pattern consisting of colors of the same value. Make a third pattern translating these colors into colors of the same hue quality, but all having the same value. Choose one of the above three patterns; use the same proportions of colors in a design, and translate it into fiber.

Keys

17. In paint or paper, make a simple illustration of the seven keys (in value only).

18. Do project 17 in a grid, stripe, plaid, or patchwork pattern. Translate each key into colors of the same value. Note the change in mood or feeling as the value relationships change. Translate this project into fiber.

19. Choose several five-color assortments in yarn or fabrics that you find pleasing. Translate each into values. Do any of these represent keys?

20. Use any five values from the value scale in a simple design. What is its key? Repeat the same design, using any five colors. Translate the color design into values. Are the keys of both the same or different?

21. Examine good black-and-white reproductions of fiber works such as Scottish tartans, carpets, dress fabrics, or upholstery fabrics. Describe them in terms of key, if appropriate.

22. Study the works of fiber artists and masters in other media, and classify their works according to key.

23. What is your own sense of key? Look at the results of exercises #19 and #20; the way you decorate your home, and so on. Are the key relationships the same or different?

Intensity

The next series of projects involves creation of essential scales that you can use as reference tools in color designing. Do them in paint or dye in both systems (RYB and MYC).

24. Tint the primary and secondary hues to make scales of from ten to fifteen steps, from hue to white. Check the undertones at the high values. In a pattern of stripes or in a grid, use one of the hues and its tints. Use the same proportions of the hue and its tints in a non grid design, (one of your own choosing) and translate it into fiber.

25. Shade the primary and secondary hues to make a scale of from ten to fifteen steps, from hue to black. Tint each of the steps to a 25 percent value, and place the 25 percent tint of each shade beside it to make a double scale. Note the effect of the blue undertone of the black when the shade is tinted. In a grid or stripe pattern, use one of the hues, its shades, and tints of its shades. Use the same proportions of the hue, its shades, and tints of its shades in a non-grid/stripe design, and translate this into fiber.

26. Tone the primary and secondary hues to make a

scale of from ten to fifteen steps, from hue to relative value of gray. In a grid or stripe pattern, use one of the hues and its tones. Use the same proportions of the hue and its tones in a non-grid/stripe design, and translate this into fiber.

27. Modulate each secondary pair (O+G, G+V, V+O, G+BV, BV+RO, RO+G) to make scales of from ten to fifteen steps, from one secondary to the other. Tint each step to 25 percent, and place the tints next to their parent colors to make a double scale. In a grid or stripe pattern, use one of the secondary modulations and its tints. Use the same proportions of the secondary modulations and its tints in a non-grid/stripe design, and translate this into fiber. For each of the scales, in its midrange, compare and label the hue dominance. For example, in the secondary pair of V(R+B) + O(R+Y), the dominance is R.

28. Modulate each complementary pair (Y/V, R/G, and B/O in the RYB system, and Y/BV, M/G, and C/RO in the MYC system) to make scales of from ten to fifteen steps, from one complement to the other. Tint each step to 25 percent, and place the tints next to their parent colors to make a double scale. Compare the chromatic neutrals in the midrange of each scale. Is there an achromatic neutral in each scale? In a grid or stripe pattern, use one of the complementary modulations and its tints. Use the same proportions in a non-grid/stripe design, and translate this into fiber. Choose a palette from the midrange colors of one of the modulations, with or without stronger accent hues, and make a pattern of stripes or a grid. Compare the two stripes or grid patterns.

29. Modulate each split complementary pair (for example, Y to RV and Y to BV) to make scales of from ten to fifteen steps. Tint each step to 15 percent and place the tints next to their parent colors to make a double scale. Select the tinted, lowest-intensity color in each of the scales. Mount them together, label each as to its parent, complement, and split complement, and compare. In a grid or stripe pattern, use one of the modulations and its tints. Use the same proportions in a non-grid/stripe design, and translate this into fiber.

30. Make scales of the following indirect modulations:

RYB System			
Y with (1) BVB;	(2) VBV;	(3) VRV;	(4) RVR.
R with (1) BGB;	(2) GRG;	(3) GYG;	(4) YGY.
B with (1) ROR;	(2) ORO;	(3) OYO;	(4) YOY.
MYC System			
Y with (1) Cbv;	(2) BVc;	(3) BVm;	(4)Mbv.
M with (1) YG;	(2) Gy;	(3) Gc;	(4) Cg.
C with (1) Yro;	(2) ROy;	(3) ROm;	(4) Mro.

Tint each step to 25 percent, and place the tints next to their parent colors to make a double scale.

31. Match scale colors to manufactured color samples. Keep these modulations displayed as a reference tool in designing.

32. From the completed scales, select one hue and compare the different ways its intensity can be broken. In a design, use only modulated colors of a hue.

33. Choose five colors you do not like. In a design, make them work successfully together by altering their value or intensity through tinting, shading, or toning.

34. Check the colors in your yarn supply, and determine which are hues and which are not. Compare them to the hues on your hue circles. Make hue circles in fiber.

35. Check the works of artists of different periods to see how many of them used hues in their works. Similarly, notice works with color palettes similar to the scales you have just completed.

36. Choose a painting you like. Using it as a reference, mix paints to match the colors of the painting. Make a bar graph showing the proportions of hues and colors used by the artist. Use these colors and proportions in a design—first in paint or paper, and then in fiber.

37. In a design, use five colors of equal value with no intensity limits.

38. In a design use high-intensity colors in the foreground and low-intensity colors in the background. Do the same design again, reversing the background and foreground intensities.

Temperature

38. Using one color, make two seven-step scales, going in opposite directions on the hue circle (for example RV, RVR, R, ROR, RO, ORO, O; and RV, VRV, V, VBV, BV, BVB, B). Compare the two RV steps, noting any apparent differences of value and temperature.

40. Make two designs of five colors each—one warm, the other cool. Compare the impact of the two.

41. Group the fibers in your studio into three groups: warm, cool, and temperate.

Combining Temperature with Other Characteristics

42. In four identical designs, use the following colors: (a) warm and cool colors, keeping the values and the intensities the same; (b) warm and cool colors, allowing value changes but no intensity changes; (c) warm and cool colors, allowing intensity changes but no value changes; (d) warm and cool colors, allowing changes in both intensity and value. Compare the differences in impact.

Contrast of Proportion

43. Translate the RYB and MYC hue circles into value circles. Notice the value differences of the two systems.

44. Using Goethe's ratios for balanced hue proportions, show the relationships of complementary pairs in a simple stripe pattern—for example, 1 yellow to 3 violet, 1 orange to 2 blue, 1 red to 1 green. Make a second more developed design in the relative values of the complementary pairs.

45. Do project 44 in the MYC system.

46. Use a protractor to measure angles, translating Goethe's proportions into a 360-degree RYB hue circle, such that $Y = 30°$, $O = 40°$, $R = 60°$, $V = 90°$, $B = 80°$, $G = 60°$ (see text). Do the same for the MYC system, using the proportions you assigned to the pairs in project 45.

47. Do a series of three stripe designs, using two to three colors in each, with the following proportions: (a) balanced proportions; (b) moderate imbalance, having a color dominance; (c) extreme imbalance, setting up afterimages and simultaneous contrast. Compare their impact.

Undertones

48. In paint or dye, tint pairs of the three primaries substitute, i.e.—two different reds, yellows, blues. Compare the higher-value tints as to the temperature of their undertones. Repeat with pairs of other colors.

49. Make all the possible combinations of the two yellows and the two blues:

> Y with a B undertone, and B with a Y undertone.
> Y with a B undertone, and B with a R undertone.
> Y with a R undertone, and B with a Y undertone.
> Y with a R undertone, and B with a R undertone.

Make all the possible combinations of the two yellows and the two reds.

Make all the possible combinations of the two reds and the two blues. If necessary tint the mixes in order to see the colors.

Observe how the undertone affects the color of the mixtures. Compare the intensity of the secondary mixtures when the undertones are the same to their intensity when the undertones are different.

The von Bezold Effect

50. Use any five colors in a striped pattern: (a) using black as one of the colors; (b) substitute a white stripe for the black one; (c) use a striped pattern with a continuous design over it such as a Greek Key. Try it first in black, then white.

Maxwell's Disks

51. For this project an electric drill with a sanding attachment will be needed as well as disks of colored paper with the same diameter as the wheel of the sanding attachment. Cut disks of the primary hues of both the RYB and MYC systems, and other colors with which to experiment. Mark each disk in the center and

cut a radius once on each. The disks can be thus fitted together to rotate to varying proportions. Mount two disks at a time on the sanding attachment and spin. Can these proportions be applied to warp/weft colors for similar optical mixtures.

Fiber Colorants

52. Dye samples of cotton, linen, wool, silk, nylon, acrylic, and polyester threads or fabrics in each of the following dyes: direct, acid, basic, disperse, pre-metallized, fiber-reactive, and light-sensitive. Use as many colors as possible. Mount the samples in a notebook, labeling each as to fiber, dye, and quantity of dye.

Using some of the samples from above, experiment with overdyeing. Keep a record of what is done.

Structural Orientation and Dye Results

53. Choose a fiber that is available in several forms—loose, roving, short staple loose-spun, long staple combed or lightly twisted, and filament—and place all of these in the same dyebath. Note the difference, if any, in dye penetration, luster, and so on.

Optical Mixing as a Dye Technique

54. In a yarn shop or in a collection of commercial samples, note the large number of fibers available that rely on optical mixing of the blend at either the carded or spun level. Collect and mount some samples, and compare them to uniformly dyed samples. The same can be done with fabrics such as shot silk and chambray.

Special Methods of Dye Application

55. Make a collection of fabrics showing special techniques of dye application: Ikat, polychromatic, tie, batik, stencil printing, silk-screen, block, roller, or discharge printing. Experiment with some of these techniques.

56. Experiment with stitching areas of a design in tight stitches, such as those in pulled thread. Areas of the design can also be worked in thick thread that disallows dye penetration. Dye the fabric and remove the stitches.

Fiber Length and Shape and Value

57. Collect, mount, and place next to one another long and short examples of the same fibers. Note if a value difference is created by the fiber length—as between woolen and worsted wools; carded-only cotton and combed cotton; line linen and tow linen; reeled silk, mawata silk, and cut staple silk; filament nylon and cut staple nylon; polyester and acrylic; and so on.

58. Compare the luster, value, and intensity of a synthetic fiber that has different cross-sectional or longitudinal shapes. Compare the difference in light reflectance and color in high- and low-twist versions of the same yarn.

Orientation of Value and Intensity

59. Make samples of various weaves (plain, twill, weft and faced, and so on) with the same yarn. Note the apparent differences in value of each.

60. Experiment with two pieces of lustrous, fine-weave damask. Mount them together at right angles to each other. Change the light source and the angle from which they are viewed, noting the dramatic change in value.

61. Quilters, clothing designers, and dressmakers should experiment with lustrous fabrics, arranging the pieces to enhance the pattern by taking advantage of light reflectance.

62. Stitchers can do the same with areas of long satin stitches, or they can use a stitch pattern whose stitches lie at right angles to each other.

63. Using corduroy, velvet, velveteen, or any other fabric that has a pile with a directional nap, design a patchwork quilt or article of clothing. Rely on light reflectance and interreflection to create areas of contrast in value and intensity.

Texture

64. Note the relative value difference in the same fabric between its smooth condition and its wrinkled condition.

65. Mount and note the differences in value and intensity of the same fabric when pleated, gathered, or smocked. Stitchers should experiment by using these contrasts in a design.

66. Using one color, stitch, quilt, or weave a design that uses the greatest variety of textures possible to create contrasts of value and intensity—for example, smooth, knotted, raised, padded, looped, and cut loops.

Texture - Gauze Effect

67. In your medium, create a fabric with areas of open and closed construction. Incorporate these differences into a design. Color can be added in some areas. Display the work in an area such as a window or room divider, where it can be lit from the front or back.

Embroidery Projects

68. Make a sampler in a single stitch or stitch pattern, using as many types of thread as possible: cotton, wool, linen, silk, metal, and so on. Note the differences in value and intensity.

69. Using one color make a sampler in a single stitch or stitch pattern, using as many weights of thread as possible. Note the differences in the look of the stitch and in the amount of background fabric showing in the pattern. In a design using a single color of thread on a different-colored background, exploit these differences.

70. Experiment with stitches or stitch patterns that require two or more steps: (a) work step one in color 1 and step two in color 2, and then reverse the color in the steps; (b) work the steps in different weight threads; (c) work the steps by reducing or expanding the size or length of the stitches; (d) work the steps by deliberately leaving out some of the steps; (e) work with background fabrics of the same color as or of different color than the threads, and then use some of the above techniques to enhance areas of contrast in a design; (f) in some areas, experiment by stitching on netting, and note how this changes the appearance of the stitch.

71. Make a sampler of stitches, some of each type of stitch made with yarn threaded with the draw and some made with yarn threaded against the draw. Compare reflectance and value. Is there a difference that can be exploited?

Optical Mixing of Colors

72. Weave five 2" x 2" squares, either in threads or in strips of paper, using two analogous hues: hue A as the warp; hue B as the weft. The hues should be of equal value. Each square is to be woven with different-width strips: 1/2", 3/16", 1/8", 1/16", and 1/32". Repeat, using any two analogous hues whose values are very different. View both sets of squares at different angles, and note any changes in the results. Note the distance required to achieve a good optical mix in all ten squares.

73. Try to achieve secondary hues by optically mixing the primaries. If necessary, adjust the values so that they get closer to each other, but keep the intensities high. Compare hue results of the mixtures.

74. Combine two very closely related reds or other hues in order to create a mixture more vibrant than either of the original two.

75. Create an optically mixed modulation of six steps from one hue to another.

76. Make hue circles of optical mixtures, using the primary hues in both systems. Hue circles can be done with embroidery or rug knotting techniques using several threads in the needle, or by carding dyed fleece together and using it spun into yarn or felted as is. Weavers can mix hues in a color blanket (grid pattern).

77. Make optically mixed grays in both the RYB system and the MYC systems, using: (a) pairs of complements; (b) all three primaries; (c) all three secondaries. When the gray has been achieved, compare it to a uniformly dyed gray thread or fabric, and note the beauty of the optical gray.

78. (For weavers and stitchers:)
Take any color A and another color B that is analogous but warmer than A (keeping in mind that blue and orange represent polarity of color temperature). A and B should be the same value. Work three adjoining areas, each at least 1½" square. The stitch should be the same in all three, and the unit of the stitch should be small in order to achieve a good blend. Work the first square in A, the second in a blend of A and B, and the third in B. Compare.

Take A and another color, C that has the same value as A and is analogous to but cooler than A. Work the same adjoining three squares, and compare.

Take A and another color D that is the complement to A and of equal value. Work the same squares, and compare.

Take A and another color E that is either higher or lower in intensity than A and is of equal value. Work the same squares, and compare.

Take A and a gray that has the same value as A. Work the same squares, and compare.

Take A and black; work the same squares, and compare.

Take A and white; work the same squares, and compare.

Of the seven mixtures, which was most easily blended by the eye?

79. In a design using no more than four colors of equal value, see how many different optical mixes you can achieve.

80. Predye areas of a fabric. Experiment in stitching with different colors and weights of threads on the dyed and undyed areas. Note how the stitch or pattern changes in the different areas. Experiment with stitches such as an eyelet: work different arms of the stitch in different color combinations. Note the optical mixing of the colors.

Successive Contrast

81. Do the experiments for demonstrating complementary and negative afterimages through successive contrast that are described on pages 54-55.

Simultaneous Contrast and Negative Afterimage

82. Do the experiments for changing value with negative afterimages as described on pages **000-00:** (a) make one value look like two; (b) make two values look like one. Reverse backgrounds to accentuate the difference.

83. Mount each of the primaries and secondaries of both the RYB and the MYC systems on black, gray, and white—1" square of the hue on a 4" square background. Observe the apparent changes in value and intensity of the hues.

84. Use four values in a striped design. Make the four values appear to be six by surrounding the darkest value with the lightest value (to make the dark appear even darker), and by surrounding the lightest value with the darkest value (to make the light appear even lighter).

85. Place a square or stripe of the primary and secondary hues on different value backgrounds. Make sure the ratio of figure (square or stripe) to ground

(background) is at least 1 to 4 to get the greatest change.

Complementary Afterimage

86. Mount a 1" gray square on a 4" background square of each primary and secondary hue of both the RYB and the MYC systems. The value of the gray square must be the same as the hue on which it is mounted. Note the apparent change of the grays from achromatic to a gray that appears to have a slight hue. In each case, mount the same gray on a white ground to see what the gray looks like without the complementary afterimage.

In a design, place several small areas of a neutral in the midst of large areas of intense hues. Notice the color changes produced on the neutrals.

87. Compare the complementary afterimages of the complements in both the RYB and the MYC systems. In the RYB system, is the complementary afterimage of V the same as its pigment complement, Y? In the MYC system, is the complementary afterimage of Y the same as its pigment complement, BV? Is the complementary afterimage of BV the same as its pigment, Y? Make the same observations about the other complementary pairs of each system.

88. Choose three colors. Mount them as narrow stripes on any fully intense hue. Mount a stripe of each on a 50 percent gray ground. Compare the two sets of stripes. By mixing paints, change the stripes on the intense ground by adding a small amount of the background color to the stripes, negating the complementary afterimage.

89. In each of the gray squares created in project 86, compensate for the complementary afterimage so as to make the gray remain gray.

90. Work a simultaneous contrast sampler in your medium or technique. Surround each of the primary and secondary hues in separate areas with every other color on the hue circle, as well as black, white, and a gray of equal value. Notice how the color changes character, depending on which color is surrounding it. The color looks less intense when surrounded by a related or analogous color or by white; the color looks more intense when surrounded by complementary color or by black. Use this project as a reference tool in designing.

Reinforcing Simultaneous Contrast

91. In a design, use large areas of intense complementary colors. The afterimage of each reinforces the intensity of the other.

92. In a design, surround colored areas with auras of low-intensity complements. The effect here is less abrasive than the effect in project 91.

93. In a design, accentuate the value contrasts by surrounding dark areas with light and light areas with dark.

94. Mount a colorful design on a black ground to increase the intensity of the colors.

Reducing Simultaneous Contrast

95. Make a low-intensity, minor-key design. Note the lack of simultaneous contrast. Take the design from project 91, and separate the colors with a 50 percent gray. Compare the feelings of intensity of the two designs. Repeat the design, using black and then white to separate the colors. Compare all three to the original, and notice which has the most simultaneous contrast.

96. Again using the design from project 91, include small areas of black and white as rest areas. Keep them small, or they will create their own negative afterimages.

97. Use the same colors as in project 91, but break up the large areas of intense color into smaller areas. Notice the change in the simultaneous contrast. Experiment with scale. Find the point at which optical mixing changes to simultaneous contrast.

98. Make a design predominantly in one hue family—for example, in all greens. Insert the relative value of gray of one of the greens into an area. The gray acquires a warm afterimage. Next, insert a small area of red into the design, and note the color of the gray. Does it turn warm or stay gray?

99. In a design, use as many methods as possible for enhancing simultaneous contrast. Using essentially the same design, use as many methods as possible for negating simultaneous contrast. These companion pieces make a comprehensive statement about the manipulation of simultaneous contrast.

Color Unity

100. Make a square of a single color. Produce color unity in the design by adding a second color of smaller proportions in a size and position that pleases you. Note how the design is enhanced.

101. Make a static design that expresses unresolved tension, by using two or three contrasting colors in equal proportion with no dominance. Make a second design using the same colors, but this time change their proportions to create unity through a dominance. Note the difference in your emotional response to these two designs.

102. Make a design that has a weak contrast of several colors with no dominance. Make a second design with the same colors as the first, but this time give unity to the design by creating a dominance of one color over the others. Note the difference in your emotional response to these two designs.

103. Make four patterns using three or four colors in stripes or a grid: (a) create a hue dominance; (b) create a value dominance; (c) create a temperature dominance; (d) create an intensity dominance.

104. Make a design with a dominance created by

organized intervals based on one of the modulations in the projects on intensity (projects 24 though 38).

105. On a multicolor background, make a design with dominance based on a pattern of hue, value, temperature, or intensity.

106. (For dyers:)

Put an assortment of reject yarn colors in a single dyebath to create a unified palette through dominance of the dyebath color over the divergent colors of the assortment.

107. (For weavers:)

Put a bright multicolored warp on your loom. Make a color dominance in the fabric by using one of the contrasting warp colors as a weft color. Weave the entire fabric with that color.

108. Make a series of five samples, using a set of complements such as red and green. In the first, use a ratio of five red to one green; in the second use a ratio of two red to one green; in the third, use a ratio of one red to one green; in the fourth, use a ratio of one red to two green; in the fifth, use a ratio of one red to four green. Which do you respond to most favorably?

Hue Systems

109. Make small colored-paper designs of as many color combinations as possible in every possible color dominance. Simple stripe patterns are effective. Mount and label each set of designs according to its system. This is an invaluable reference tool for color designing. Begin with the RYB hue circle, and then repeat with the MYC hue circle. Mount and compare the two systems.

Hue Systems - Dyads

110. Make two designs in each of the twelve complementary pairs around the twenty-four-hue circle, changing the color dominance of each pair of dyads; for example, make two blue-and-orange designs—one with a dominance of blue, and one with a dominance of orange. Note your responses to each of the designs.

Hue Systems - Triads

111. With paper or bristol board, make an equilateral triangle and mount it on your hue circle. Rotate it so that its corners point to the primaries. Make four simple designs using just the primaries, so that each primary has dominance in one of the designs and the fourth design is balanced. If in any of these exercises you strongly dislike a particular combination of hues, try changing the proportions to create a very strong dominance of one hue and a much smaller amount of the other hues. This technique of creating a strong dominance tends to lessen the high color contrast characteristic of work that uses all three primaries; it may also shift the value key to one you find more comfortable.

112. Rotate the triangle to the secondaries, and do the same with them. Do your responses toward these designs differ from your responses toward the designs made with the primaries and the complementary dyads?

113. Move the triangle, and repeat the process with all eight sets of equilateral triads. Note the differences in emotional impact of these color palettes, and try to determine how value, keys, hue, temperature, balance, and so on may have affected your response.

114. Make an isosceles triangle on the hue circle, and move it around the circle. As in the previous exercise, make four designs for every position on the hue circle, experimenting with shifts in color dominance. How do these differ in impact from the dyads and the triads?

Hue Systems - Tetrads

115. Make a long rectangle from two of the elongated isosceles triangles in the above exercises, and rotate this tetrad around the hue circle. At each position on the circle, make five designs—one design each with a dominance of each of the four colors of the palette, and one with equal amounts of the four colors.

116. Make a square within the hue circle. It will form a double complement with its diagonal corners. Rotate it in the hue circle and make the series of palettes formed by each tetrad. Change the color dominance with each palette. How does the impact of the double complement differ from the palettes that have gone before, especially from those of the simple complementary dyad?

Hue Systems - Hexads

117. Make a hexagonal shape within the hue circle, and rotate it to each of the four possible sets of hexads. Make six designs from any hexad, each with a different color dominance. Examine the one you respond to most in terms of its hue, value, and temperature.

Hue Systems - Analogs

118. Choose a range of analogous hues contained within a primary arc—for example, between red and blue. Expand the selection past the limits of the single primary arc, and note the difference in harmony, drama, impact, contrast, and balance caused by the introduction of a temperature difference. Note, too, how these changes affect the general color unity of the selection. Repeat with the other two primary arcs.

Hue Systems - Modulated Colors

119. Review the intensity modulations you have made. For each of the primary and secondary hues: (a) make a one-color design of a hue and its tints; (b) make a similar design of a hue and its tones; (c) make a similar design of a hue, its shades, and tints of its shades.

120. Make a design from each of the three comple-

mentary modulations, and include the tints.

121. Make a design from each of the secondary modulations, and include their tints.

Emotional Impact

122. Produce four subjective designs that interpret seasonal changes: winter, spring, summer, and fall.

123. Design a color palette for a piece of fiber art for the following: (a) a bedroom; (b) a living room; (c) a study; (d) a kitchen; (e) a quiet child; (f) an overly active child.

124. Choose six yarn colors. Analyze each as to hue, value, temperature, and intensity. Wind them on a card, and establish a dominance. On a second card, reverse the relative quantities of each. Compare.

Space

125. Produce a design with a feeling of deep space by means of a gradation of value (from very dark to light). Produce another design with a feeling of deep space by means of a gradation of intensity. Create a similar feeling of deep space by means of a gradation of temperature. Combine all of the above methods to achieve deep space. Change the color characteristics in the last design so that the strong advancing and receding characteristics in the colors oppose one another, canceling out the spatial effect.

126. Create a feeling of flat space in a design through minor value relationships: (a) with all cool colors; (b) with all warm colors; (c) with all high-intensity colors; (d) with all low-intensity colors; (e) with the least degree of contrast in value, intensity, and temperature.

127. In three designs: (a) place the warm colors in the foreground and the cool colors in the background; (b) place the cool colors in the foreground and the warm colors in the background. (c) change the quantities, value, and intensity. See if you can make the warm colors recede and the cool colors advance.

128. Design a small work containing five values, each in clearly defined shapes. Make four more designs, shifting each value to another position in the design. Notice how the different positions of the same values in each design change the emphasis of light and space.

129. Make a design that achieves the effect of rounded surfaces through chiaroscuro or modulating in gradual steps from light to dark.

130. Study works of painters who distort or flatten space, such as Picasso, Gris, Braque, Leger, or Stuart Davis. Identify areas in which space has been flattened. What methods were used?

131. Make a design with overlapping areas, shapes, or objects. Choose and arrange colors to create deep space by the use of contrasts in temperature, value, and intensity. Do it again, trying to flatten the space this time by arranging the temperature, value, and intensity of the colors you choose in opposition to the spatial clues given by the overlapping shapes; that is, put receding colors on a shape that appears to be in the foreground, and put advancing colors on a shape that appears to be behind it.

132. Choose a modulation of five colors: two parent colors (1 and 5), and three steps in the modulation between them (2, 3, and 4). Make three simple, identical designs of two partially overlapping shapes, using the parent colors in the areas that do not overlap. Use color 2 in the overlap area of the first design; use color 3 in the overlap area in the second design; use color 4 in the overlap area in the third design. Compare the feeling of transparency in all three. In the first design, color 1 appears to be overlapping color 5; in the second, the overlapping is ambiguous; in the third, color 5 appear to be overlapping color 1.

133. Using the information gained in project 132, make two designs that use advancing and receding characteristics of color (a) to show flat space, and (b) to show deep space in transparent overlapping shapes.

134. Based on skills gained from the two previous projects, develop a design that uses the illusion of transparency and the sense of space to their fullest expressive limits.

135. Choose three or four colors in either fabrics or threads. Lay a piece of colored gauze, net, or colored film on top of the colors. Match another set of colors to what you see. In a design, use these two sets of colors to achieve the illusion of transparency.

136. Make a color design on a light box, using various shapes cut out of colored transparent film. Match these colors exactly in either fabric or thread, and translate the design into fiber.

137. Produce a design in any technique, using texture and the absence of texture to make some areas advance and others recede. Embroiders should experiment with using layers of net or organdy for a spatial effect; try stitches either under or on top of the netting.

Structural Color

138. Before you imitate the structural colors of iridescense, opalescence, or luminescence, make a list of things you observe. Include the following information:

    a. What is its overall key?

    b. What kind of color pattern do you see? Is it massed in one place or loosely spread about?

    c. What are the hue relationships? Are they complementary or analogous? Are they ordered, or do they shift back and forth between complements?

    d. What is the surface texture? Is there any type of pattern to the different textures?

    e. Can you see contrasts of value, intensity, or temperature in any areas?

240

f. Note the apparent differences in hue as the object is viewed in daylight, under a tungsten bulb, and under a fluorescent light. Exhibition light and production light ideally should be the same.

g. Hold the object at various angles, and identify differences in the colors you see at different angles.

h. Hold the object up against commercial yarn color cards, and identify and choose the colors.

i. Produce small samples at first. Use techniques you think may work to achieve the actual effect. Analyze the samples. Are the threads or stitches that work best long and parallel or short and multidirectional, raised or flat, smooth or rough?

j. Try combining different types of fibers together: metallic and nonmetallic, shiny and matte, loosely twisted and tightly twisted. Some combinations will be more successful than others.

k. Make a collection of shells, feathers, insects, or stones that show structural color.

139. Imitate an example of iridescence in nature.

140. Using project 139 as a starting point, design a work in your medium that translates the exact copy you made above into an abstract interpretation of the color relationships.

141. Imitate opalescence from nature.

142. Imitate luminescence—a phosphorescence found in minerals or something as simple as patterns of city lights glowing in the dark.

143. Using the information contained in chapter 7, experiment with your medium to reproduce the sense of moving, shimmering, or changing color characteristic of iridescence or opalescence. Experiment with several different methods before choosing the one that works best for you.

Glossary

Acid Dyes. A large group of chemical dyes usually (but not always) applied from an acid dyebath. They are called acid dyes because an acid chemical group is present in each dye molecule.

Additive Mixing. Color mixing using wavelengths of light.

Additive Primaries. The largest divisions of the visible spectrum red, green, and blue-violet. When the three light primaries (red, green, and blue-violet) are added together, they produce white light.

Additive Secondaries. The products of the mixng of two additive primaries: yellow (red + green), cyan (green + blue-violet), and magenta (red + blue-violet).

Advancing Color. Planes of color in a design that appear to come toward the viewer. Usually the warm colors in a work have this characteristic, but the effect depends on color usage.

Afterimage. Any phenomenon that is seen as a response to a visual stimulus but that does not actually exist.

Analogous Hues. Hues that lie next to one another on the hue circle.

Artificial Light. Any light produced by incandescence, fluorescence, phosphorescence, or other means than natural radiation.

Auxochrome. A chemical group present in dye that imparts intensity to the dye color, makes the dye water soluble, and enables the dye to bond with the fiber.

Azoic Dyes (naphthol dyes). A group of dyes consisting of two chemically reactive colorless compounds (a diazonium compound and a phenolic compound) that combine to form a colored dye molecule inside the fiber.

Basic Dyes (cationic dyes). The first of the synthetic dyes. In basic dyes, the chromophore is positively charged and attracts a negative group to form the molecule—the opposite situation from acid dyes.

Basket Weave. A variation on plain weave in which two or more warp threads are woven as one unit with one or more weft threads, giving the fabric a softer drape.

Bast Fibers. Fibers made from plant stems, such as linen, ramie, and jute.

Batik. A resist method of dyeing fabric perfected by the javanese; the areas not to be dyed are covered with wax before immersion of the fabric in the dyebath.

Beetling. A smooth finish produced by pounding a fabric with large hammers; often applied to cotton and linen fabric to flatten fabric surfaces, increase luster, and close the weave.

Bengaline. A warp-faced weave that uses a heavier weft yarn than warp yarn, creating a noticeable horizontal rib texture on the fabric surface; used for dresses, coats, trimmings, and draperies.

Binder. In novelty yarn construction, the yarn that holds the effect yarn in position on the core yarn; in colorants, a glue substance that holds paint to a surface.

Bioluminescence. Light produced by living creatures; usually cool in color temperature.

Blackwork. A counted embroidery technique in which a strong value contrast is maintained between thread and fabric. The stitches can be counted (for creating geometric patterns) or not counted (as in free embroidery).

Body Tone. The color effect of a pigment or dye without any adulteration—that is, before mixing with white, black, or some other modifying, color.

Bouclé Yarn. A novelty yarn that has a looped appearance.

Brightness. A synonym for the intensity of color.

Brilliance. A synonym for the intensity of color.

Broadcloth. A fine warp-faced weave in which the fine weft yarn creates a very small horizontal rib and little texture on the fabric surface.

Brocade. A double-element fabric created by adding an extra warp or extra weft element (often a different color) to the basic warp or weft of a plain weave.

Cable Yarn. A yarn produced when two (or more) ply yarns are twisted together, with each successive twist (single ply and cable) going in the same direction.

Calendering. A smooth finish applied to fabrics, in which fabric passes through heated rollers to remove wrinkles, the industrial equivalent to ironing.

Carding. A process by which fibers are sorted, separated, and partially aligned.

Card Sliver. A ropelike strand of fibers about ¾″ to 1″ in diameter—the form in which fibers emerge from the carding machine.

Cationic Dyes. See basic dyes.

Cellulosic Fibers. Fibers made from plant materials. They can be natural (cotton, linen) or man-made (rayon).

Chemical Affinity. An attraction between substances or particles that causes them to enter into and remain in chemical combination.

Chenille. A complex or novelty yarn with a pilelike surface texture.

Chiaroscuro. The technique of using light and dark contrast within a work to show form.

Chroma. A synonym for the intensity of color; coined by Munsell at the turn of the twentieth century.

Chromatic Neutral. A low-intensity color produced by modulations of complementary hues; also any low-intensity color that approaches gray but has a warm/cool character.

Chromatic Reflection. The reflection of specific wavelengths of light, producing a color sensation. A red surface reflects only red wavelengths of light, and so on.

Chromatic Transmission. The transmission of a specific wavelength of light, producing a color sensation. Orange glass allows only orange light to travel through it, and so on.

Chromophore. A chemical group that gives rise to color in a molecule.

Cire. A high-polish finish sometimes applied to silk and silk blends, in which the fabric is impregnated with wax or thermoplastic material and passed through a friction calendar (two rollers, one rotating faster than the other), resulting in a polished, wet look.

Colorant. Any substance that produces a color change in or on another substance, such as a dye, a paint, or a stain.

Color Key. The dominant color in a work, or a group of colors that appears to be dominant (for example, red-violet, red-orange, and red, centered about one color common to all).

Color System. A specific means of obtaining color effects. Complementary and analogous systems, for example produce different effects.

Color Temperature (of light). The color quality of light, measured in degrees Kelvin.

Combed Cotton. A strong, fine yarn made from long staple cotton fibers that are carded and combed before being spun.

Combing. A process by which fibers are sorted and straightened; a more refined treatment that follows carding.

Complementary Hues. Hues that lie opposite one another on the hue circle.

Complex Yarn. See Novelty Yarn.

Cones. The photoreceptors in the retina that are sensitive to green, blue-violet, and red wavelengths of light.

Cool Colors. Green. violet, and blue, and colors that contain greens, violets, and blues, such as cool neutrals.

Corduroy (commercial). A ribbed, high-luster, cut-pile fabric made with two sets of weft yarn and one warp. The extra weft yarns are woven into the fabric as floats arranged above each other so that they form vertical rows of pile when the weft floats are cut.

Corduroy (handwoven). A cut-pile fabric woven with a flat weave that leaves long weft floats on the surface that can be cut to form a pile.

Cord Yarn. A yarn resulting from two (or more) ply yarns twisted together, with each successive twist (single ply and cord) going in the opposite direction.

Core Yarn. The base yarn in novelty yarn construction; controls the length and stability of the finished yarn.

Corkscrew Yarn. A novelty yarn made by twisting together yarns of different diameters, varying the speed and direction of twist.

Crepe. A lightweight fabric of silk rayon, cotton, wool. manmade or blended fibers characterized by a crinkled surface that is produced by using hard-twist yarn and by weaving S and Z twists in alternating patterns.

Crepe Yarn. A high-twist simple yarn.

Crimp. The waviness of a fiber.

Crock. To transfer color under rubbing.

Cross Dyeing. Dyeing a fabric constructed from a blend of two or more fibers in such a way that each fiber type accepts a different dyestuff, resulting in either a multicolored fabric or an optically mixed fabric color.

Crystallinity. The degree to which fiber molecules are parallel to each other (though not necessarily parallel to the longitudinal fiber axis).

Damask. A firm-textured, lustrous fabric with patterns that are created by light reflectance on areas of warp floats juxtaposed with areas of weft floats on the same face of the fabric.

Daylight Bulb. An incandescent bulb with a blue coating that serves to neutralize the warm color temperature of the filament.

Decating. A smooth finish applied to wool, silk, and rayon blends through a pressing process using heat, pressure, and moisture.

Decorative Yarn (effect yarn). The design yarn (in novelty yarn construction) that forms the design, color appearance, or texture of the finished yarn by the way it is attached to the core yarn.

Develop. To treat with an agent to cause color to appear.

Direct Dyes (substantive dyes). A group of dyes that are absorbed directly into the fiber structure without the aid of complicated application procedures or chemical assistance.

Direct Modulation. The addition of one complement to another— usually done in steps, to visualize the change more clearly.

Discharge Printing. A method of printing fabric in which pattern areas are bleached out of previously printed fabric.

Disperse Dyes. Dyes (developed from azoic dyes) that disperse in water and migrate from suspension in water to suspension in the fiber.

Dope Dyeing (solution dyeing). A method of dyeing man-made fibers in which the colorant is added to the viscous raw material before it is formed into fibers.

Double Cloth. A plain-weave fabric made with two or more elements, in which two fabrics are woven simultaneously (one above the other on the same loom) and either connected at one edge to form a flat cloth of double width or connected at both edges to form a tubular weave or cloth cylinder.

Doup Weave (leno weave). A lace weave in which warp yarns are at certain points and held in place by the weft shot. Called *doup* after the doup attachment used for changing warp position on commercial power looms.

Drawing. The process by which slivers of natural fibers are pulled out after carding or combing; also, the process of pulling fibers out to a thin thread as they are spun into yarn.

Drawn Fabric Work. See Pulled thread embroidery.

Dyad. Any pair of complementary hues.

Dye. A colorant that will go into solution (dissolve in water or another solvent).

Effect Yarn. See Decorative yarn.

Electromagnetic Radiation Spectrum. The total range of electromagnetic wavelengths or frequencies, extending from the longest radio waves to the shortest cosmic rays.

Elongation. The amount of stretch or extension that a fiber yarn or fabric will accept.

English Quilting. A type of quilting in which the decorated top layer is made of many small pieces of fabric sewn together in a pattern or design (pieced work) or in which smaller pieces are applied on top of a larger piece of fabric in order to create a pattern or design (appliquéd work).

Faille. A soft, slightly glossy silk, rayon, or cotton warp-faced fabric that uses a heavier weft yarn than warp yarn, creating a noticeable horizontal rib texture on the fabric surface.

Felt. A thick, dense, nonwoven wool fabric made by applying boiling water, soap, pressure, and agitation to a pile of loose, carded fleece, which causes the wool fibers to intermigrate and interlock into a firm mat of fabric.

Felting (fulling). A washing finish in which hot water, soap and agitation are applied to wool fabrics to cause the wool fibers to intermigrate and interlock, creating a denser, tighter fabric.

Filament Fibers. Long, continuous fibers that can be measured in feet, yards, or (in the case of man-made fibers) miles.

Filament Yarn. A yarn made from several continuous filaments held together with a twist.

Finish. A commercial or hand process that alters fibers or fabric structure in some way that, in turn, alters the behavior of the fabric.

Fleece. Wool sheared from a living sheep.

Float. A segment of warp or weft in a woven fabric that crosses over at least two threads before again interlocking in the fabric weave.

Flocking. A raised fabric finish that creates what appears to be a nap on certain areas of a fabric or on a whole fabric; produced by gluing short fibers onto the fabric.

Fluorescence. The emission of light from a substance during the absorption of some other kind of radiation.

Fulling. See Felting.

Full-Spectrum Light. Artificial or natural light that contains all wavelengths of the visible spectrum.

Gauze. A plain-weave fabric with widely spaced warp and weft.

Gauze Effect. The effect caused by lighting an open weave from the front (same side as viewer) or from behind (opposite side from viewer). Lit from the front, the threads reflect light back to the viewer making the fabric appear solid; lit from behind, the fabric appears to be a thin diaphanous web.

Gel. The colored sheets of acetate placed over lamps in theatrical lighting; coined from the word gelatin.

Gimp Yarn (guimpe yarn). A novelty yarn produced when a bulky yarn is looped around a core yarn and held in place by a binder yarn.

Hand. The feel of a fabric; the qualities that can be ascertained by touching it.

Heat Setting. A finish produced by using heat on thermoplastic fabrics to set the dimensional stability of the fabric, to press out wrinkles, or to make pleats or creases permanent, involves heating the fabric until the fibers are soft and malleable, pressing it into a new shape, and cooling it.

Hexad. A system of colors or hues found by placing a six-pointed shape within a hue circle to determine three sets of complements.

High-Intensity Color. Color that is pure (a hue) or almost pure, with no adulterants added.

Hue. The family name of a color (for example, blue, yellow, or orange); also, a color that is entirely pure.

Ikat. A resist method of hand dyeing in which certain areas of the yarn are wrapped to resist dye, producing a pattern that will be developed later in the weave.

Incandescence. The emission of visible radiation (light) by a heated substance.

Indirect Modulation. Any mixture of two noncomplementary hues (containing all three primaries, but not producing a neutral) that results in a temperature shift. For example, a mixture of yellow-orange and red-violet.

Inlay. Discontinuous brocade; the extra or brocade yarn does not run full length of warp or weft but is added discontinuous in certain areas to the plain weave from an extra shuttle.

Intensity. The relative purity of a color.

Interreflection. A color shift due to light absorption into a deeply textured yarn or fabric surface; particularly evident in a nap or pile surface texture.

Iridescence. A color effect produced by a physical structure or structures rather than by a colorant.

Italian Quilting. A stitched and padded type of quilting similar to trapunto, except that the padding takes the form of a thick yarn padding inserted between two parallel rows of stitching, creating a linear type of raised design.

Kasuri. See Ikat.

Kelvin Temperature Scale. A temperature scale based on the same unit as the centigrade scale, but beginnning with O at absolute zero rather than at the freezing point of water; the scale used to describe the color of light.

Key. See Color Keys.

Lace. An open-work cloth with a design formed by a network of threads.

Lace Weaves. Open weaves created by distortion of either warp or weft yarns.

Leno Weave. See Doup Weave.

Light. The visible spectrum, consisting of electromagnetic radiation ranging from 400 to 700 nanometers.

Light Level. The degree of ambient light, the intensity of which may be high or low.

Light Primaries. See Additive Primaries.

Light Secondaries. See Additive Secondaries.

Line Linen. A strong linen yarn made from staple linen that has been carded and combed before being spun.

Loft. The springiness or fluffiness of a fiber or yarn.

Low-Intensity Color. Color that shows little of its original purity because it is a broken color—a hue that has been mixed with white, black, gray, or its own complement.

Luminescence. Light not associated with heat.

Luster. The gloss, sheen, or shine of a fiber yarn or fabric.

Major Key. The organization of values in a work that produces high contrast.

Maxwell's Disks. Rapidly spun disks or wheels that produce color effects depending on the proportions of colors originally placed on them.

Mercerization. A finish produced by applying caustic soda under tension to cotton fibers, improving the luster, strength, and dye receptiveness of the fiber.

Minor Key. The organization of value in a work that produces low contrast.

Moiré. A lustrous, patterned finish whose appearance depends on changes of light reflectance and resembles the patterns seen on water; used primarily on ribbed silks and synthetic fabrics such as taffeta, faille, and bengaline. The pattern is created by flattening the fabric ribs in some areas and leaving them rounded in others.

Molecule Orientation. The degree to which fiber molecules are parallel to each other and to the longitudinal axis of the fiber.

Monk's Cloth. A heavy loosely woven basket-weave in solid colors, stripes, or plaids, used chiefly for draperies and slipcovers.

Monomer. A single unit or molecule from which polymers are formed.

Mordant. A chemical that fixes a dye in a fiber by combining with the dye to form an insoluble compound.

Mordant Dyes. A group of dyes (also called metallized or pre-metallied dyes) that cannot be applied to fiber without the help of metallic salts or chemical assistants called mordants.

MYC System. A pigment system in which magenta, yellow, and cyan are the primary colors.

Nanometer. A measurement equal to 1 billionth of a meter; used to express the length of waves of electromagnetic radiation in the visible spectrum.

Nap. A hairy or downy surface, as on a woven fabric.

Naphthol Dyes. See Azoic Dyes.

Non-Spectral Color. Any color not found in the spectrum such as brown, black, or gray.

Novelty Yarn. A yarn made with irregularities in size, twist, or construction, but not necessarily having a complicated construction.

Nub Yarn. A novelty yarn made by wrapping a decorative strand repeatedly around a core to form an enlarged segment.

Opalescence. A color effect produced by a physical structure or structures rather than colorants; like iridescence but milkier in appearance.

Optical Finishes. Chemical finishes that either raise or lower the light reflectance and luster of a fiber.

Optical Mixtures. Color combinations perceived as mixtures by the eye/brain, produced by juxtaposing small dots or slashes of color.

Oriented. Aligned parallel with the length of the fiber.

Ottoman. A heavy warp-faced silk or synthetic fabric that uses a heavier weft yarn than warp yarn, to create a noticeable horizontal rib texture on the fabric surface; commonly used for coats, skirts, and trimmings.

Oxford Cloth. A fine basket-weave fabric in which two warp threads are used as one unit equal in size to one thicker weft yarn, giving the fabric a softer drape than is produced in plain weave.

Palette. A particular range, quality, selection, or use of colors; also, surface on which to place colors.

Partitive Mixing. The same as optical mixing. See Optical Mixtures.

Patchwork (piecing; pieced work). The sewing together of small pieces of fabric to form a large piece.

Perspective (aerial). The technique of making a two-dimensional surface appear three-dimensional through the use of value.

Perspective (Linear). The techinque of making a two dimensional surface appear three-dimensional through the use of line.

Phosphor. A substance (usually of mineral origin) that becomes luminescent when bombarded with radiation.

Phosphorescence. Fluorescence that continues to be visible after radition has ceased.

Piece Dyeing. A commercial practice of dyeing solid-color fabric to order.

Piqué. A ribbed or corded cotten in which an extra warp element is used as a detaining backing float to force the woven face of the fabric into raised, rounded, curved ribs that run horizontally across the fabric.

Plain Weave. See Tabby.

Plangi (tie dyeing). A resist method of printing fabric or yarn in which the fabric or yarn is first tied with waxed thread wherever it is to resist the dye, and is then dipped into the dyebath.

Ply Yarn. A yarn in which two or more single strands are twisted together.

Pointillism. A system of painting based on the juxtaposition of dots of color that blend optically.

Polychromatic Dyeing. A dyeing process in which streams of different colored dyes are poured over a moving piece of fabric, resulting in a colored pattern.

Polymer. A long chain molecule made by linking many monomers together.

Poplin. A fine, tightly woven, warp-faced fabric that has a heavier weft yarn than warp yarn to create a noticeable horizontal rib texture on the fabric surface.

Primary Arc. Any arc consisting of hues that fall between a pair of primary hues on a hue circle; for example, an arc of hues between red and yellow in an RYB hue circle.

Primaries. See Additive Primaries, Subtractive Primaries.

Prismatic Hues. Colors seen in the visible spectrum; that is, colors seen when light is refracted through a prism.

Protein Fibers. Fibers made from animal or plant proteins, either natural (wool, silk) or manmade (azion).

Pulled Thread Embroidery (drawn fabric work). A counted embroidery technique in which the values and hue of thread and of fabric are the same. The stitches are pulled tight so that the warp and weft are either pulled together or pulled apart to form geometric patterns.

Purkinje Shift. An adaptation of the eye to low light levels.

Quilting. Various techniques that involve sandwiching two or three layers of fabric (or a top and bottom layer of fabric *with a nonwoven batting for the middle layer*), and holding these *together* with small running stitches or with knots sewn through all of the layers.

Ratine Yarn. A novelty yarn produced when a bulky yarn is looped around a core yarn and held in place by a binder yarn.

Raw Cotton. Cotton in its natural (unmercerized) state.

Raw Silk. Silk that has not been degummed.

Reactive Dyes. Dyes that react chemically with fiber to form a permanent bond.

Receding Color. Planes of color in a design that appear to move away from the viewer. Usually the cool colors in a work have this characteristic, but the effect depends on color usage.

Recovery. The degree to which a fiber will return to its original length after elongation.

Reeled Silk. A fine silk-filament yarn made from several perfect silk filaments held together with a twist.

Reflected Color. Wavelengths of light that reflect off a surface and give that surface an identifiable color, such as red, orange, or blue; also, the ambient color effect from one surface to another.

Refraction. The bending of white light to produce spectral hues.

Relative Value. A gray whose ability to absorb or reflect light matches that of a specfic hue.

Resilience. The ability of a fiber yarn or fabric to stretch or bend under pressure and to snap back to its original position when the pressure is released.

Retina. The sensory membrane lining the eye, containing rods and cones and connected to the brain by the optic nerve.

Rods. The photoreceptors in the retina that are sensitive to low light levels and colorless vision.

Roving. The process by which a sliver of natural fiber is attenuated to between one-quarter and one-eighth of its original diameter; also, the product of this operation.

RYB System. A pigment system in which red, yellow, and blue are the primary colors.

Sateen. A lustrous fabric characterized by floats running in the weft direction; often made of cotton.

Satin. A lustrous fabric characterized by floats running in the warp direction, usually made of silk, rayon and cotton.

Satin Stitch. A long, straight embroidery stitch that resembles a weaving float in its ability to reflect light.

Saturation. The purity of a color.

Schreinering. A softly lustrous finish sometimes applied to cotton and linen fabric; a roller engraved with fine lines at an angle parallel to the twist of the yarns is used to flatten the yarns and make a smoother, more compact cloth.

Scrooping. A finish used to add luster to silk; mild acids are applied to the silk fibers, which are then dried under tension and steamed.

Secondaries. See Additive Secondaries, Subtractive Secondaries.

Seed Yarn. A novelty yarn produced when a decorative strand is wrapped repeatedly around a core yarn to form an enlarged segment; similar to a nub yarn, but with smaller segments.

Seersucker. A lightweight cotton or cotton blend fabric characterized by crinkled stripes that are woven into the fabric by setting regular groups of the warp yarns tight and alternating these with other groups of warp ends set slack.

Selective Reflection. Specific wavelengths of light reflected from a surface, giving that surface an identifiable color.

Sericin. A natural gum (produced by a silkworm) that coats a silk filament and holds the two halves of the silk strand together.

Shade. Any hue or color mixed with black.

Shot. In fabric, having changeable and contrasting color effects similar to iridescence. In weaving technique one passage of weft yarn through a shed of warp yarn; one weft yarn.

Shuttle. A device used in weaving to pass weft thread between the threads of the warp.

Simple Yarn. A smooth, even, uniform yarn that has an even twist (an equal number of turns per inch) throughout the length of the yarn.

Simultaneous Contrast. The phenomenon of an afterimage seen while the viewer is still looking at a color stimulus.

Singeing. A smooth fabric finish that is created by burning off the fuzz of fiber ends sticking out of a fabric made from staple-length fibers.

Singles Yarn. A basic yarn strand; a continuous length of fibers held together with a unidirectional twist.

Size (sizing). A transparent glue solution used on fabric or paper in order to make metallic powder, leafing, or any other substance adhere to it.

Solution Dyeing. See Dope Dyeing.

Space Dyeing. A method of dyeing yarn in which different areas of the yarn are dyed different colors so as to produce a pattern on the fabric made from it.

Spectral Hue Circle. A projection of the spectrum seen as a circle—that is, a rainbow.

Spectrum. See Electromagnetic Radiation Spectrum, Visible Light Spectrum.

Spinerette. One of two small holes in a silkworms's head through which silk strands are extruded by the worm; also, a device resembling a shower head through which viscous raw material is extruded to form man-made fibers.

Spiral Yarn. A novelty yarn made by twisting a bulky low-twist yarn around a fine hard-twist yarn.

Split Complement. A triad of hues (or colors) made up of a hue and the two hues that lie adjacent to its complement.

Spun Yarns. Yarns composed of staple fibers held together with a twist.

Staple Fibers. Short fibers measured in inches or fractions of inches.

Staple Yarn. A yarn constructed from short fibers held together with a twist.

Stock Dyeing. Dyeing fibers before they are spun into yarn.

Striations. Lengthwise grooves on a fiber.

Substantive Dyes. See Direct Dyes.

Subtractive Complementary Mixtures. Complementary mixes of colorants.

Subtractive Mixing. Color mixing using colorants (paints, dyes, and inks).

Subtractive Primaries. The pigments magenta, yellow, and cyan of the MYC system, which when added together produce black. In the RYB system, red, yellow, and blue are designated as primaries although when added together they do not produce black.

Subtractive Secondaries. The products of the mixing of any two subtractive primaries: in the MYC system, red-orange (yellow + magenta), green (yellow + cyan) and blue-violet (magenta + cyan); in the RYB system, orange (yellow + red), green (yellow + blue), and violet (red + blue).

Successive Contrast. The phenomenon of an afterimage seen after the viewer looks away from a color stimulus.

Synthetic Fibers. Fibers made from chemicals that were never fibrous in form (also called man-made or synthesized fibers).

Tabby (plain weave). The simplest way warp and weft can be interlaced, consisting of the alternate interlacing of warp and weft yarns.

Tapestry. A weft-faced fabric in which the pattern is woven with colored weft threads; used extensively for wall hangings and table covers.

Temperate Colors. Hues that fall between red-violet and green-yellow on the hue circle.

Temperature (of hue). The characteristic of color that describes its relative warmth or coolness.

Tent Stitch. A common counted thread stitch that can be worked in either horizontal or diagonal rows. Each stitch is taken diagonally over one thread of both the warp and the weft, at the intersection of the two.

Tertiary Colors. Colors produced by a combination (modulation) of two secondary colors.

Tetrad. A system of colors or hues found by placing a rectangle, square, or trapezoid within the hue circle.

Thermoplastic. Capable pf softening or fusing when heated and of rehardening when subsequently cooled.

Tie Dyeing. See plangi.

Tinctorial Power. A colorant's ability to change the character of another color.

Tint. Any hue or color mixed with white.

Tonality. The feeling or mood that the organization of values in a work produces.

Tonal Range. The total range of values within a work.

Tone. Any hue or color mixed with its relative value.

Top. A loose, untwisted, ropelike roll of staple fibers suitable for spinning, somewhat more attenuated and thinner or finer in diameter than a carder sliver but less attenuated and thicker in diameter than a roving.

Tow Linen. A linen yarn made from short staple linen fibers that are carded but not combed before being spun.

Trapunto. A type of quilting in which the fabric layers are stitched together with a design, after which some or all areas of the design are stuffed to create a bas-relief surface.

Triad. Any combination of three colors or hues within a work.

Twist. To form yarn or a strand of fibers into a spiral shape by rotating one end.

Ultraviolet Light. Radiation that lies beyond the visible spectrum at the violet end, having shorter wavelengths than visible violet. Ultraviolet light is actinic—that is, produces photochemical changes (such as fading) in pigments and dyes.

Undertone. The color effect of a hue when tinted; the result may look like the body tone or it may show a temperature change.

Union Dyeing. Dyeing a fabric that is composed of a blend of two or more fibers with different dyes to achieve a single, uniform color.

Unity. A feeling of wholeness or completeness inherent in a work of art.

Value. A color's relative degree of lightness or darkness.

Value Scale. A scale of grays ranging to and limited by black and white.

Vat Dyes. A group of dyes that are made soluble in water by the addition of a reduction chemical and then returned to insoluble form inside the fiber by oxidation.

Velour. A soft, closely woven fabric with a short thick pile.

Velvet. A warp-pile fabric with a short, soft, thick pile surface, usually made of silk or of man-made pile fiber with a cotton back, woven with a double-cloth method.

Velveteen. A cut-pile fabric made with two sets of weft and one warp. The extra weft is woven in floats that are staggered unevenly over the fabric and later cut and brushed up to form a pile.

Visible Light Spectrum. The band of radiation in the electro-magnetic spectrum that we perceive as light and that, when refracted, produces a spectral hue.

Von Bezold Effect (spreading effect). The phenomenon in which by adding or changing one color in a design, one alters the total color effect.

Warm Colors. Red, orange, and yellow, and colors that contain reds, oranges, and yellows, such as warm neutrals.

Warp. Yarns that run parallel to the length of the fabric or selvage.

Warp-Faced Weave. An unbalanced weave (more warp ends per inch than weft ends) in which only the warp shows on the surface of the fabric; for example, inkle weaving.

Weft (filling yarns; woof yarn; picks). Yarns that run perpendicular to the length of the fabric or selvage.

Weft-Faced Weave. An unbalanced weave (more weft ends per inch than warp ends) in which only the weft shows on the surface of the fabric; for example, traditional tapestry.

Welts. A textured weave in which an extra warp element is used as a detaining backing float to force the woven face of the cloth into straight, raised ribs that run horizontally to the cloth.

White Light. Visible radiation—that is natural light or daylight.

Woolen Yarn. A soft, fluffy, low-twist yarn made from short staple wool fibers that are carded and spun.

Worsted Yarn. A strong, compact, tightly twisted yarn made from long staple wool fibers that are carded and combed before being spun.

Bibliography

Albers, Josef. *The Interaction of Color.* New Haven, Conn.: Yale University Press, 1963.

"A Quarterly Review of the Fiber Arts." *Textile Artists' Newsletter* 1 (3) (1978), 2 (1) (1979), 2 (4) (1980), and 3 (1) (1980).

Birrell, Verla. *The Textile Arts: A Handbook of Fabric Structure and Design Processes.* New York: Harper & Row, 1959.

Birren, Faber. *Color Psychology and Color Therapy.* Secaucus, N.J.: Citadel Press, 1978.

_____ . *Color: A Survey in Words and Pictures.* New Hyde Park, N.Y.: University Books, 1963.

_____ . *History of Color in Painting.* New York: Reinhold, 1965.

Brasch, R. *How Did It Begin?* New York: David McKay, 1965.

Burnham, Dorothy K. *Warp and Weft: A Dictionary of Textile Terms.* New York: Charles Scribner's, 1981.

Buzan, Tony. *Use Both Sides of Your Brain.* New York: E.P. Dutton, 1974.

Chamberlain, Marcia, and Crockett, Candace. *Beyond Weaving.* New York: Watson-Guptil, 1974.

Chevreul, M.E. *The Principles of Harmony and Contrast of Colors and Their Applications to the Arts.* 1854. New York: Van Nostrand Reinhold, 1981.

Clark, R.T.R. *Myth and Symbol in Ancient Egypt.* 1959. Reprint. London: Thames & Hudson, 1978.

"Color." *Life Library of Photography.* New York: Time-Life Books, 1970.

Coren, S., and Girgus, J.S. *Seeing Is Deceiving: The Psychology of Visual Illusions.* Hillsdale, New Jersey: Lawrence Erlbaum, 1978.

Crockett, Candace. *The Complete Spinning Book.* New York: Watson-Guptil, 1977.

Dawson, Barbara. *Metal Thread Embroidery.* New York: Watson-Guptil, 1976.

Eastman Kodak Co. *Color as Seen and Photographed.* 2d ed. Rochester: Eastman Kodak, 1972.

Emery, Irene. *The Primary Structures of Fabrics: An Illustrated Classification.* Washington, D.C.: Textile Museum, 1966.

Evans, Ralph. *An Introduction to Color.* New York: John Wiley, 1948.

_____ . *The Perception of Color.* New York: John Wiley, 1974.

Ferguson, George. *Signs and Symbols in Christian Art.* New York: Oxford University Press, 1961.

Gerritsen, Frans. *Theory and Practice of Color.* New York: Van Nostrand Reinhold, 1975.

Gibson, James J. *The Senses Considered as Perceptual Systems.* Boston: Houghton Mifflin, 1966.

Goethe, Johann Wolfgang von. *Theory of Colours.* 1810. Translated by Charles Lock Eastlake. Cambridge, Mass.: M.I.T. Press, 1973.

Gordon, Beverly. *Feltmaking: Traditions, Techniques, and Contemporary Explorations.* New York: Watson-Guptil, 1980.

Graham, Clarence H., and Brown, John L. *Vision and Visual Perception.* New York: John Wiley, 1965.

Graves, Maitland. *The Art of Color and Design.* New York: McGraw-Hill, 1951.

Gregory, R.L. *Eye and Brain: The Psychology of Seeing.* 3d ed. New York: McGraw-Hill, 1978.

Held, Shirley E. *Weaving: A Handbook of the Fiber Arts.* New York: Holt, Rinehart & Winston, 1978.

Helmholtz, Hermann von. *Treatise on Physiological Optics.* 1867. Reprint of English ed. New York: Dover Publications, 1962.

Homer, William I. *Seurat and the Science of Painting.* 2d ed. Cambridge, Mass.: M.I.T. Press, 1970.

Itten, Johannes. *The Art of Color.* New York: Reinhold, 1961.

Jacobson, Egbert. *Basic Color.* Chicago: Paul Theobald, 1948.

Joseph, Marjory. *Introductory Textile Science.* New York: Holt, Rinehart & Winston, 1981.

Jung, Carl G. *Man and His Symbols.* Garden City, N.Y.: Doubleday & Co., 1964.

Kuehni, Rolf G. *Color: Essence and Logic.* New York: Van Nostrand Reinhold, 1983.

Küppers, Harold. *Colour: Origins, Systems, Uses.* New York: Van Nostrand Reinhold, 1974.

Land, Edwin H. "The Retinex Theory of Color Vision." *Scientific American* 237 (6): 108-128 (December 1977).

LeGrand, Y. *Light, Colour, and Vision.* Translated by R.W.G. Hunt, J.W.T. Walsh, and S.R.W. Hunt. New York: John Wiley, 1957.

Linton, George L. *Natural and Man-made Textile Fibers, Raw Material to Finished Fabric.* New York: Duel, Sloan & Pearce, 1966.

Mackenzie, Clinton D. *New Design in Crochet.* New York: Van Nostrand Reinhold, 1972.

Maier, Manfred. *Basic Principles of Design.* New York: Van Nostrand Reinhold, 1977.

"Macramé Techniques and Projects." *Sunset Books.* Menlo Park, Calif.: Lane Publishing, 1976.

Marx, Ellen. *Optical Color and Simultaneity.* New York: Van Nostrand Reinhold, 1983.

Mayer, Ralph. *The Artist's Handbook of Materials and Techniques.* New York: Viking Press, 1970.

_____ . *A Dictionary of Art Terms and Techniques.* New York: Thomas Y. Crowell, 1969.

Meilach, Dona Z. *Macramé: Creative Design in Knotting.* New York: Crown Publishers, 1971.

Milam, Betsy. *Macramé.* New York: Grosset & Dunlap, 1977.

Minnaert, M. *The Nature of Light and Color in the Open Air.* Translated by H.M. Kremer-Priest. New York: Dover Publications, 1954.

Munsell, A.H. *A. Color Notation.* 10th ed. Baltimore: Munsell Color Co., 1947.

Nassau, Kurt. "The Causes of Color." *Scientific American.* Vol. 243, No. 4, 124-154 (October 1980).

_____ . *The Physics and Chemistry of Color.* New York: John Wiley, 1983.

Newhall, Beaumont. *The History of Photography.* Rev. ed. New York: Museum of Modern Art, 1982.

Oren, Linda Lowe. "Do It Yourself." *Shuttle, Spindle, and Dyepot.* Vol. 11, No. 1:59-62 (Winter 1979).

Ott, John N. *Health and Light.* New York: Pocket Books, 1976.

Rood, Ogden N. *Modern Chromatics.* New York: Van Nostrand Reinhold, 1973.

Seagroatt, Margaret. *A Basic Textile Book.* New York: Van Nostrand Reinhold, 1975.

Sharpe, Deborah T. *The Psychology of Color and Design.* Totowa, N.J.: Littlefield, Adams & Co., 1975.

Simon, Hilda. *The Splendor of Iridescence.* New York: Dodd, Mead, 1971.

Sinkankas, John. *Mineralogy.* Princeton, N.J.: D. Van Nostrand, 1964.

Thorpe, Azalea S., and Larsen, Jack L. *Elements of Weaving: A Complete Introduction to the Art and Techniques.* Garden City, N.Y.: Doubleday & Co., 1967.

Verity, Enid. *Color Observed.* New York: Van Nostrand Reinhold, 1980.

Vinroot, Sally, and Crowder, Jennie. *The New Dyer.* Loveland, Colo.: Interweave Press, 1981.

Walch, Margaret. *Color Source Book.* New York: Charles Scribner's Sons, 1979.

Waller, Irene. *Designing with Thread: From Fiber to Fabric.* New York: Viking Press, 1973.

Ward, Michael. *Art and Design in Textiles.* New York: Van Nostrand Reinhold, 1973.

Watson, William. *Textile Design and Color.* 6th ed. New York: Longmans, Green & Co., 1954.

Wright, W.D. *The Rays Are Not Colored.* London: Hilger, 1967.

Zimmerman, Jane. *Techniques of Metal Thread Embroidery.* Rev. ed. Richmond, Calif.: Jane D. Zimmerman, 1980.

Index